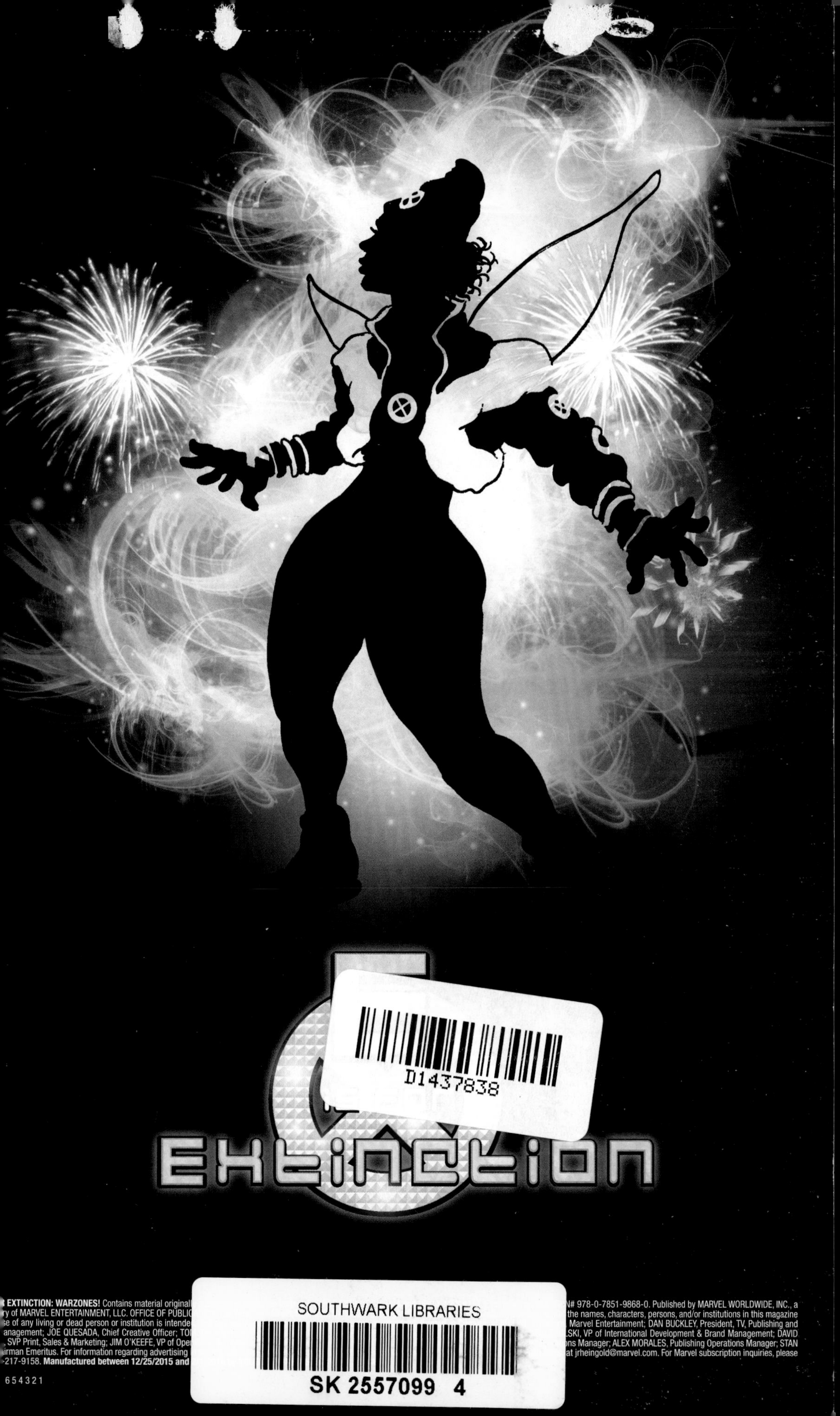

EXTINCTION

EXTINCTION: WARZONES! Contains material originall … N# 978-0-7851-9868-0. Published by MARVEL WORLDWIDE, INC., a
ry of MARVEL ENTERTAINMENT, LLC. OFFICE OF PUBLIC … the names, characters, persons, and/or institutions in this magazine
se of any living or dead person or institution is intende … Marvel Entertainment; DAN BUCKLEY, President, TV, Publishing and
anagement; JOE QUESADA, Chief Creative Officer; TO … LSKI, VP of International Development & Brand Management; DAVID
, SVP Print, Sales & Marketing; JIM O'KEEFE, VP of Ope … ons Manager; ALEX MORALES, Publishing Operations Manager; STAN
irman Emeritus. For information regarding advertising … at jrheingold@marvel.com. For Marvel subscription inquiries, please
-217-9158. **Manufactured between 12/25/2015 and**
654321

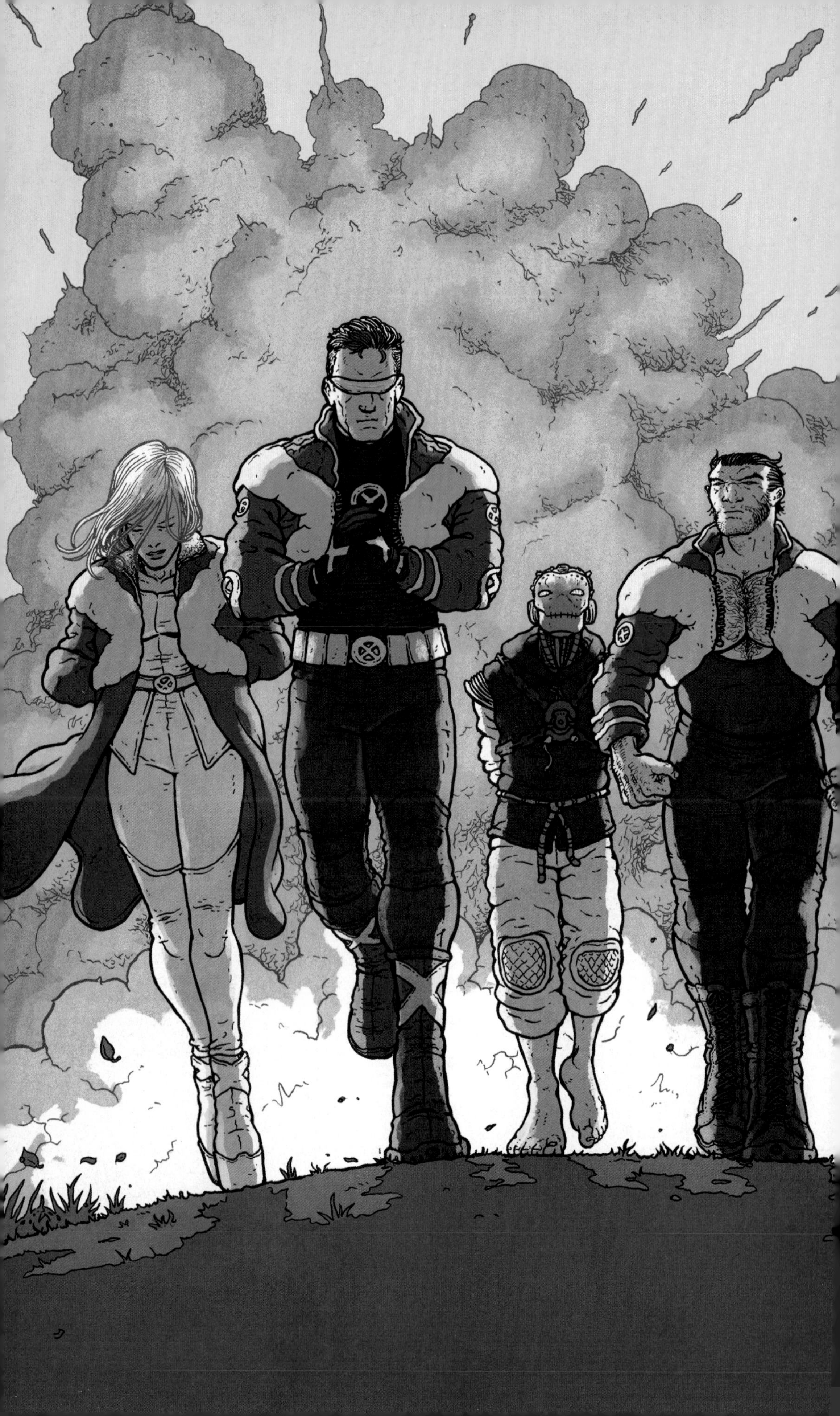

THE MULTIVERSE WAS DESTROYED

THE HEROES OF EARTH-616 AND EARTH-1610 WERE POWERLESS TO SAVE IT!

NOW, ALL THAT REMAINS...IS BATTLEWORLD!

A MASSIVE, PATCHWORK PLANET COMPOSED OF THE FRAGMENTS OF
WORLDS THAT NO LONGER EXIST, MAINTAINED BY THE IRON WILL OF
ITS GOD AND MASTER, VICTOR VON DOOM!

EACH REGION IS A DOMAIN UNTO ITSELF!

E is for EXTINCTION

BATTLEWORLD DOMAIN MUTOPIA
21+ ONLY | X-GENE+ ONLY

Chris Burnham & Dennis Culver
WRITERS

Ramon Villalobos
ARTIST

Ian Herring
COLOR ARTIST

VC's Clayton Cowles
LETTERER

Ian Bertram & Dave Stewart
COVER ART

Christina Harrington
ASSISTANT EDITOR

Katie Kubert
EDITOR

COLLECTION EDITOR
JENNIFER GRÜNWALD

ASSISTANT EDITOR
SARAH BRUNSTAD

ASSOCIATE MANAGING EDITOR
ALEX STARBUCK

EDITOR, SPECIAL PROJECTS
MARK D. BEAZLEY

SENIOR EDITOR, SPECIAL PROJECTS
JEFF YOUNGQUIST

SVP PRINT, SALES & MARKETING
DAVID GABRIEL

BOOK DESIGNER
JAY BOWEN

EDITOR IN CHIEF
AXEL ALONSO

CHIEF CREATIVE OFFICER
JOE QUESADA

PUBLISHER
DAN BUCKLEY

EXECUTIVE PRODUCER
ALAN FINE

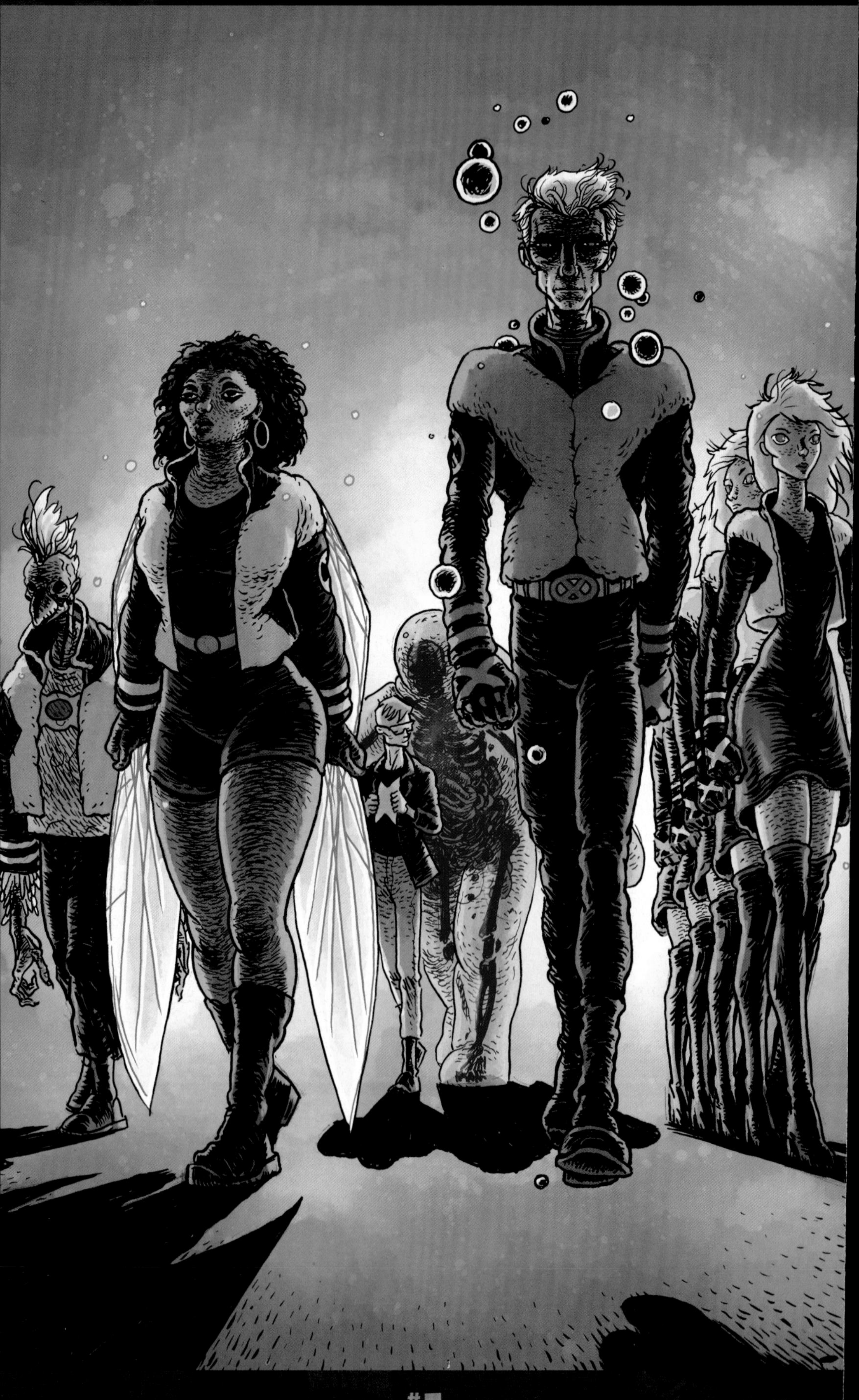

#1

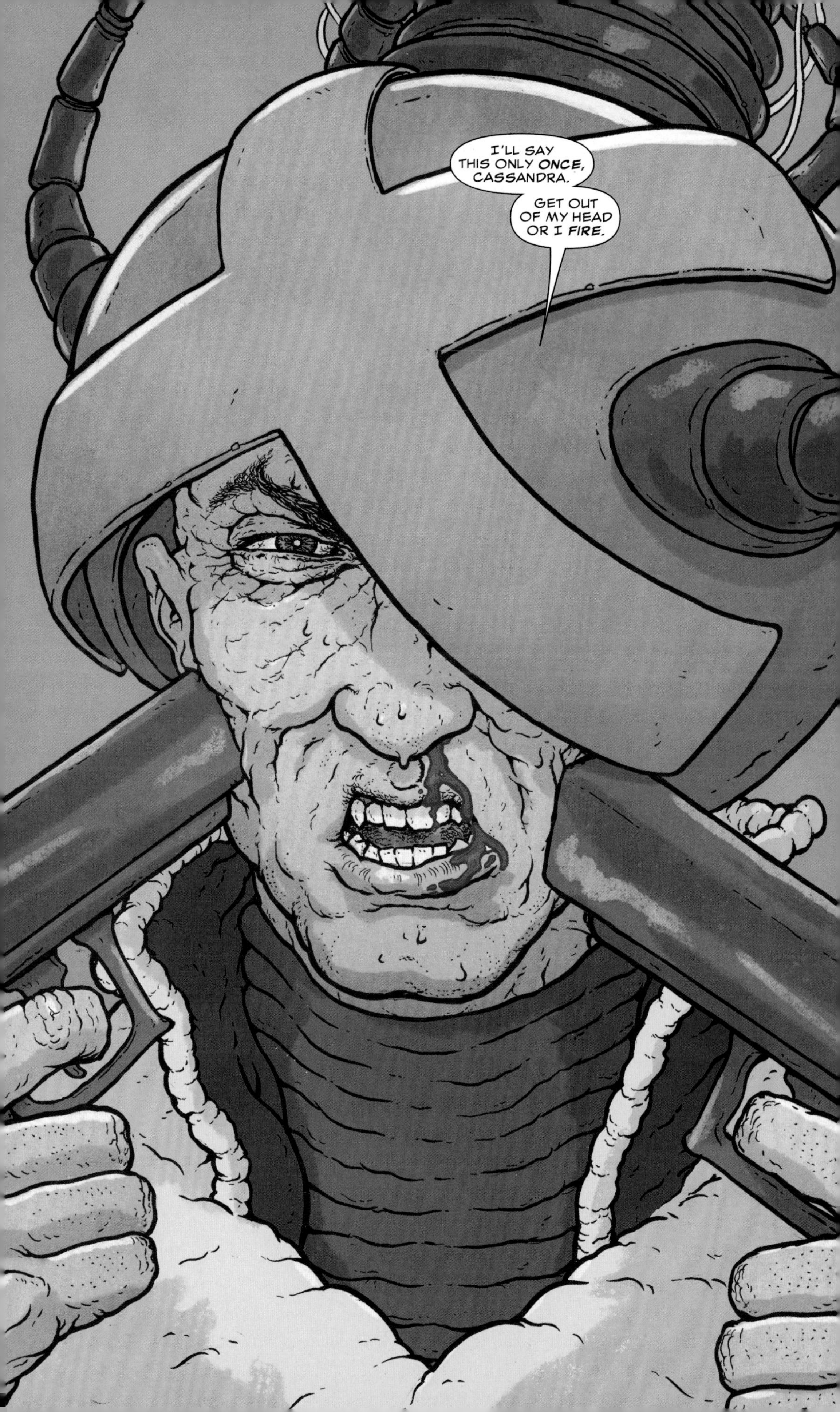
I'LL SAY THIS ONLY ONCE, CASSANDRA.
GET OUT OF MY HEAD OR I FIRE.

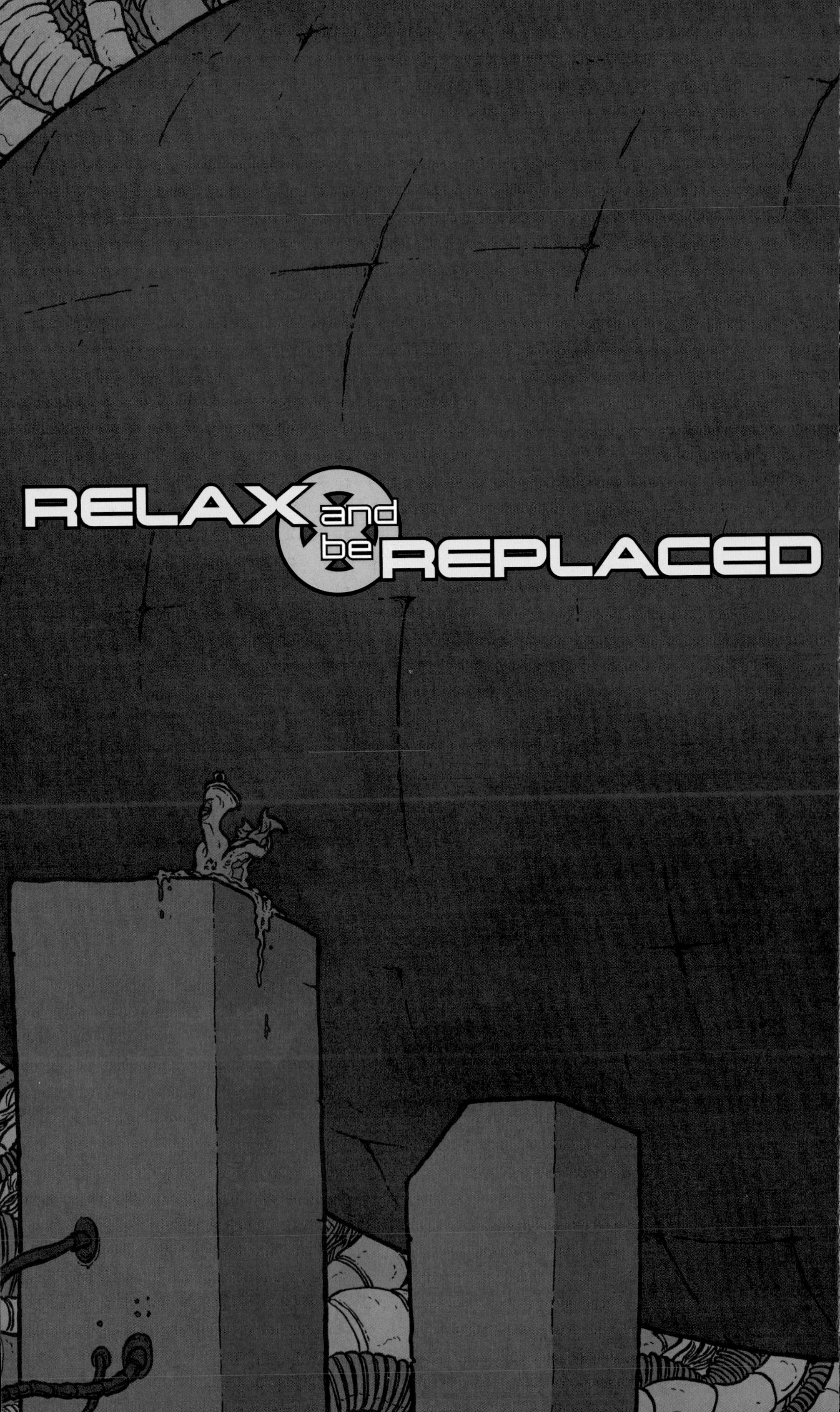
RELAX and be REPLACED

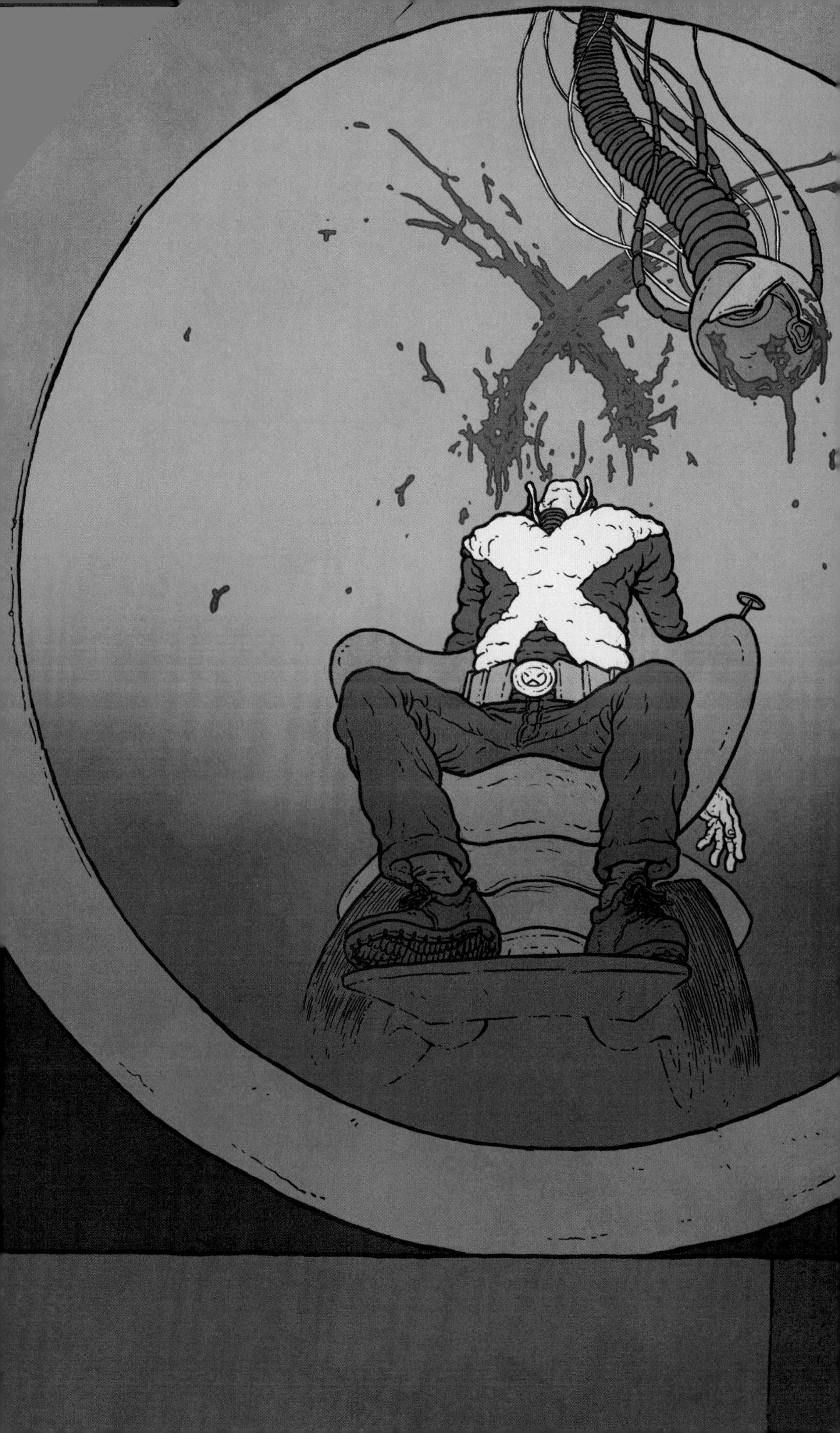

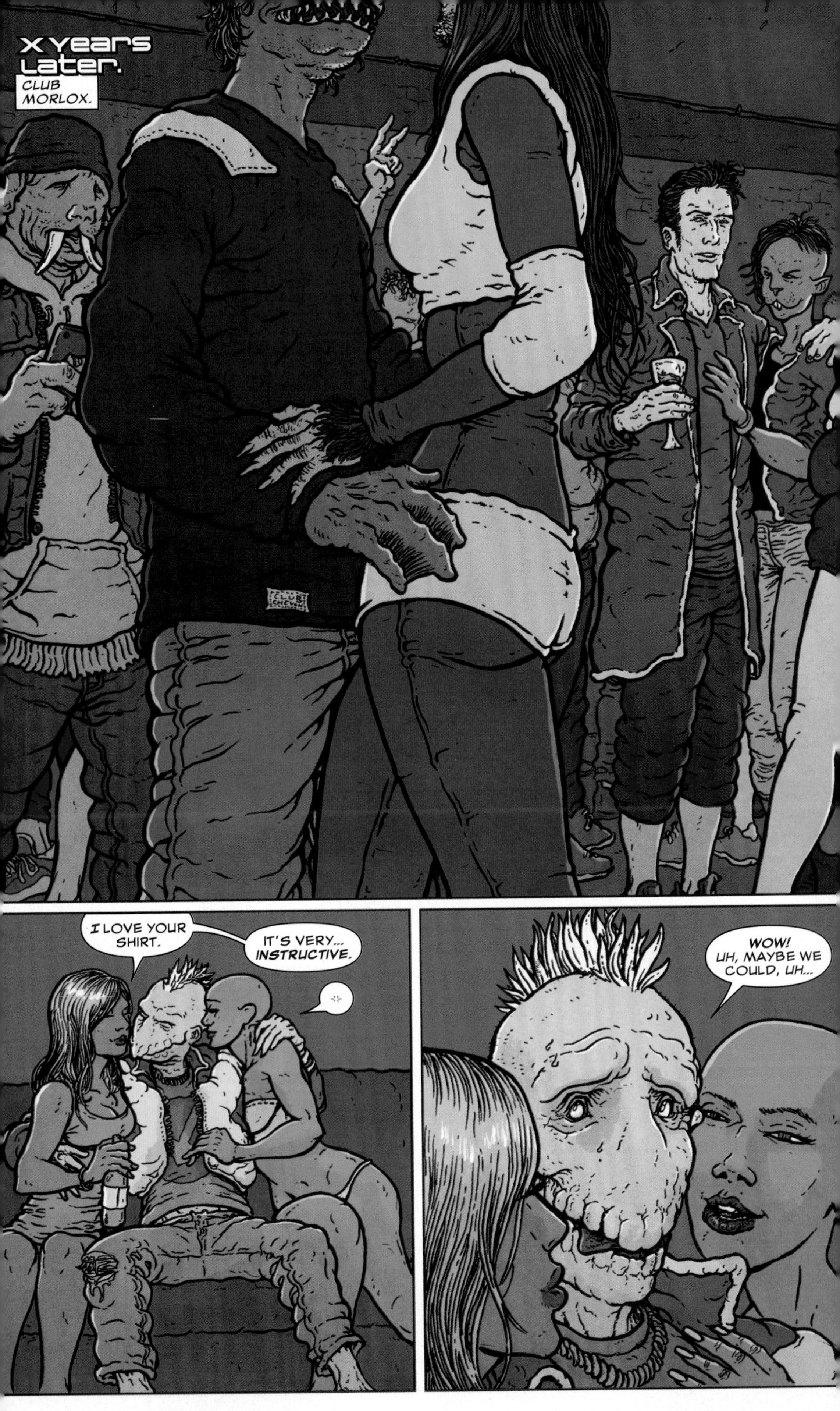
X Years Later.
CLUB MORLOX.
I LOVE YOUR SHIRT.
IT'S VERY... INSTRUCTIVE.
WOW! UH, MAYBE WE COULD, UH...

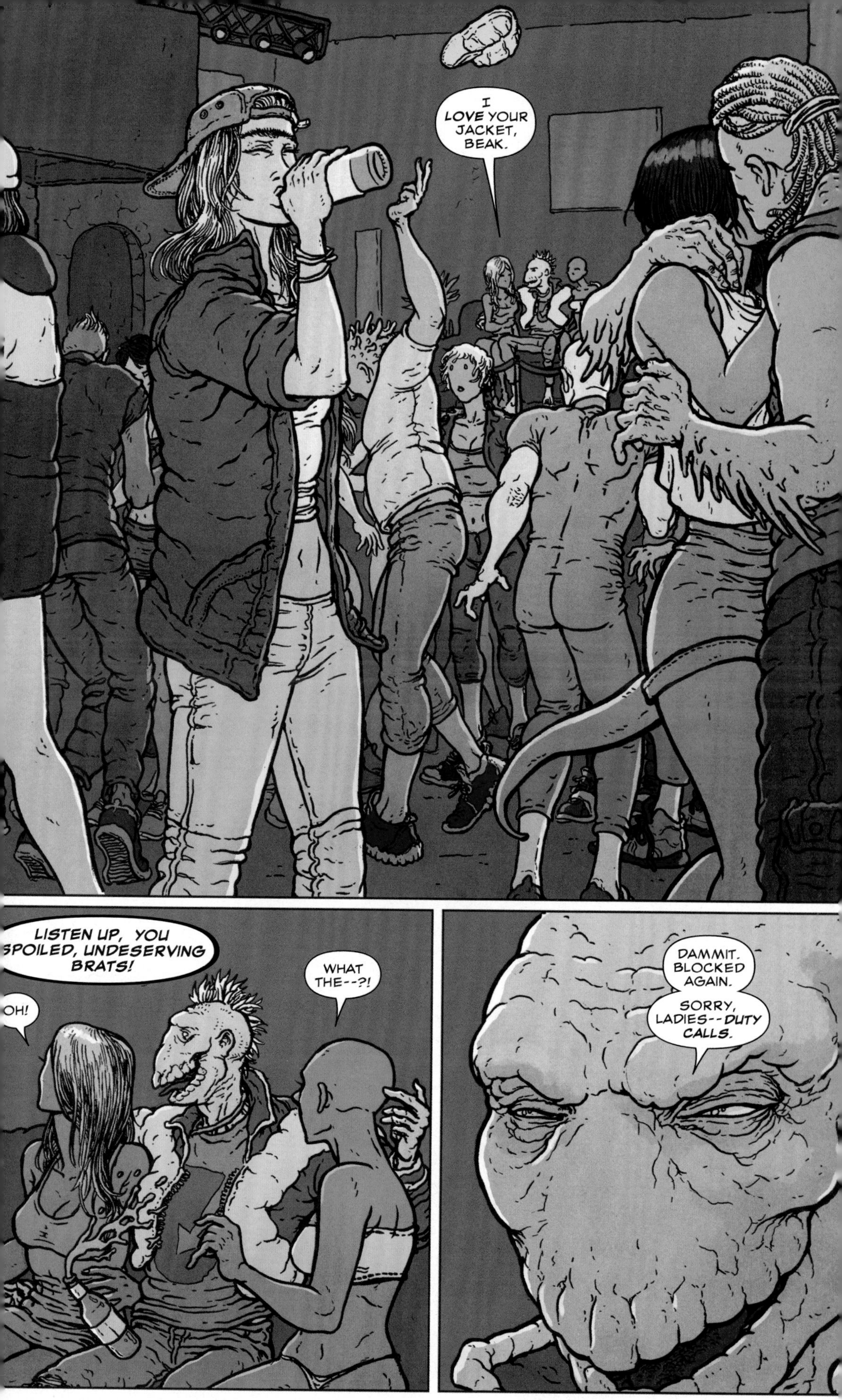
I LOVE YOUR JACKET, BEAK.
LISTEN UP, YOU SPOILED, UNDESERVING BRATS!
OH!
WHAT THE--?!
DAMMIT. BLOCKED AGAIN.
SORRY, LADIES--DUTY CALLS.

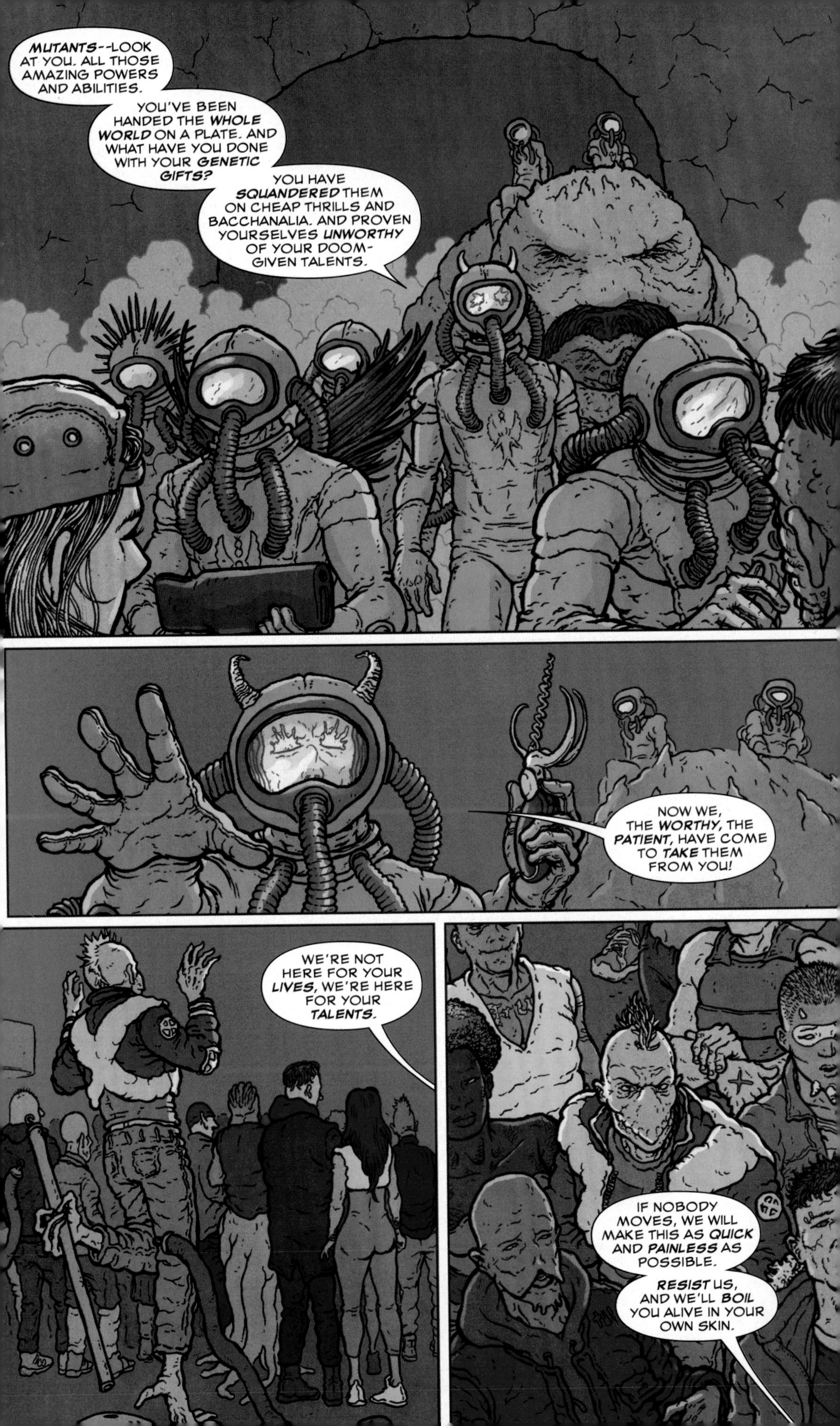
MUTANTS--LOOK AT YOU. ALL THOSE AMAZING POWERS AND ABILITIES.
YOU'VE BEEN HANDED THE WHOLE WORLD ON A PLATE. AND WHAT HAVE YOU DONE WITH YOUR GENETIC GIFTS?
YOU HAVE SQUANDERED THEM ON CHEAP THRILLS AND BACCHANALIA. AND PROVEN YOURSELVES UNWORTHY OF YOUR DOOM-GIVEN TALENTS.
NOW WE, THE WORTHY, THE PATIENT, HAVE COME TO TAKE THEM FROM YOU!
WE'RE NOT HERE FOR YOUR LIVES, WE'RE HERE FOR YOUR TALENTS.
IF NOBODY MOVES, WE WILL MAKE THIS AS QUICK AND PAINLESS AS POSSIBLE.
RESIST US, AND WE'LL BOIL YOU ALIVE IN YOUR OWN SKIN.

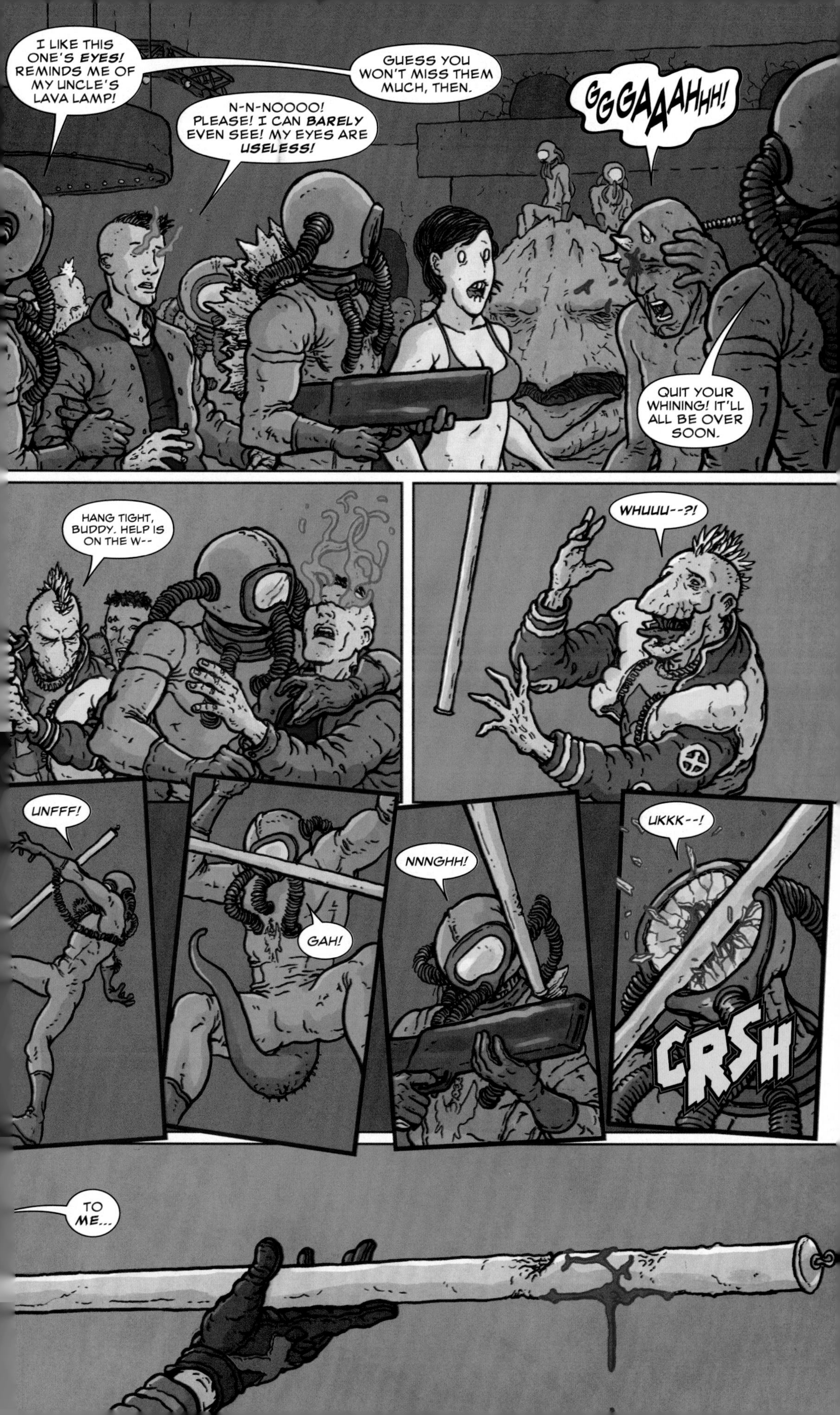

I LIKE THIS ONE'S EYES! REMINDS ME OF MY UNCLE'S LAVA LAMP!
GUESS YOU WON'T MISS THEM MUCH, THEN.
N-N-NOOOO! PLEASE! I CAN BARELY EVEN SEE! MY EYES ARE USELESS!
GGGAAAHHH!
QUIT YOUR WHINING! IT'LL ALL BE OVER SOON.
HANG TIGHT, BUDDY. HELP IS ON THE W--
WHUUU--?!
UNFFF!
GAH!
NNNGHH!
UKKK--!
CRSH
TO ME...

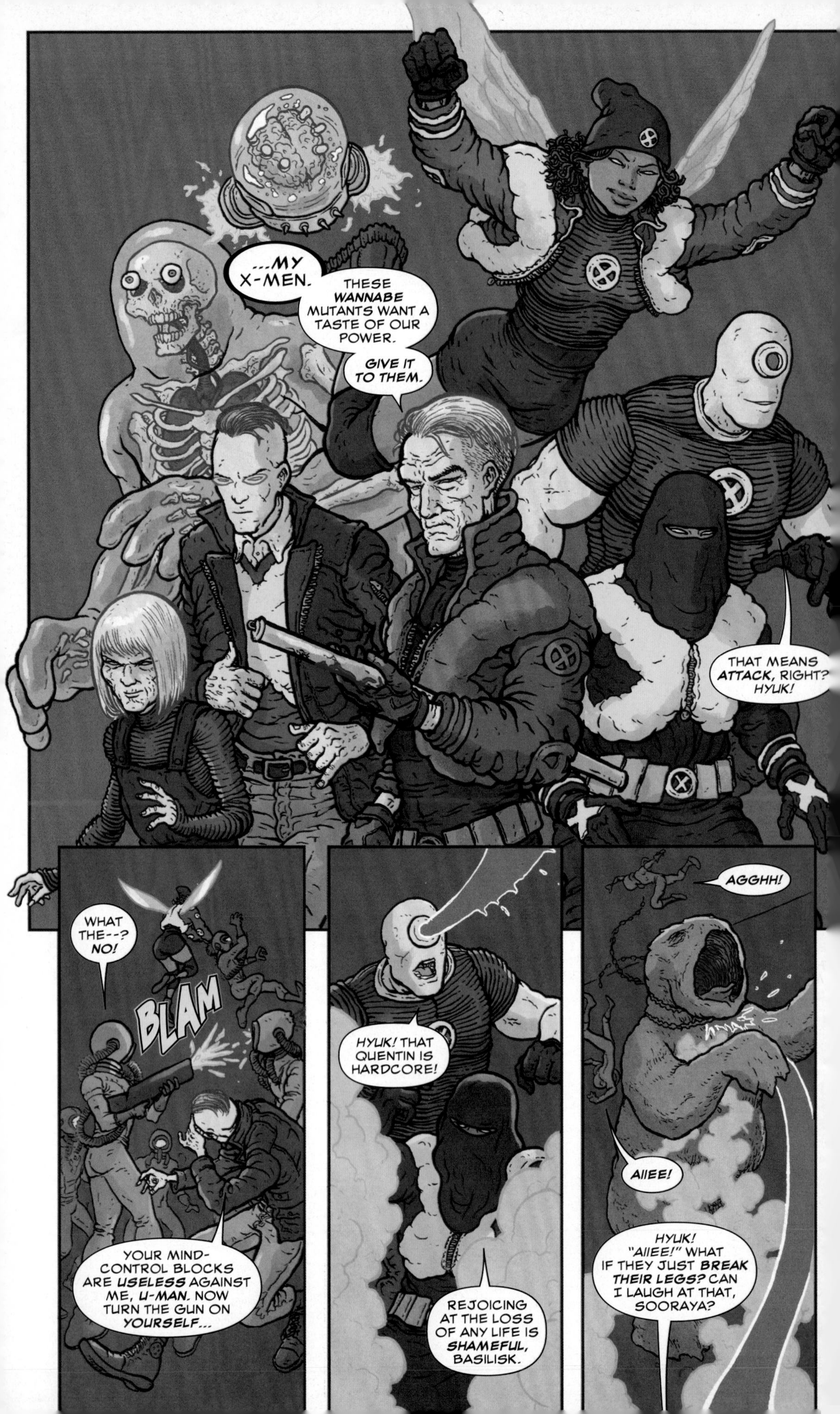
...MY X-MEN.
THESE WANNABE MUTANTS WANT A TASTE OF OUR POWER.
GIVE IT TO THEM.
THAT MEANS ATTACK, RIGHT? HYUK!
WHAT THE--? NO!
BLAM
YOUR MIND-CONTROL BLOCKS ARE USELESS AGAINST ME, U-MAN. NOW TURN THE GUN ON YOURSELF...
HYUK! THAT QUENTIN IS HARDCORE!
REJOICING AT THE LOSS OF ANY LIFE IS SHAMEFUL, BASILISK.
AGGHH!
AIIEE!
HYUK! "AIIEE!" WHAT IF THEY JUST BREAK THEIR LEGS? CAN I LAUGH AT THAT, SOORAYA?

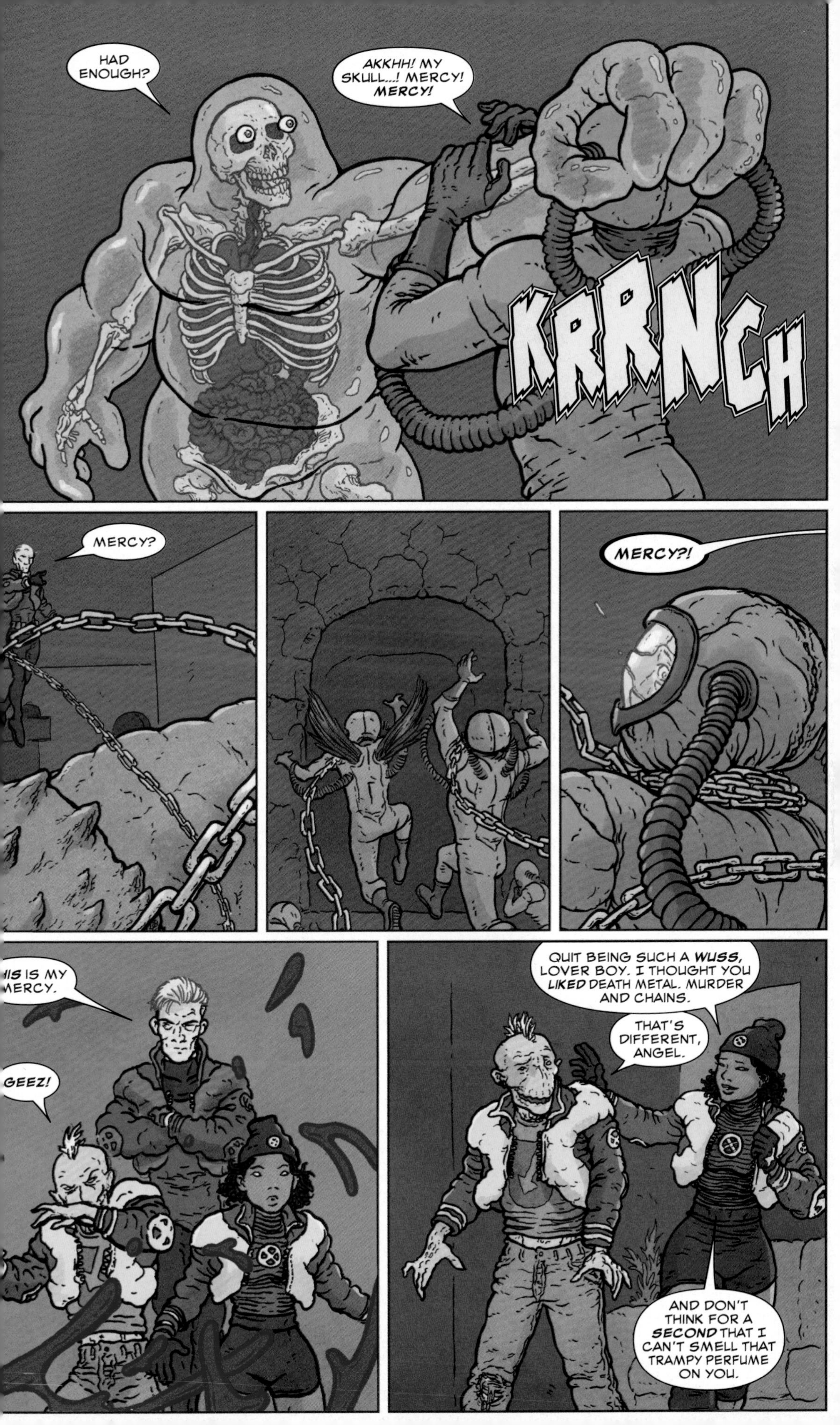
HAD ENOUGH?
AKKHH! MY SKULL...! MERCY! MERCY!
KRRNCH
MERCY?
MERCY?!
IS IS MY ERCY.
GEEZ!
QUIT BEING SUCH A WUSS, LOVER BOY. I THOUGHT YOU LIKED DEATH METAL. MURDER AND CHAINS.
THAT'S DIFFERENT, ANGEL.
AND DON'T THINK FOR A SECOND THAT I CAN'T SMELL THAT TRAMPY PERFUME ON YOU.

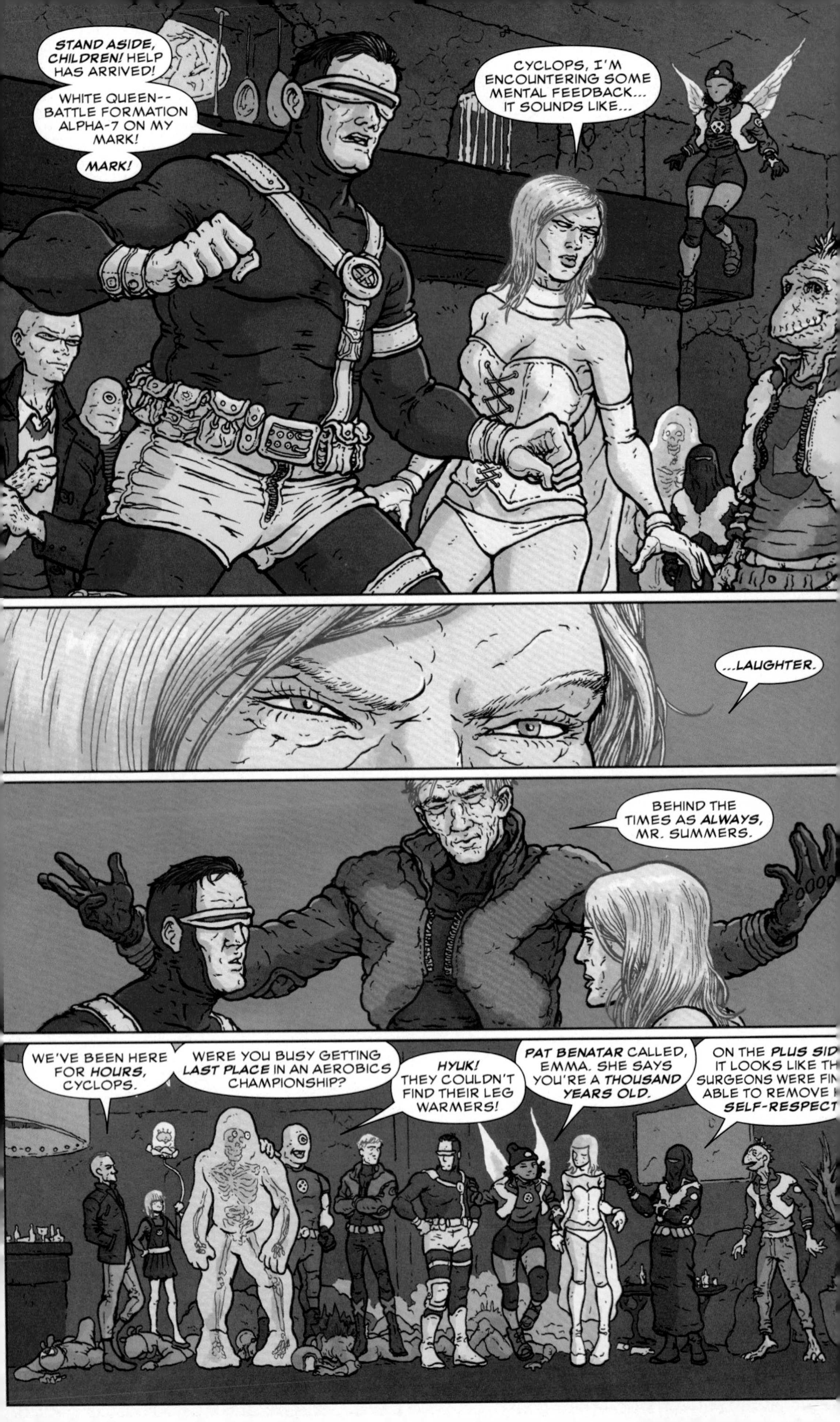
STAND ASIDE, CHILDREN! HELP HAS ARRIVED!
WHITE QUEEN-- BATTLE FORMATION ALPHA-7 ON MY MARK!
MARK!
CYCLOPS, I'M ENCOUNTERING SOME MENTAL FEEDBACK... IT SOUNDS LIKE...
...LAUGHTER.
BEHIND THE TIMES AS ALWAYS, MR. SUMMERS.
WE'VE BEEN HERE FOR HOURS, CYCLOPS.
WERE YOU BUSY GETTING LAST PLACE IN AN AEROBICS CHAMPIONSHIP?
HYUK! THEY COULDN'T FIND THEIR LEG WARMERS!
PAT BENATAR CALLED, EMMA. SHE SAYS YOU'RE A THOUSAND YEARS OLD.

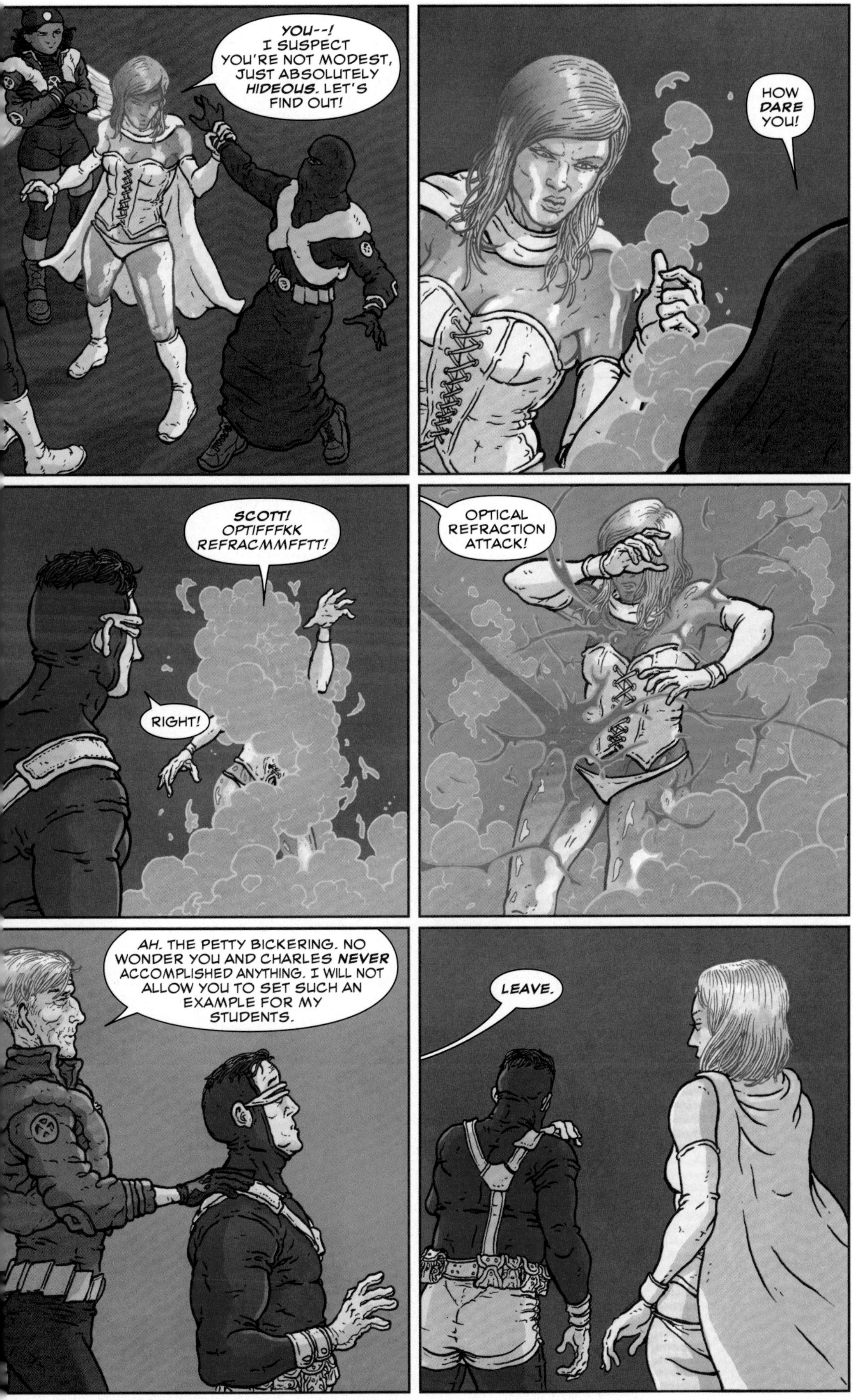
YOU--! I SUSPECT YOU'RE NOT MODEST, JUST ABSOLUTELY HIDEOUS. LET'S FIND OUT!
HOW DARE YOU!
SCOTT! OPTIFFFKK REFRACMMFFTT!
RIGHT!
OPTICAL REFRACTION ATTACK!
AH. THE PETTY BICKERING. NO WONDER YOU AND CHARLES NEVER ACCOMPLISHED ANYTHING. I WILL NOT ALLOW YOU TO SET SUCH AN EXAMPLE FOR MY STUDENTS.
LEAVE.

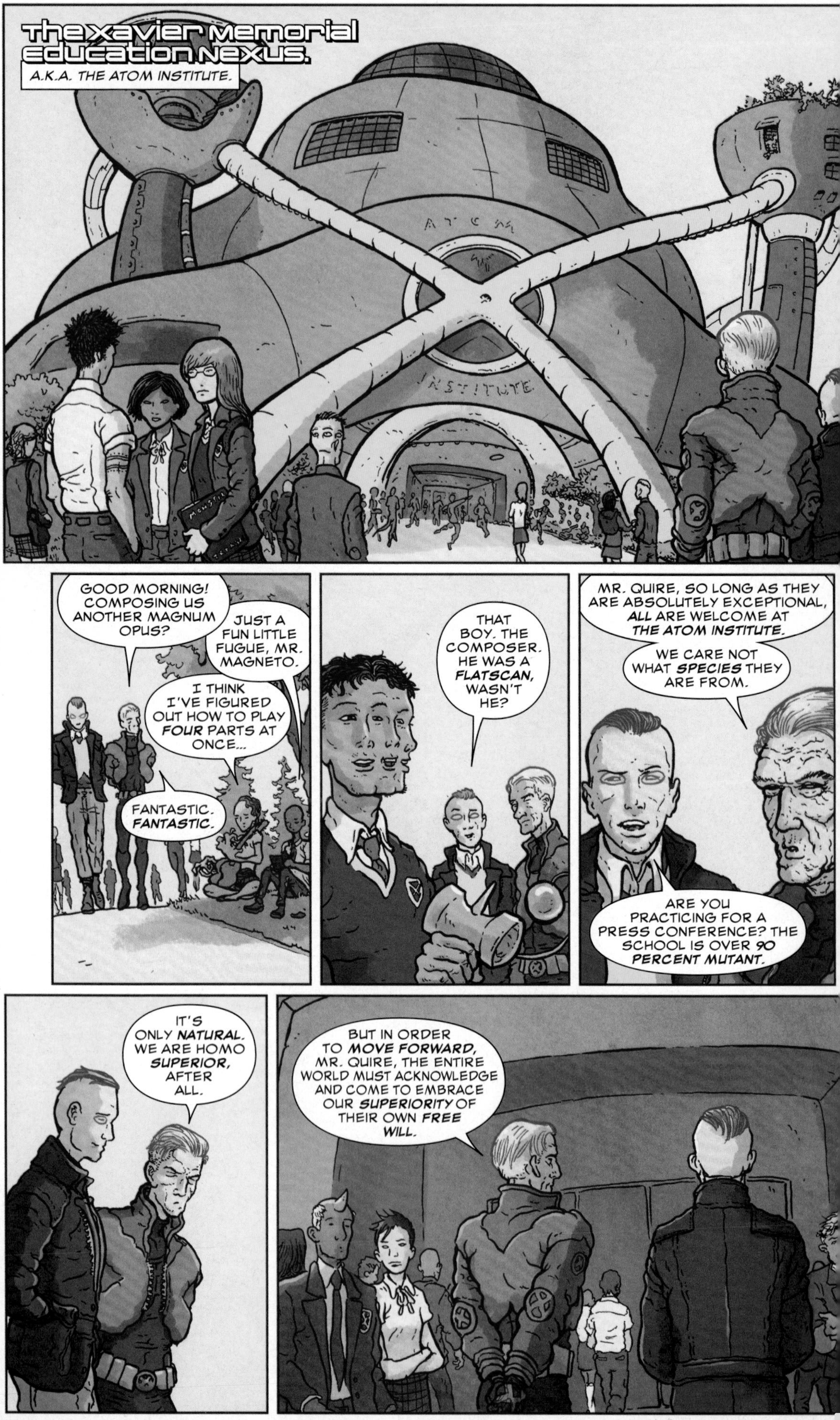

The Xavier Memorial Education Nexus.
A.K.A. THE ATOM INSTITUTE.
ATOM
INSTITUTE
GOOD MORNING! COMPOSING US ANOTHER MAGNUM OPUS?
JUST A FUN LITTLE FUGUE, MR. MAGNETO.
I THINK I'VE FIGURED OUT HOW TO PLAY FOUR PARTS AT ONCE...
FANTASTIC. FANTASTIC.
THAT BOY. THE COMPOSER. HE WAS A FLATSCAN, WASN'T HE?
MR. QUIRE, SO LONG AS THEY ARE ABSOLUTELY EXCEPTIONAL, ALL ARE WELCOME AT THE ATOM INSTITUTE.
WE CARE NOT WHAT SPECIES THEY ARE FROM.
ARE YOU PRACTICING FOR A PRESS CONFERENCE? THE SCHOOL IS OVER 90 PERCENT MUTANT.
IT'S ONLY NATURAL. WE ARE HOMO SUPERIOR, AFTER ALL.
BUT IN ORDER TO MOVE FORWARD, MR. QUIRE, THE ENTIRE WORLD MUST ACKNOWLEDGE AND COME TO EMBRACE OUR SUPERIORITY OF THEIR OWN FREE WILL.

I WASTED **DECADES** TRYING TO SET MUTANTKIND APART FROM HUMANITY.

WHAT **WAS I** THINKING?

DON'T BE SO HARD ON YOURSELF, MAGNETO. IT'S NOT *YOUR* FAULT THAT YOU'RE SO OLD.

NO, I SUPPOSE NOT.

QUENTIN, WHAT YOU ARE ABOUT TO SEE, I'VE NEVER SHOWN TO ANYONE ALIVE. *I TRUST YOU.* AS A MATTER OF FACT, YOU REMIND ME OF *ME*.

MY ACTUAL CHILDREN HAVE ALL BEEN **DISAPPOINTMENTS** THUS FAR.

YOU, I HAVE FAITH IN.

WHEN CHARLES *KILLED HIMSELF*, HE WAS IN MENTAL CONTACT WITH JEAN GREY, THE IDEAL FEMALE FORM AND CONTAINER OF *THE PHOENIX FORCE*. THE PSYCHIC FEEDBACK KNOCKED HER INTO A *COMA.*

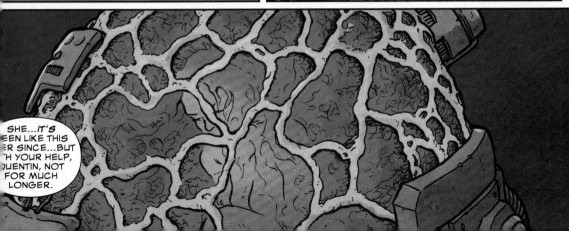

SHE...*IT'S* BEEN LIKE THIS EVER SINCE...BUT WITH YOUR HELP, QUENTIN, NOT FOR MUCH LONGER.

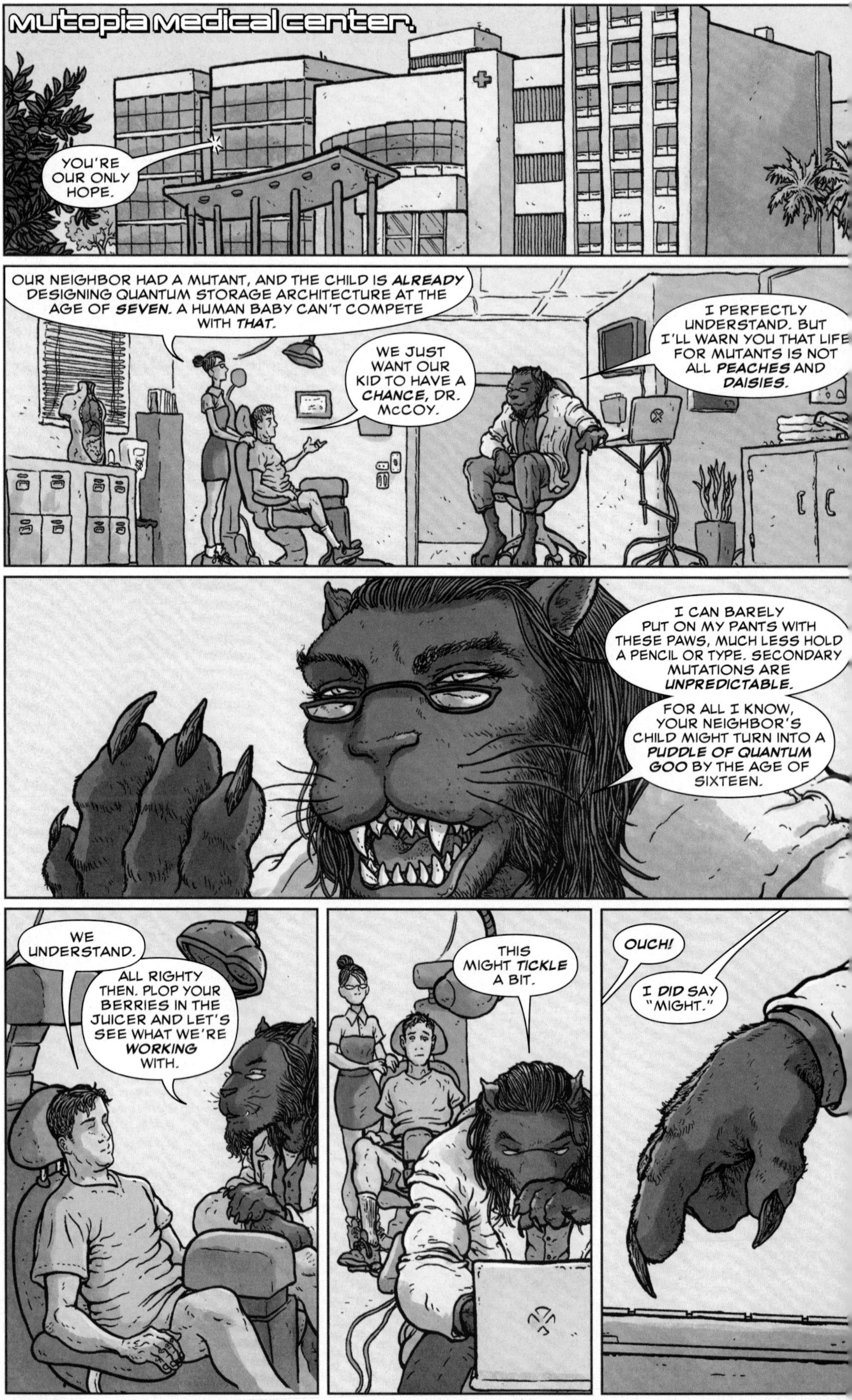
MUTOPIA MEDICAL CENTER.
YOU'RE OUR ONLY HOPE.
OUR NEIGHBOR HAD A MUTANT, AND THE CHILD IS ALREADY DESIGNING QUANTUM STORAGE ARCHITECTURE AT THE AGE OF SEVEN. A HUMAN BABY CAN'T COMPETE WITH THAT.
WE JUST WANT OUR KID TO HAVE A CHANCE, DR. McCOY.
I PERFECTLY UNDERSTAND. BUT I'LL WARN YOU THAT LIFE FOR MUTANTS IS NOT ALL PEACHES AND DAISIES.
I CAN BARELY PUT ON MY PANTS WITH THESE PAWS, MUCH LESS HOLD A PENCIL OR TYPE. SECONDARY MUTATIONS ARE UNPREDICTABLE.
FOR ALL I KNOW, YOUR NEIGHBOR'S CHILD MIGHT TURN INTO A PUDDLE OF QUANTUM GOO BY THE AGE OF SIXTEEN.
WE UNDERSTAND.
ALL RIGHTY THEN. PLOP YOUR BERRIES IN THE JUICER AND LET'S SEE WHAT WE'RE WORKING WITH.
THIS MIGHT TICKLE A BIT.
OUCH!
I DID SAY "MIGHT."

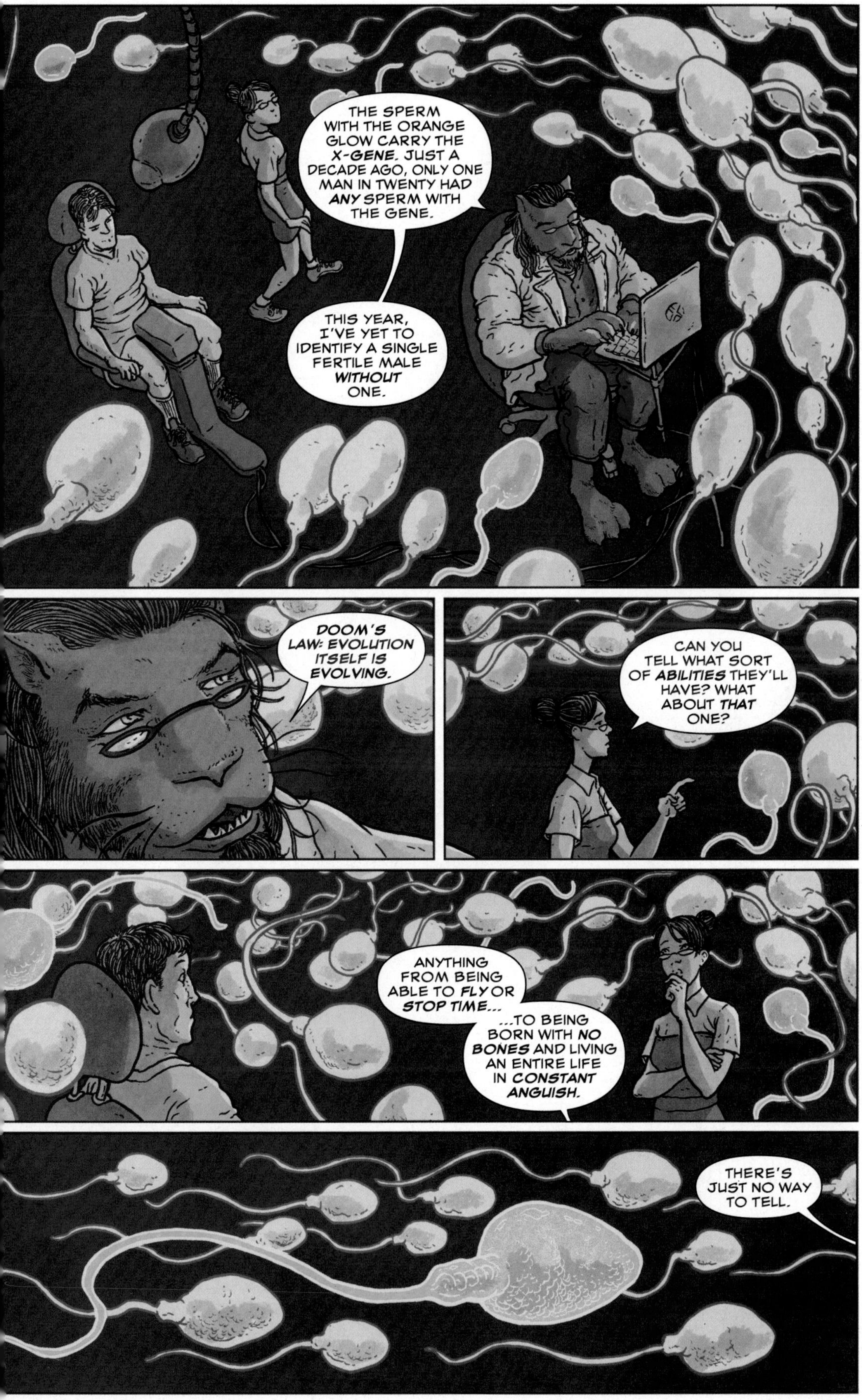
THE SPERM WITH THE ORANGE GLOW CARRY THE X-GENE. JUST A DECADE AGO, ONLY ONE MAN IN TWENTY HAD ANY SPERM WITH THE GENE.
THIS YEAR, I'VE YET TO IDENTIFY A SINGLE FERTILE MALE WITHOUT ONE.
DOOM'S LAW: EVOLUTION ITSELF IS EVOLVING.
CAN YOU TELL WHAT SORT OF ABILITIES THEY'LL HAVE? WHAT ABOUT THAT ONE?
ANYTHING FROM BEING ABLE TO FLY OR STOP TIME...
...TO BEING BORN WITH NO BONES AND LIVING AN ENTIRE LIFE IN CONSTANT ANGUISH.
THERE'S JUST NO WAY TO TELL.

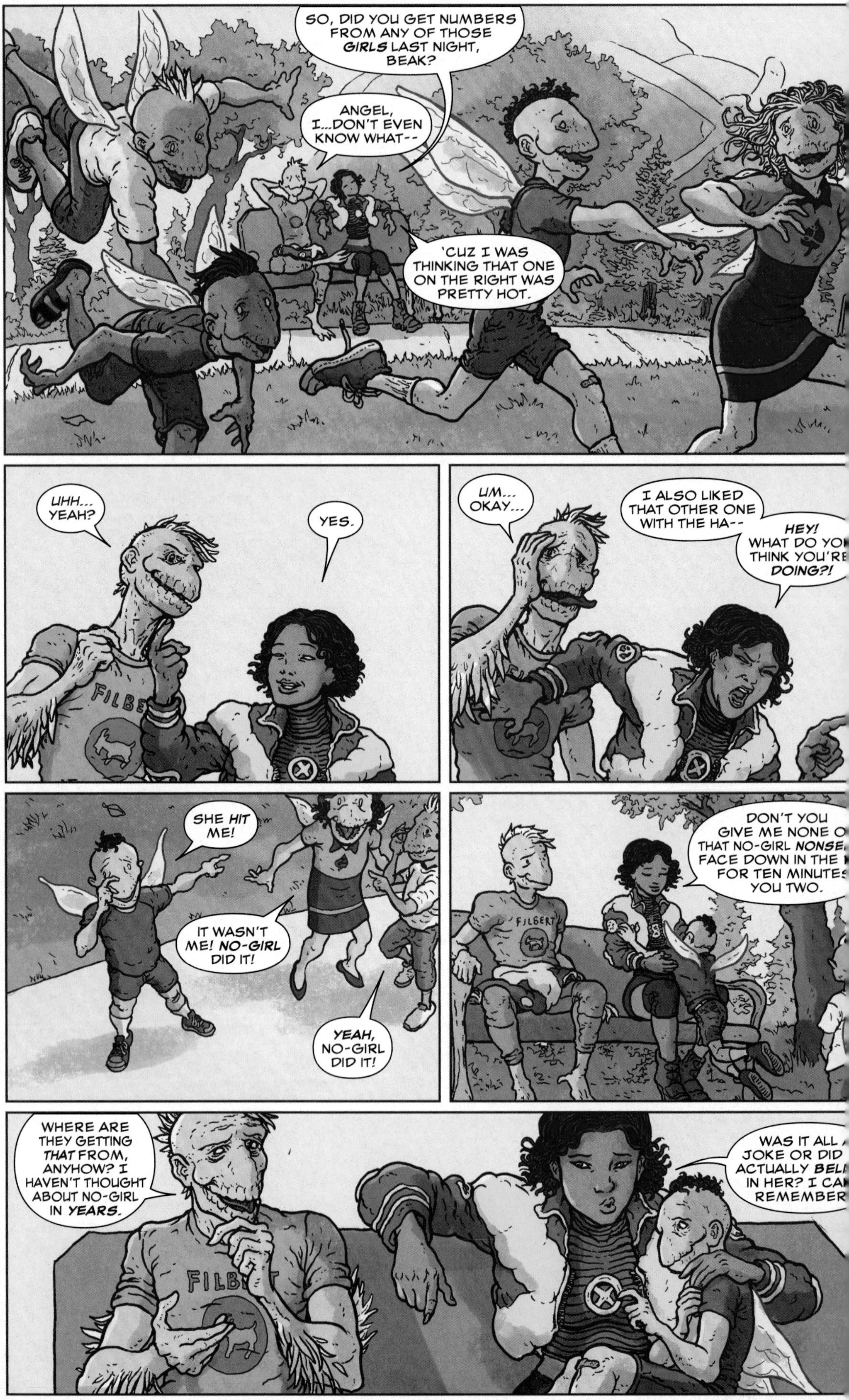
SO, DID YOU GET NUMBERS FROM ANY OF THOSE GIRLS LAST NIGHT, BEAK?
ANGEL, I...DON'T EVEN KNOW WHAT--
'CUZ I WAS THINKING THAT ONE ON THE RIGHT WAS PRETTY HOT.
UHH... YEAH?
YES.
UM... OKAY...
I ALSO LIKED THAT OTHER ONE WITH THE HA--
HEY! WHAT DO YO THINK YOU'RE DOING?!
SHE HIT ME!
IT WASN'T ME! NO-GIRL DID IT!
YEAH, NO-GIRL DID IT!
DON'T YOU GIVE ME NONE O THAT NO-GIRL NONSE FACE DOWN IN THE FOR TEN MINUTE YOU TWO.
WHERE ARE THEY GETTING THAT FROM, ANYHOW? I HAVEN'T THOUGHT ABOUT NO-GIRL IN YEARS.
WAS IT ALL JOKE OR DID ACTUALLY BEL IN HER? I CA REMEMBER

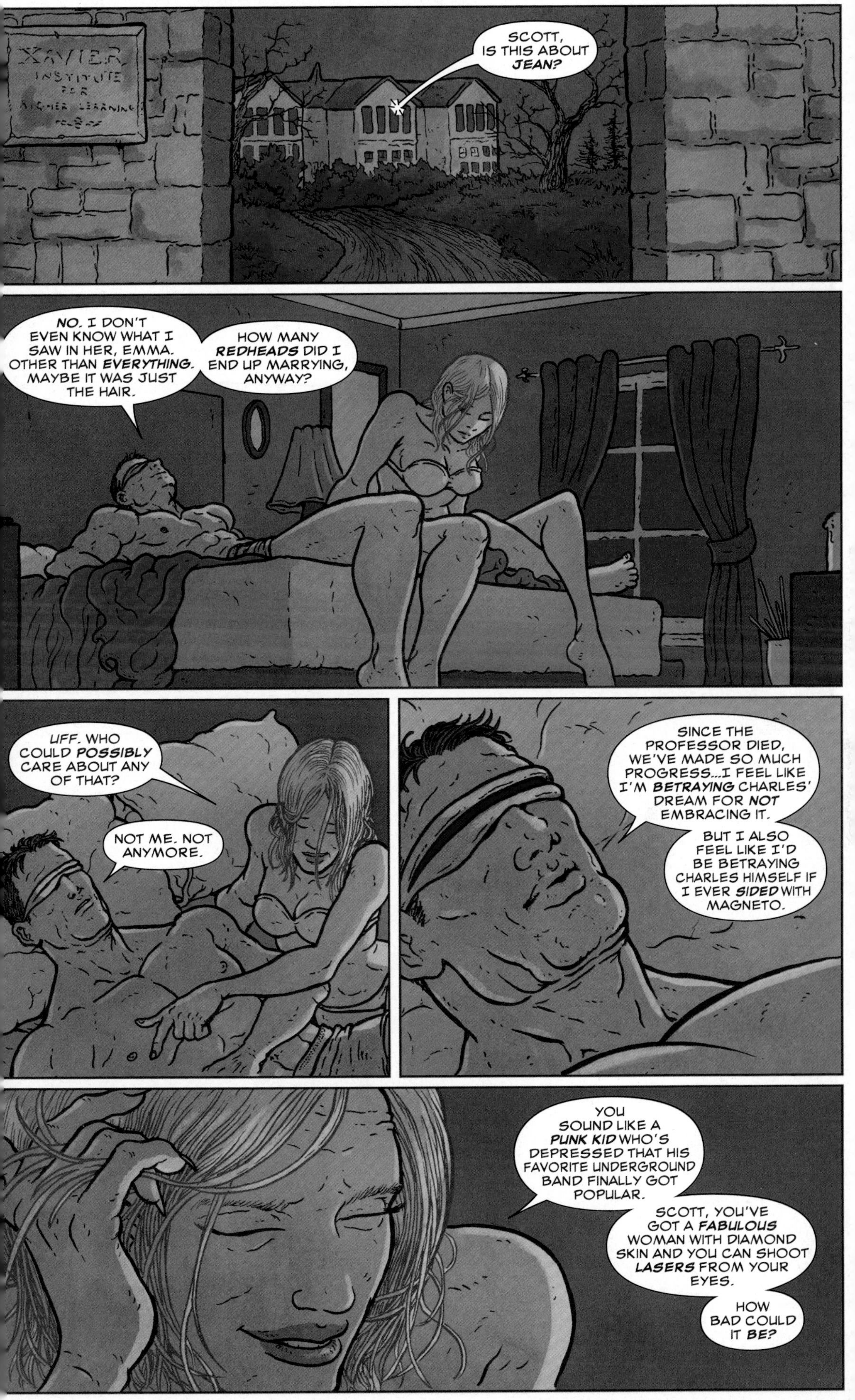
XAVIER INSTITUTE FOR HIGHER LEARNING
SCOTT, IS THIS ABOUT JEAN?
NO. I DON'T EVEN KNOW WHAT I SAW IN HER, EMMA. OTHER THAN EVERYTHING. MAYBE IT WAS JUST THE HAIR.
HOW MANY REDHEADS DID I END UP MARRYING, ANYWAY?
UFF. WHO COULD POSSIBLY CARE ABOUT ANY OF THAT?
NOT ME. NOT ANYMORE.
SINCE THE PROFESSOR DIED, WE'VE MADE SO MUCH PROGRESS...I FEEL LIKE I'M BETRAYING CHARLES' DREAM FOR NOT EMBRACING IT.
BUT I ALSO FEEL LIKE I'D BE BETRAYING CHARLES HIMSELF IF I EVER SIDED WITH MAGNETO.
YOU SOUND LIKE A PUNK KID WHO'S DEPRESSED THAT HIS FAVORITE UNDERGROUND BAND FINALLY GOT POPULAR.
SCOTT, YOU'VE GOT A FABULOUS WOMAN WITH DIAMOND SKIN AND YOU CAN SHOOT LASERS FROM YOUR EYES.
HOW BAD COULD IT BE?

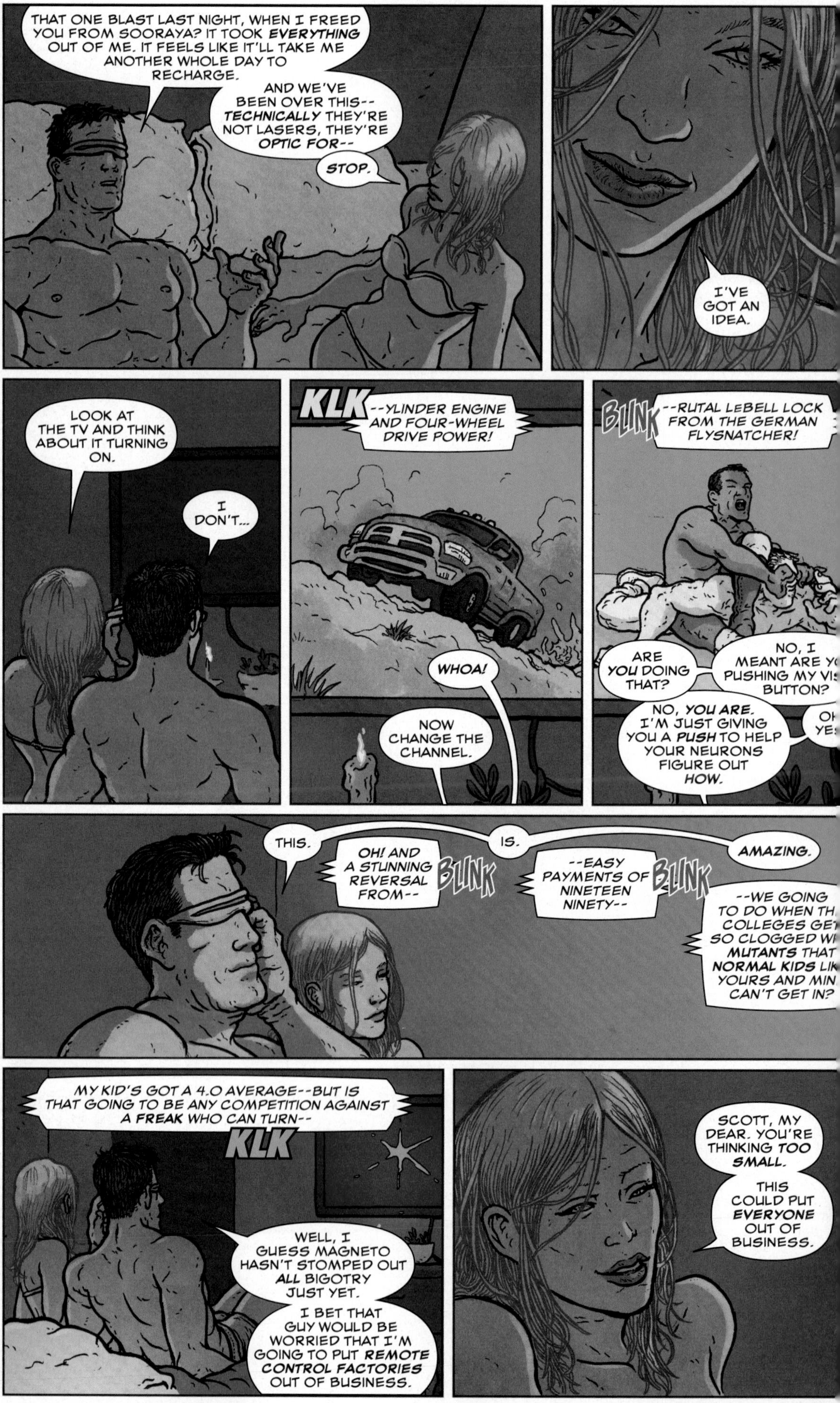
THAT ONE BLAST LAST NIGHT, WHEN I FREED YOU FROM SOORAYA? IT TOOK EVERYTHING OUT OF ME. IT FEELS LIKE IT'LL TAKE ME ANOTHER WHOLE DAY TO RECHARGE.
AND WE'VE BEEN OVER THIS--TECHNICALLY THEY'RE NOT LASERS, THEY'RE OPTIC FOR--
STOP.
I'VE GOT AN IDEA.
LOOK AT THE TV AND THINK ABOUT IT TURNING ON.
I DON'T...
KLK
--YLINDER ENGINE AND FOUR-WHEEL DRIVE POWER!
WHOA!
NOW CHANGE THE CHANNEL.
BLINK
--RUTAL LEBELL LOCK FROM THE GERMAN FLYSNATCHER!
ARE YOU DOING THAT?
NO, I MEANT ARE Y PUSHING MY VI BUTTON?
NO, YOU ARE. I'M JUST GIVING YOU A PUSH TO HELP YOUR NEURONS FIGURE OUT HOW.
OH YE
THIS.
IS.
AMAZING.
OH! AND A STUNNING REVERSAL FROM--
BLINK
--EASY PAYMENTS OF NINETEEN NINETY--
BLINK
--WE GOING TO DO WHEN TH COLLEGES GE SO CLOGGED W MUTANTS THAT NORMAL KIDS LI YOURS AND MIN CAN'T GET IN?
MY KID'S GOT A 4.0 AVERAGE--BUT IS THAT GOING TO BE ANY COMPETITION AGAINST A FREAK WHO CAN TURN--
KLK
WELL, I GUESS MAGNETO HASN'T STOMPED OUT ALL BIGOTRY JUST YET.
I BET THAT GUY WOULD BE WORRIED THAT I'M GOING TO PUT REMOTE CONTROL FACTORIES OUT OF BUSINESS.
SCOTT, MY DEAR. YOU'RE THINKING TOO SMALL.
THIS COULD PUT EVERYONE OUT OF BUSINESS.

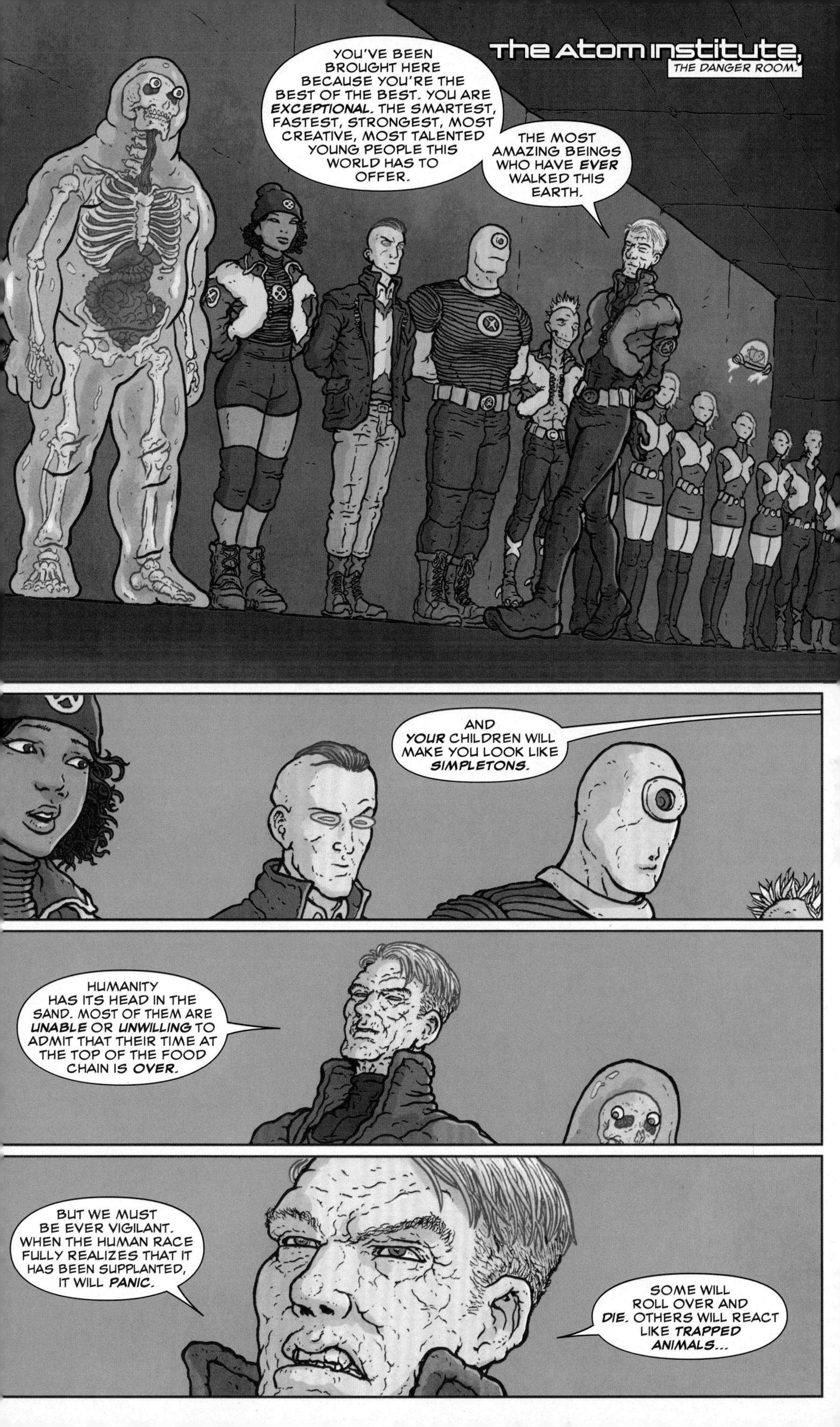
The Atom Institute,
THE DANGER ROOM.
YOU'VE BEEN BROUGHT HERE BECAUSE YOU'RE THE BEST OF THE BEST. YOU ARE EXCEPTIONAL. THE SMARTEST, FASTEST, STRONGEST, MOST CREATIVE, MOST TALENTED YOUNG PEOPLE THIS WORLD HAS TO OFFER.
THE MOST AMAZING BEINGS WHO HAVE EVER WALKED THIS EARTH.
AND YOUR CHILDREN WILL MAKE YOU LOOK LIKE SIMPLETONS.
HUMANITY HAS ITS HEAD IN THE SAND. MOST OF THEM ARE UNABLE OR UNWILLING TO ADMIT THAT THEIR TIME AT THE TOP OF THE FOOD CHAIN IS OVER.
BUT WE MUST BE EVER VIGILANT. WHEN THE HUMAN RACE FULLY REALIZES THAT IT HAS BEEN SUPPLANTED, IT WILL PANIC.
SOME WILL ROLL OVER AND DIE. OTHERS WILL REACT LIKE TRAPPED ANIMALS...

...AND ATTACK!

SOORAYA! SET UP A SAND SCREEN!

AS YOU WISH.

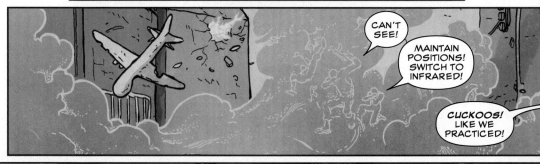

CAN'T SEE!

MAINTAIN POSITIONS! SWITCH TO INFRARED!

CUCKOOS! LIKE WE PRACTICED!

WE

DON'T

NEED

YOUR

INSTRUCTIO

QUENTIN!

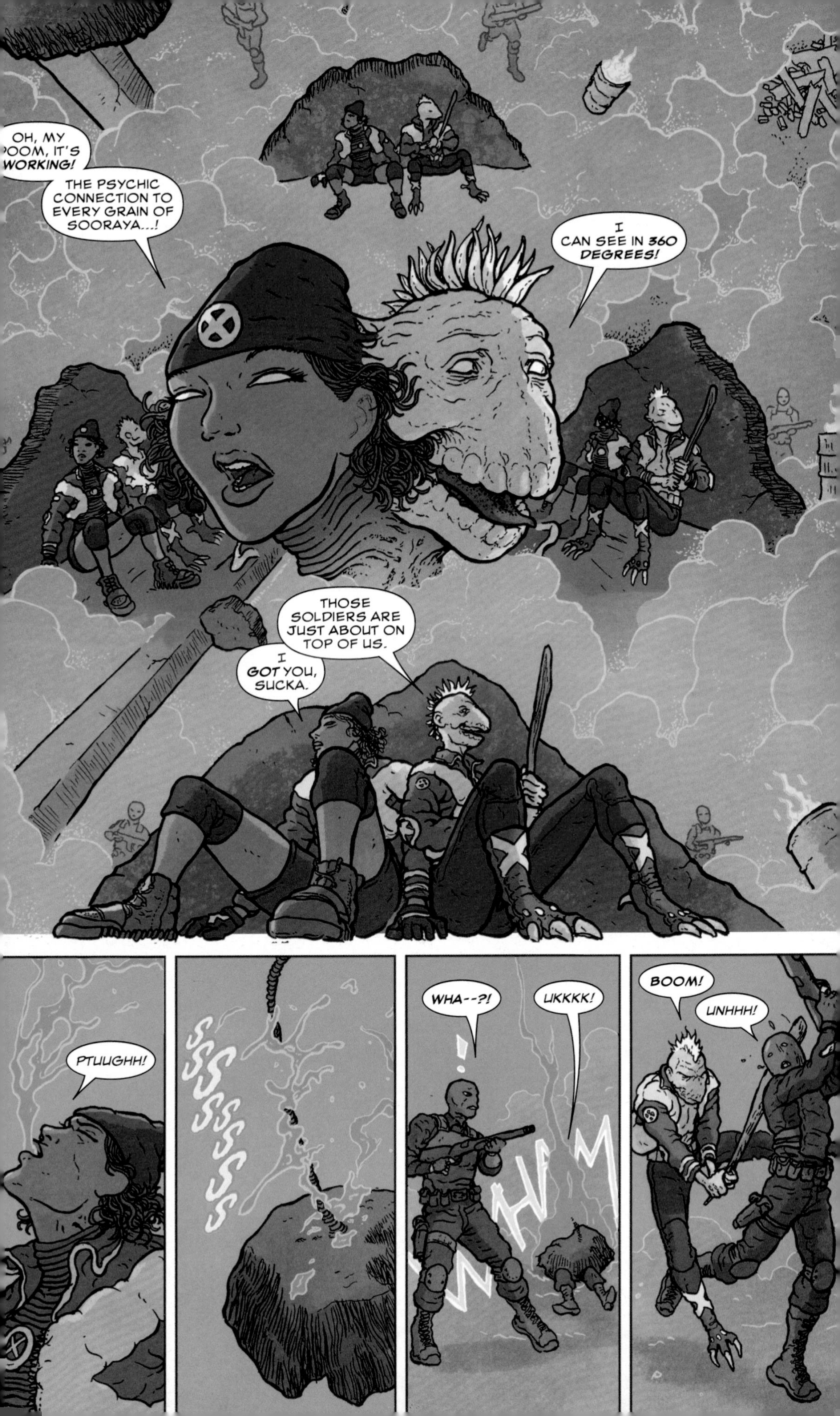
OH, MY DOOM, IT'S WORKING!
THE PSYCHIC CONNECTION TO EVERY GRAIN OF SOORAYA...!
I CAN SEE IN 360 DEGREES!
THOSE SOLDIERS ARE JUST ABOUT ON TOP OF US.
I GOT YOU, SUCKA.
PTUUGHH!
SSSSSSSSS
WHA--?!
!
UKKKK!
WHAM
BOOM!
UNHHH!

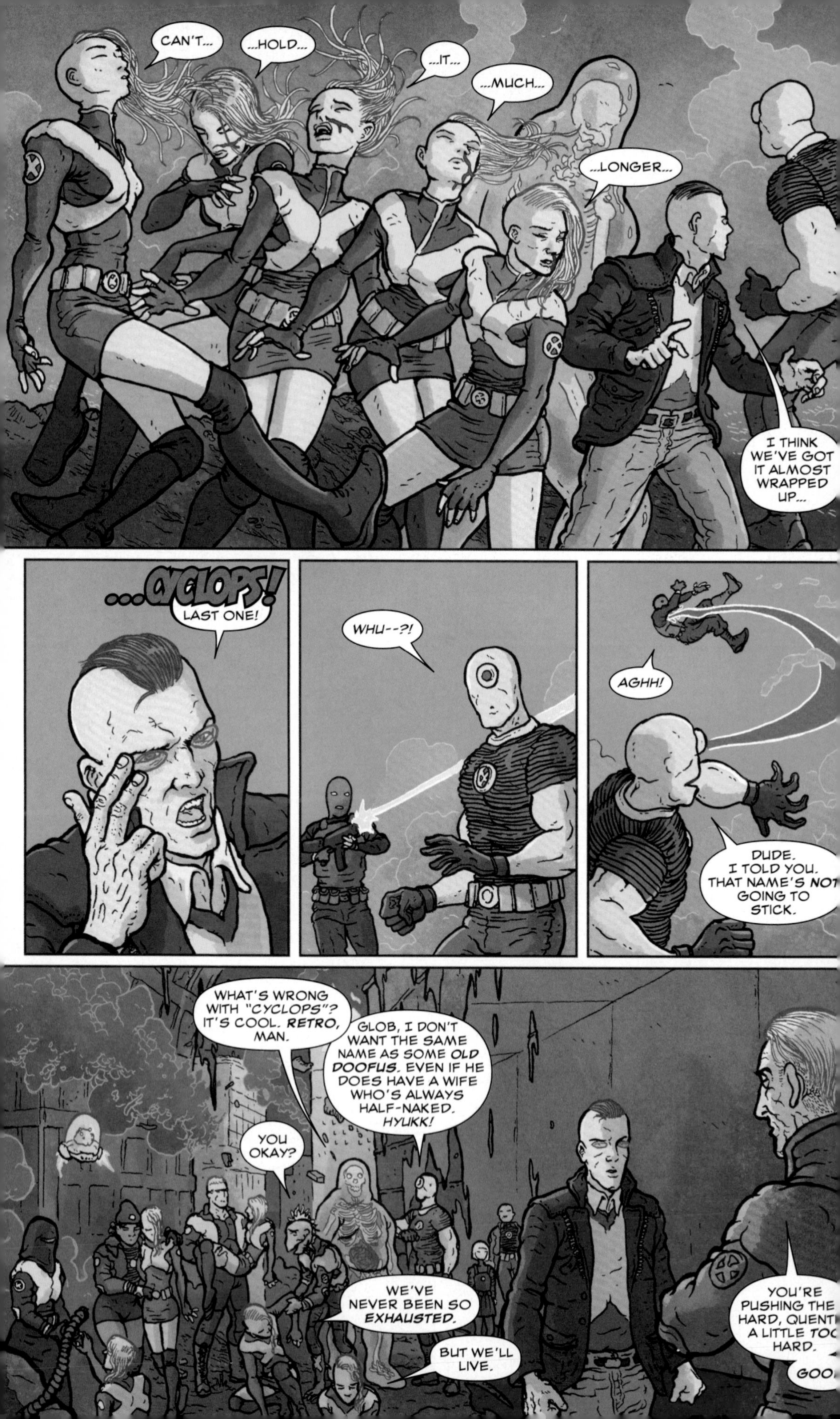
CAN'T...
...HOLD...
...IT...
...MUCH...
...LONGER...
I THINK WE'VE GOT IT ALMOST WRAPPED UP...
...CYCLOPS!
LAST ONE!
WHU--?!
AGHH!
DUDE. I TOLD YOU. THAT NAME'S NOT GOING TO STICK.
WHAT'S WRONG WITH "CYCLOPS"? IT'S COOL. RETRO, MAN.
GLOB, I DON'T WANT THE SAME NAME AS SOME OLD DOOFUS. EVEN IF HE DOES HAVE A WIFE WHO'S ALWAYS HALF-NAKED. HYUKK!
YOU OKAY?
WE'VE NEVER BEEN SO EXHAUSTED.
BUT WE'LL LIVE.
YOU'RE PUSHING THE HARD, QUENT A LITTLE TOO HARD.
GOO

YOU'RE THE *WOLVERINE*, AIN'T CHA?

...

I TELL YOU WHAT, *WOLVIE*, WHOEVER GAVE YOU THAT NAME MUSTA BEEN *BLIND*...

...'CUZ YOU LOOK LIKE A FREAKIN' *OWL!*

HAHAHAHA! SPIN YOUR HEAD AROUND! *SPIN YOUR HEAD AROUND!*

IT AIN'T THE HAIRDO THAT GAVE ME THE NAME, BUB.

ANYHOW, YOU LOOK LIKE *THIS* BOTTLE.

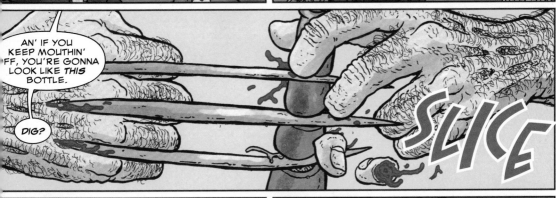

AN' IF YOU KEEP MOUTHIN' FF, YOU'RE GONNA LOOK LIKE *THIS* BOTTLE.

DIG?

SLICE

GEEZ, PAL. SOMEONE MAKES A JOKE AND YOUR FIRST INSTINCT IS TO *THREATEN MURDER?*

IF YOU WEREN'T, LIKE, EIGHT FEET TALL, I'D SAY YOU GOT A SERIOUS *NAPOLEON COMPLEX.*

WHAT IS THE DEAL WITH THAT, ANYWAY? WAS YOUR SECONDARY MUTATION JUST A *GROWTH SPURT?*

I'LL HAVE YOU KNOW MY SECONDARY MUTATION IS THE *ABILITY TO GET WASTED.*

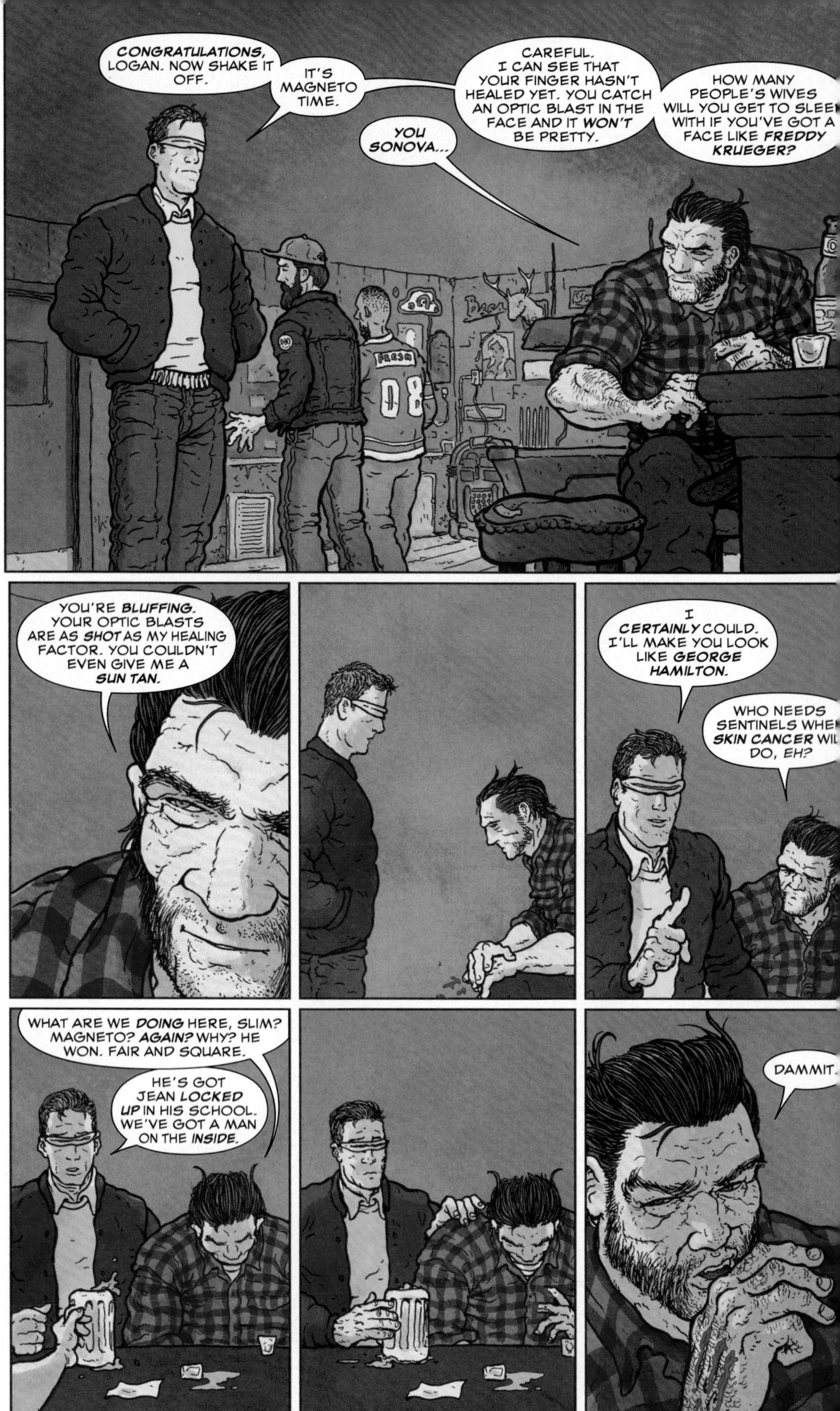
CONGRATULATIONS, LOGAN. NOW SHAKE IT OFF.
IT'S MAGNETO TIME.
YOU SONOVA...
CAREFUL. I CAN SEE THAT YOUR FINGER HASN'T HEALED YET. YOU CATCH AN OPTIC BLAST IN THE FACE AND IT WON'T BE PRETTY.
HOW MANY PEOPLE'S WIVES WILL YOU GET TO SLEE WITH IF YOU'VE GOT A FACE LIKE FREDDY KRUEGER?
YOU'RE BLUFFING. YOUR OPTIC BLASTS ARE AS SHOT AS MY HEALING FACTOR. YOU COULDN'T EVEN GIVE ME A SUN TAN.
I CERTAINLY COULD. I'LL MAKE YOU LOOK LIKE GEORGE HAMILTON.
WHO NEEDS SENTINELS WHE SKIN CANCER WI DO, EH?
WHAT ARE WE DOING HERE, SLIM? MAGNETO? AGAIN? WHY? HE WON. FAIR AND SQUARE.
HE'S GOT JEAN LOCKED UP IN HIS SCHOOL. WE'VE GOT A MAN ON THE INSIDE.
DAMMIT.

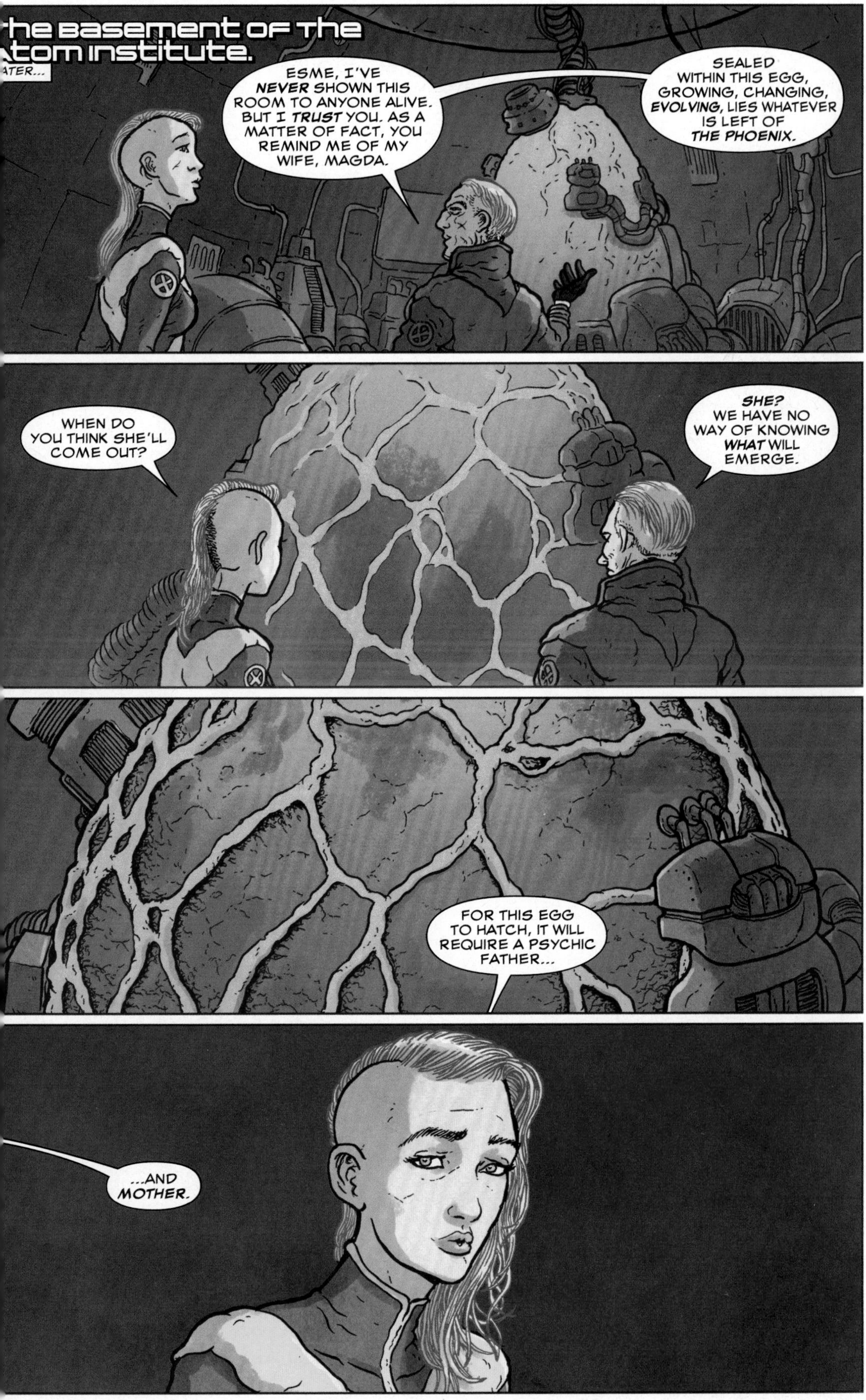
he basement of the
tom institute.
ATER...
ESME, I'VE NEVER SHOWN THIS ROOM TO ANYONE ALIVE. BUT I TRUST YOU. AS A MATTER OF FACT, YOU REMIND ME OF MY WIFE, MAGDA.
SEALED WITHIN THIS EGG, GROWING, CHANGING, EVOLVING, LIES WHATEVER IS LEFT OF THE PHOENIX.
WHEN DO YOU THINK SHE'LL COME OUT?
SHE? WE HAVE NO WAY OF KNOWING WHAT WILL EMERGE.
FOR THIS EGG TO HATCH, IT WILL REQUIRE A PSYCHIC FATHER...
...AND MOTHER.

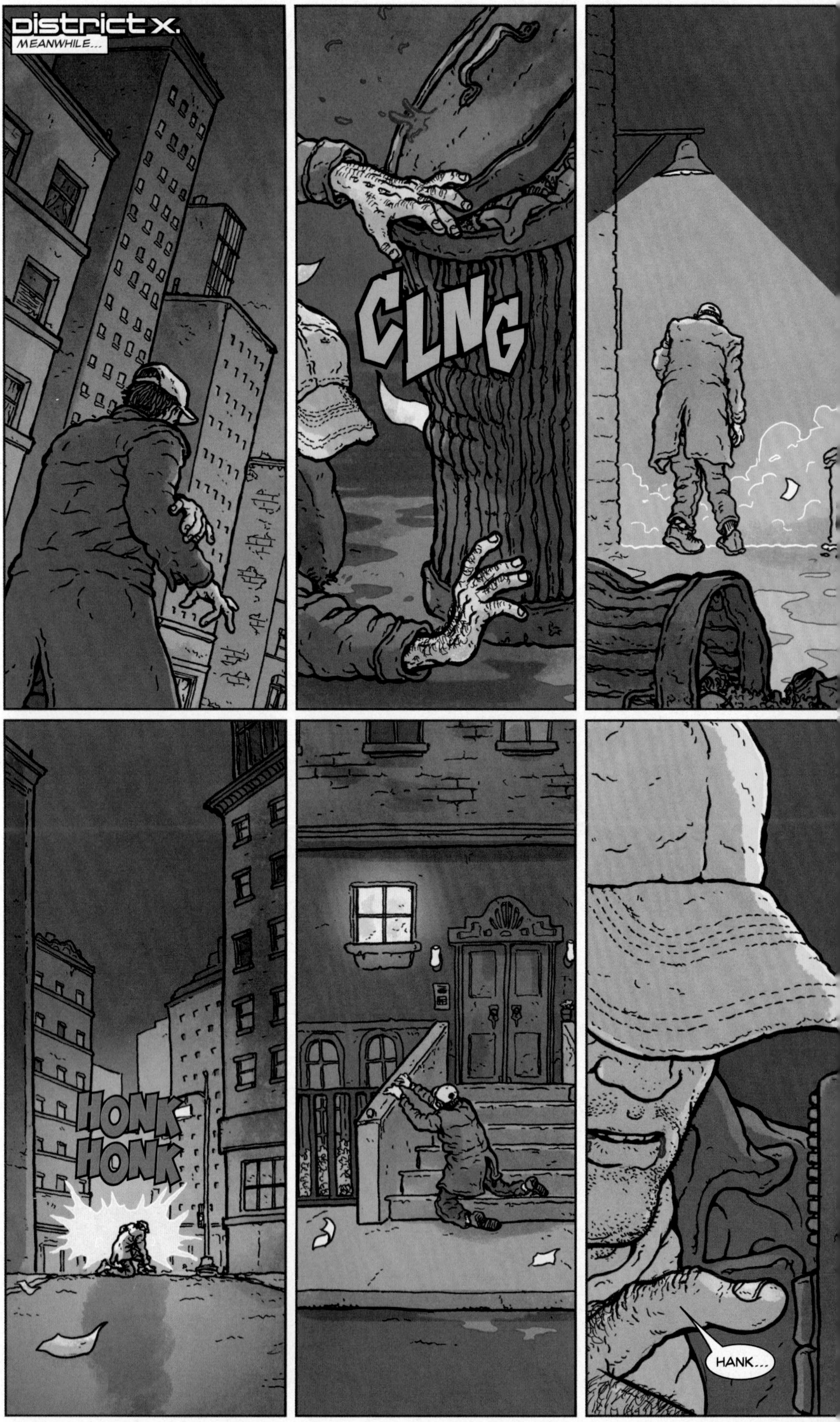
district X.
MEANWHILE...
CLNG
HONK
HONK
HANK...

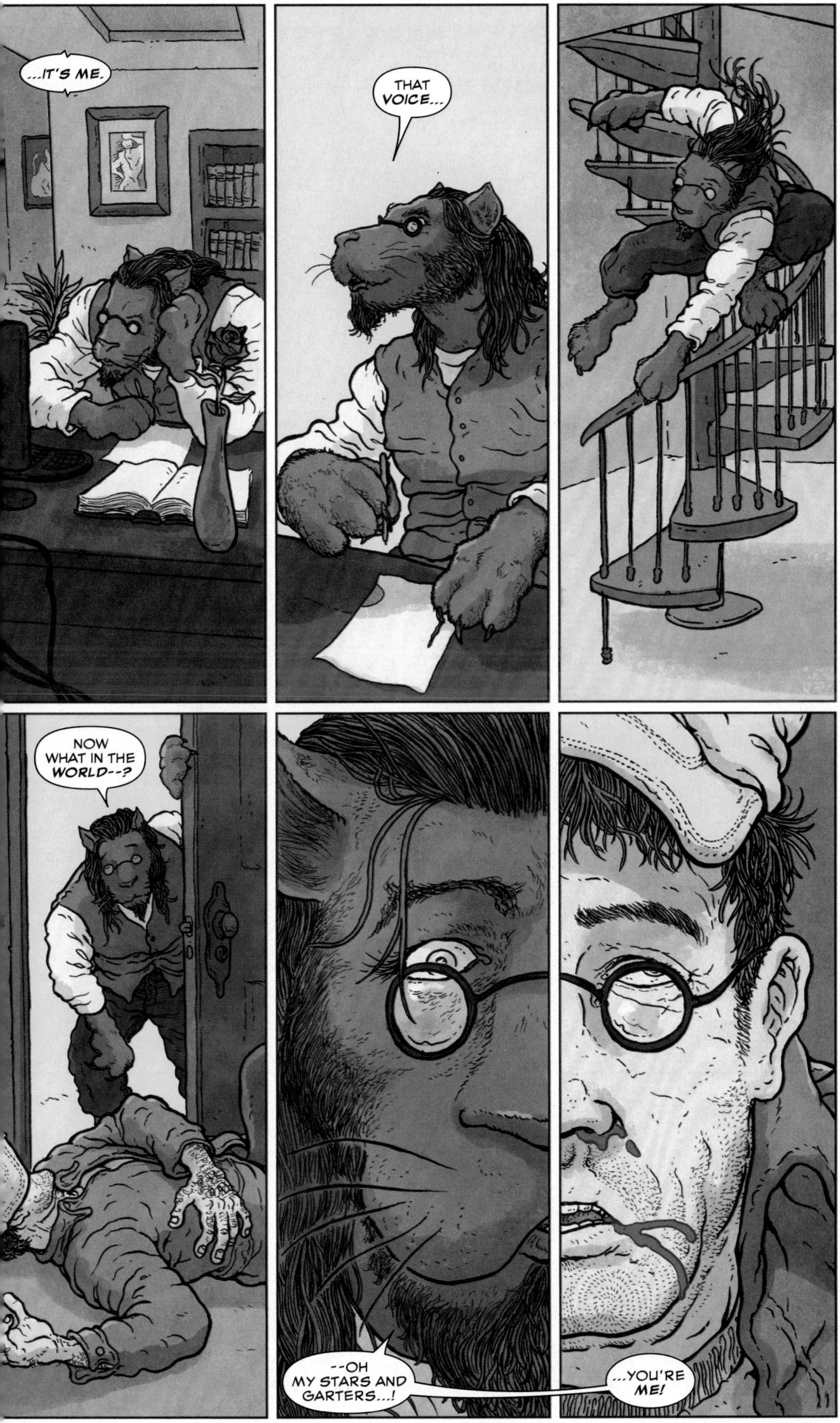
...IT'S ME.
THAT VOICE...
NOW WHAT IN THE WORLD--?
--OH MY STARS AND GARTERS...!
...YOU'RE ME!

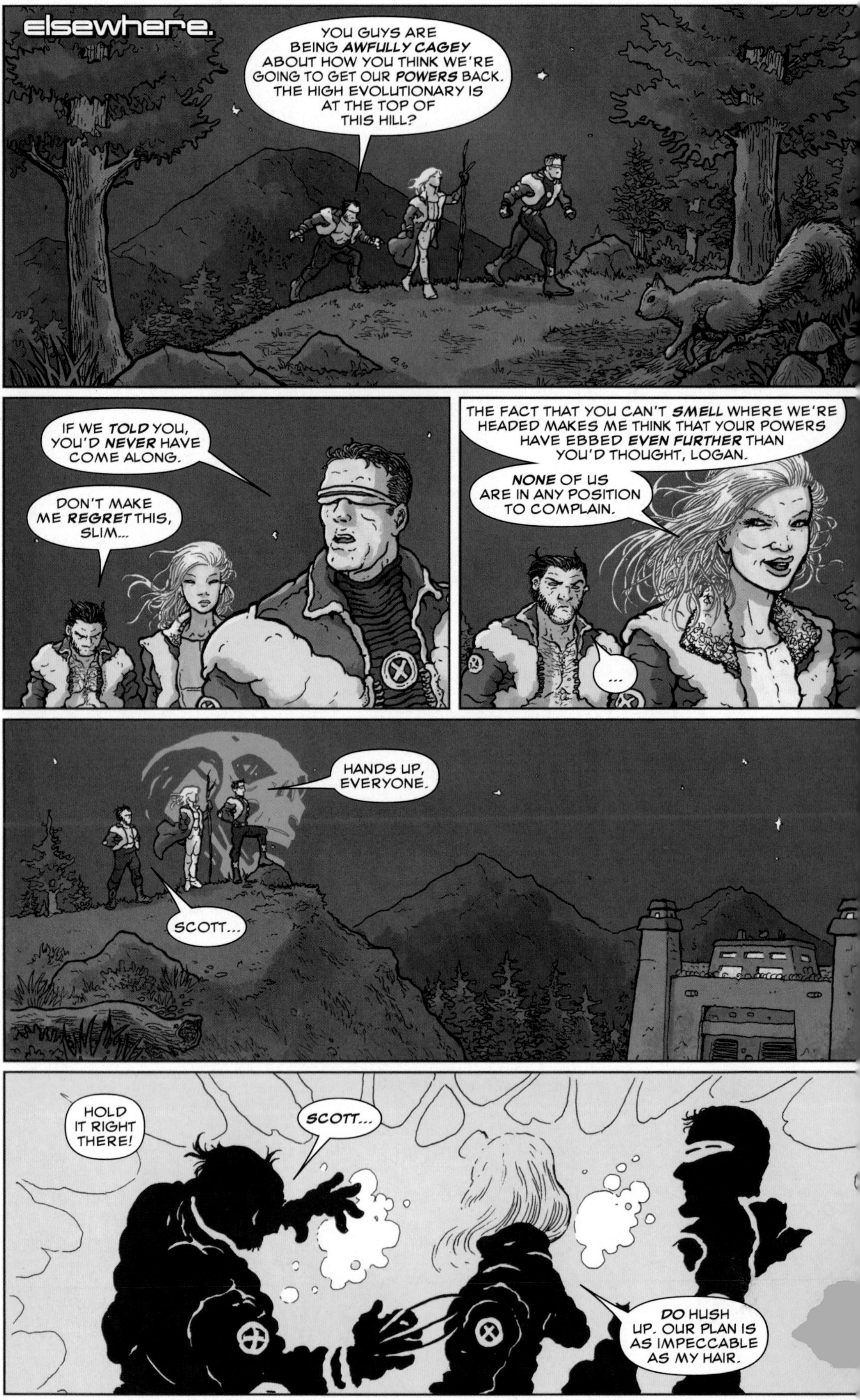
elsewhere.
YOU GUYS ARE BEING AWFULLY CAGEY ABOUT HOW YOU THINK WE'RE GOING TO GET OUR POWERS BACK. THE HIGH EVOLUTIONARY IS AT THE TOP OF THIS HILL?
IF WE TOLD YOU, YOU'D NEVER HAVE COME ALONG.
DON'T MAKE ME REGRET THIS, SLIM...
THE FACT THAT YOU CAN'T SMELL WHERE WE'RE HEADED MAKES ME THINK THAT YOUR POWERS HAVE EBBED EVEN FURTHER THAN YOU'D THOUGHT, LOGAN.
NONE OF US ARE IN ANY POSITION TO COMPLAIN.
...
HANDS UP, EVERYONE.
SCOTT...
HOLD IT RIGHT THERE!
SCOTT...
DO HUSH UP. OUR PLAN IS AS IMPECCABLE AS MY HAIR.

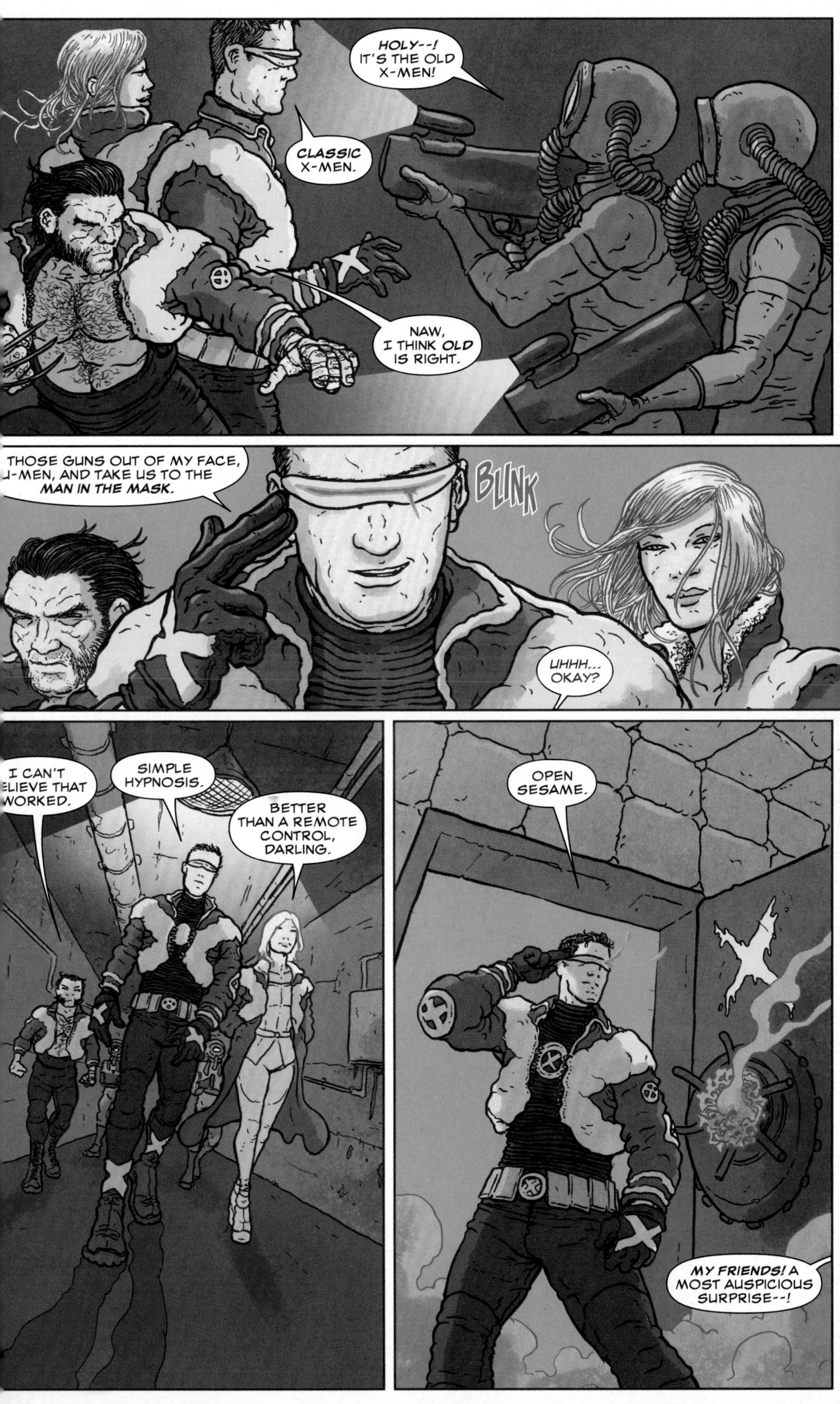
HOLY--! IT'S THE OLD X-MEN!
CLASSIC X-MEN.
NAW, I THINK OLD IS RIGHT.
THOSE GUNS OUT OF MY FACE, -MEN, AND TAKE US TO THE MAN IN THE MASK.
BLINK
UHHH... OKAY?
I CAN'T ELIEVE THAT WORKED.
SIMPLE HYPNOSIS.
BETTER THAN A REMOTE CONTROL, DARLING.
OPEN SESAME.
MY FRIENDS! A MOST AUSPICIOUS SURPRISE--!

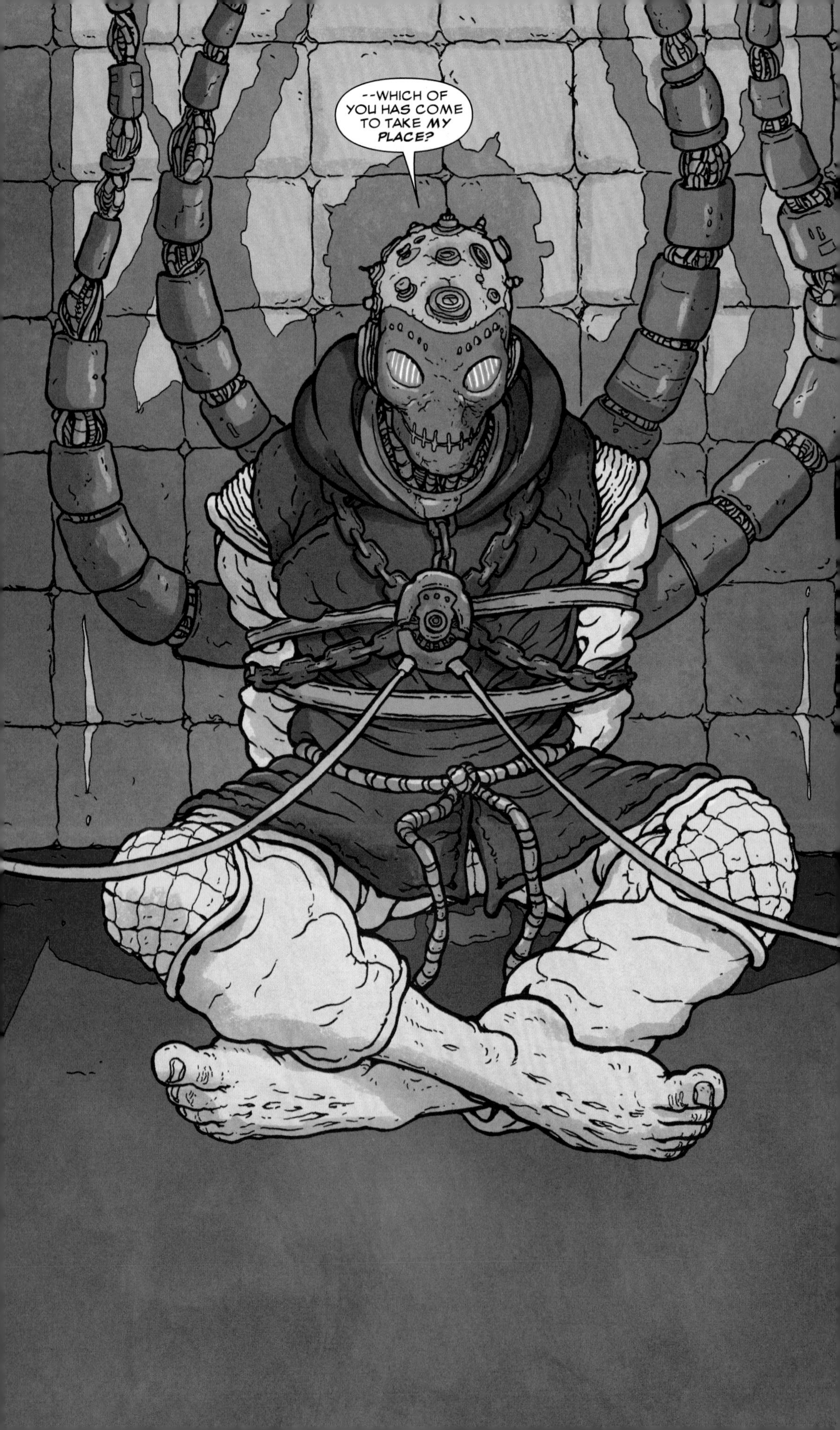
--WHICH OF YOU HAS COME TO TAKE MY PLACE?

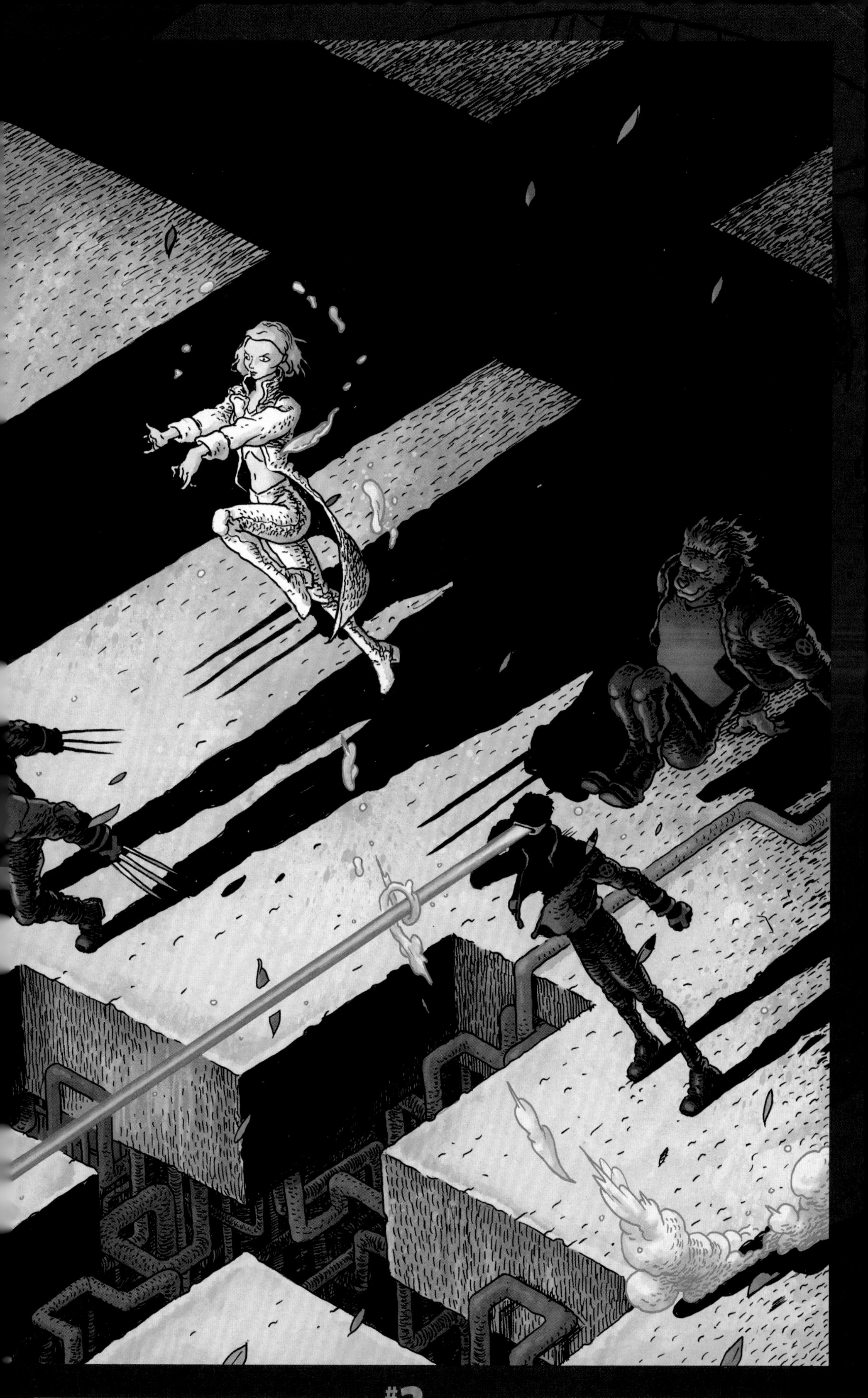

#2

AND THEY JUST *OFFERED* TO TRADE PLACES WITH *XORN?*

YES, SIR.

XORN IS ONE OF THE MOST *POWERFUL* MUTANTS IN THE WORLD, AND YOU *TRADED* HIM FOR THREE WASHED-UP *HAS-BEEN* MUTANTS?

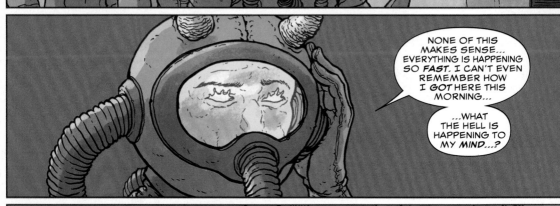

NONE OF THIS MAKES SENSE... EVERYTHING IS HAPPENING SO *FAST.* I CAN'T EVEN REMEMBER HOW I *GOT* HERE THIS MORNING...

...WHAT THE HELL IS HAPPENING TO MY *MIND...?*

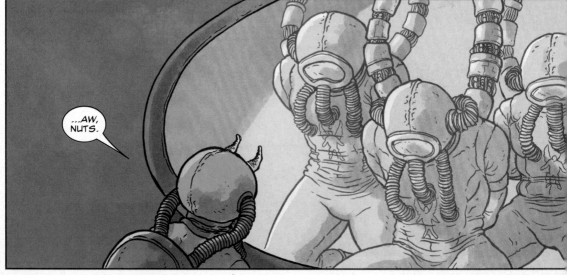

...AW, NUTS.

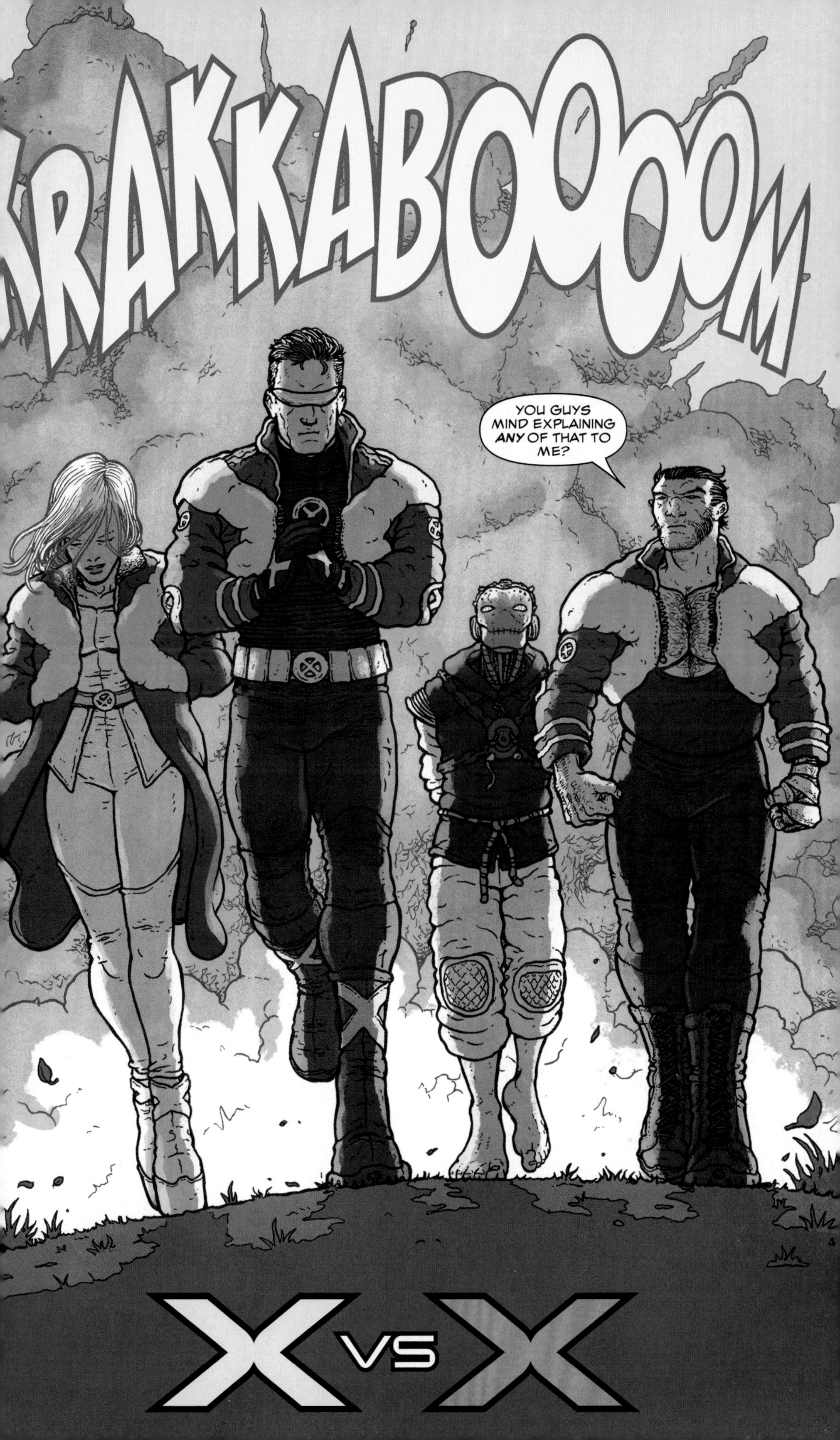
RAKKABOOOOM
YOU GUYS MIND EXPLAINING ANY OF THAT TO ME?
X VS X

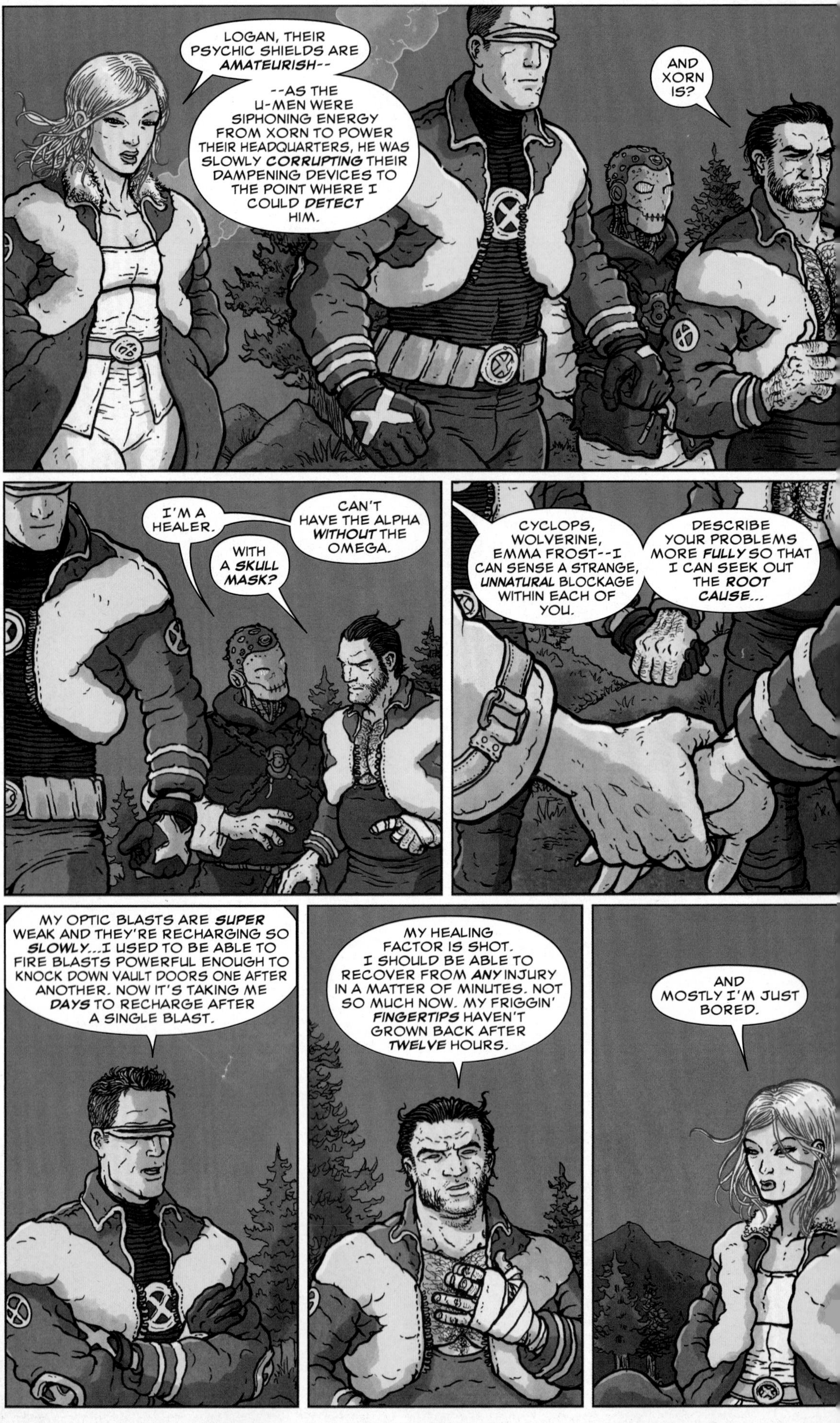
LOGAN, THEIR PSYCHIC SHIELDS ARE AMATEURISH--
--AS THE U-MEN WERE SIPHONING ENERGY FROM XORN TO POWER THEIR HEADQUARTERS, HE WAS SLOWLY CORRUPTING THEIR DAMPENING DEVICES TO THE POINT WHERE I COULD DETECT HIM.
AND XORN IS?
I'M A HEALER.
CAN'T HAVE THE ALPHA WITHOUT THE OMEGA.
WITH A SKULL MASK?
CYCLOPS, WOLVERINE, EMMA FROST--I CAN SENSE A STRANGE, UNNATURAL BLOCKAGE WITHIN EACH OF YOU.
DESCRIBE YOUR PROBLEMS MORE FULLY SO THAT I CAN SEEK OUT THE ROOT CAUSE...
MY OPTIC BLASTS ARE SUPER WEAK AND THEY'RE RECHARGING SO SLOWLY...I USED TO BE ABLE TO FIRE BLASTS POWERFUL ENOUGH TO KNOCK DOWN VAULT DOORS ONE AFTER ANOTHER. NOW IT'S TAKING ME DAYS TO RECHARGE AFTER A SINGLE BLAST.
MY HEALING FACTOR IS SHOT. I SHOULD BE ABLE TO RECOVER FROM ANY INJURY IN A MATTER OF MINUTES. NOT SO MUCH NOW. MY FRIGGIN' FINGERTIPS HAVEN'T GROWN BACK AFTER TWELVE HOURS.
AND MOSTLY I'M JUST BORED.

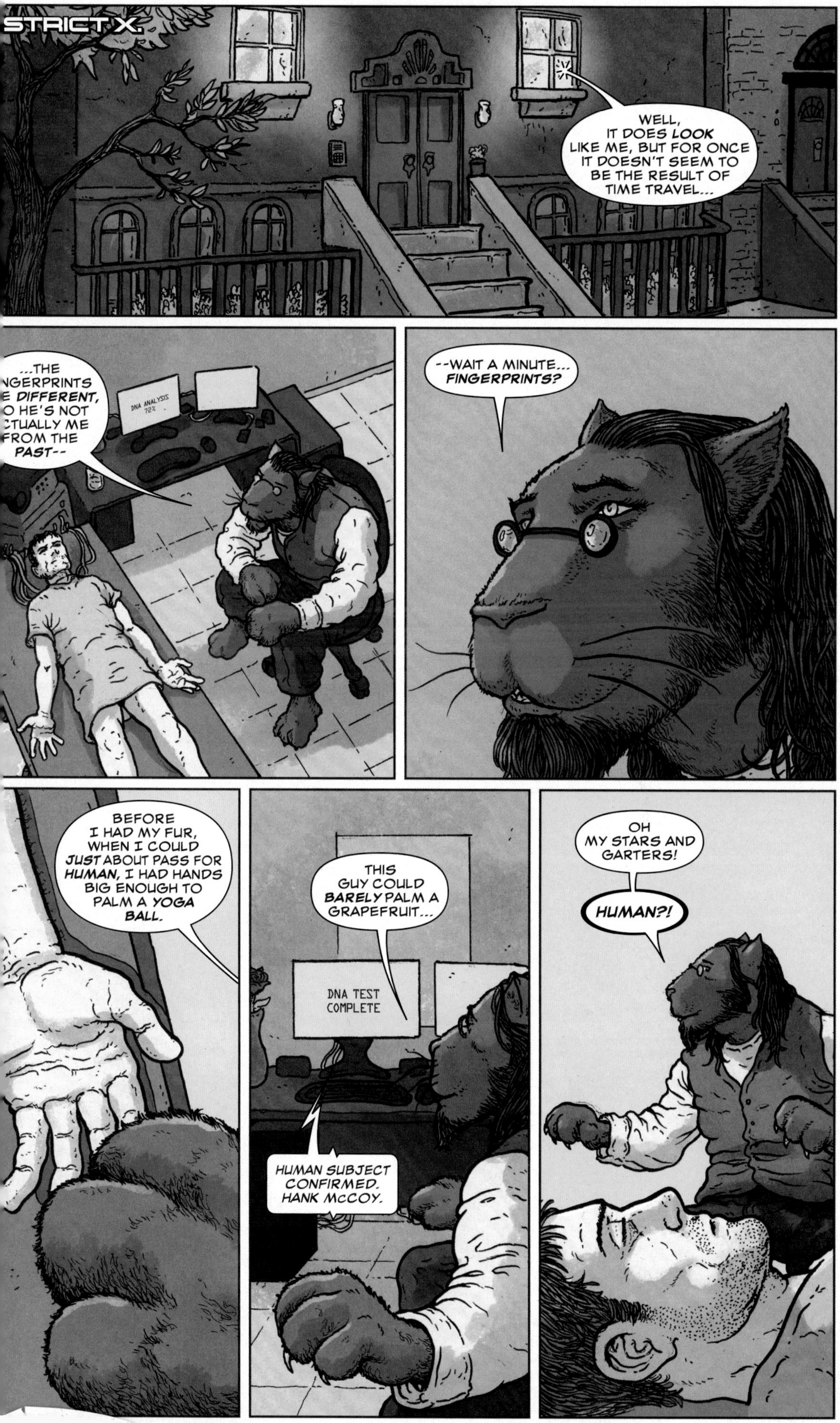
STRICT X.
WELL, IT DOES LOOK LIKE ME, BUT FOR ONCE IT DOESN'T SEEM TO BE THE RESULT OF TIME TRAVEL...
...THE NGERPRINTS E DIFFERENT, O HE'S NOT CTUALLY ME FROM THE PAST--
DNA ANALYSIS 72%
--WAIT A MINUTE... FINGERPRINTS?
BEFORE I HAD MY FUR, WHEN I COULD JUST ABOUT PASS FOR HUMAN, I HAD HANDS BIG ENOUGH TO PALM A YOGA BALL.
THIS GUY COULD BARELY PALM A GRAPEFRUIT...
DNA TEST COMPLETE
HUMAN SUBJECT CONFIRMED. HANK McCOY.
OH MY STARS AND GARTERS!
HUMAN?!

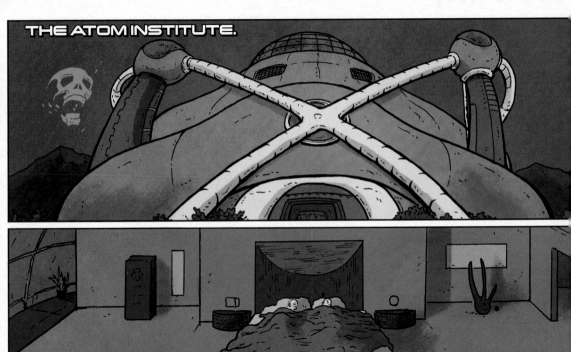

THE ATOM INSTITUTE.

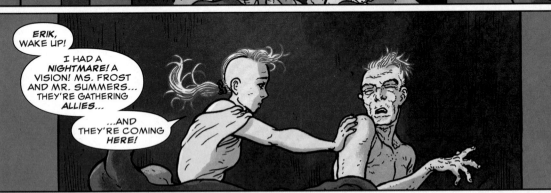

NOOO!

ERIK, WAKE UP!

I HAD A *NIGHTMARE!* A *VISION!* MS. FROST AND MR. SUMMERS... THEY'RE GATHERING *ALLIES...*

...AND THEY'RE COMING *HERE!*

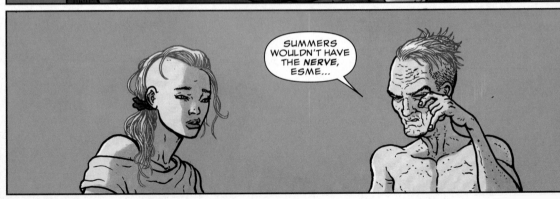

SUMMERS WOULDN'T HAVE THE *NERVE,* ESME...

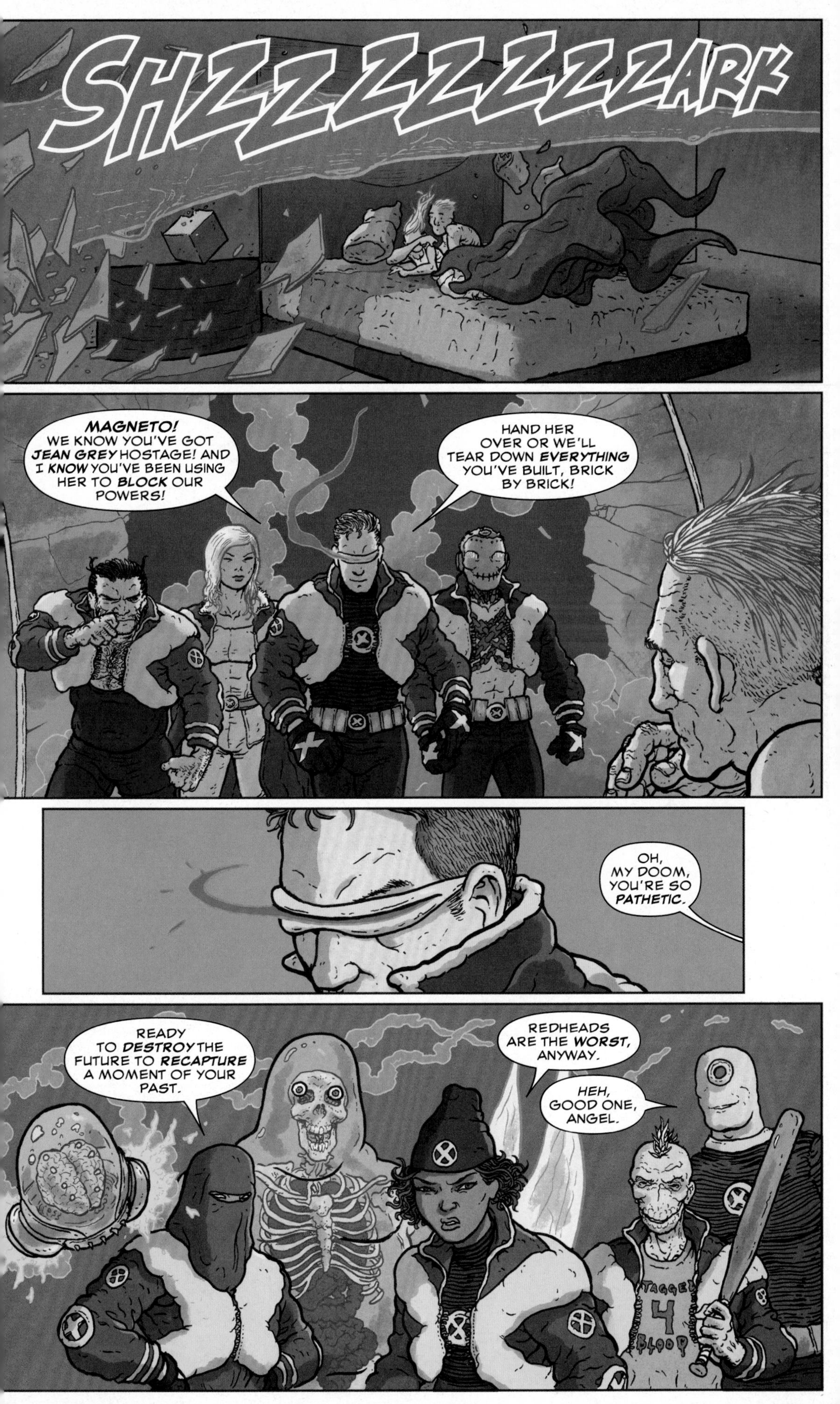
SHZZZZZZZZARK
MAGNETO! WE KNOW YOU'VE GOT JEAN GREY HOSTAGE! AND I KNOW YOU'VE BEEN USING HER TO BLOCK OUR POWERS!
HAND HER OVER OR WE'LL TEAR DOWN EVERYTHING YOU'VE BUILT, BRICK BY BRICK!
OH, MY DOOM, YOU'RE SO PATHETIC.
READY TO DESTROY THE FUTURE TO RECAPTURE A MOMENT OF YOUR PAST.
REDHEADS ARE THE WORST, ANYWAY.
HEH, GOOD ONE, ANGEL.
TAGGED
4
BLOOD

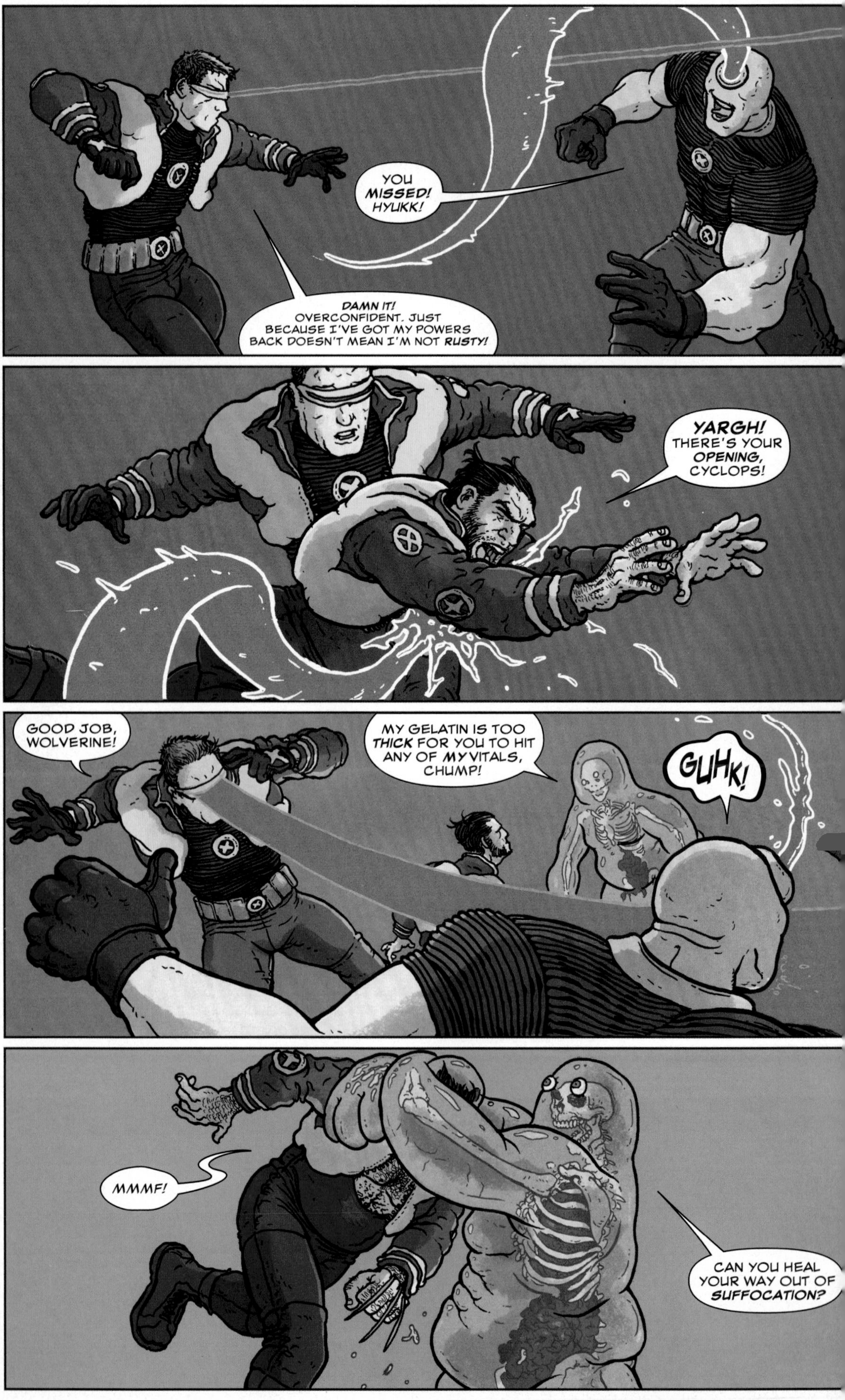
YOU MISSED! HYUKK!
DAMN IT! OVERCONFIDENT. JUST BECAUSE I'VE GOT MY POWERS BACK DOESN'T MEAN I'M NOT RUSTY!
YARGH! THERE'S YOUR OPENING, CYCLOPS!
GOOD JOB, WOLVERINE!
MY GELATIN IS TOO THICK FOR YOU TO HIT ANY OF MY VITALS, CHUMP!
GUHK!
MMMF!
CAN YOU HEAL YOUR WAY OUT OF SUFFOCATION?

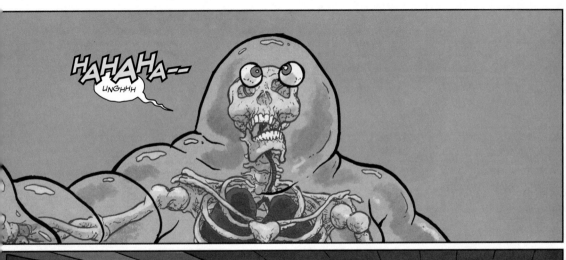

HAHAHA--

UNGHHH

SHAME YOUR GELATIN *WASN'T* THICK ENOUGH TO BLOCK MY *PSYCHIC* ATTACK, GLOB. NIGHTY NIGHT.

THANKS FOR THAT, EMMA. I OWE YA ONE.

WUMP

IT'S A SHAME XORN COULDN'T HEAL YOUR *HORRIBLE HAIRCUT*.

GIRLS, JUST LISTEN TO--

WE'RE YOUR *WORST* NIGHTMARE, MS. FROST.

FIVE REMINDERS OF YOUR *FORMER* GLORY.

OOH! PSYCHI
ASSAULT! I WA
TO HELP!

AGGHH!

YOU'LL *NEVER* BE AS *YOUNG* OR AS *PRETTY* AS WE ARE EVER AGAIN.

AW, ARE THE MEAN *QUINTUPLETS* GANGING UP ON YOU, EMMA? THAT'S NOT VERY *FAIR*, IS IT?

UGH--

--NOT FAIR AT ALL!

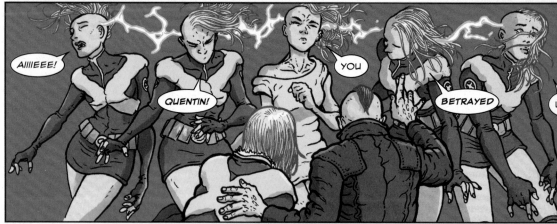

AIIIIEEE!

QUENTIN!

YOU

BETRAYED

YOU CHOSE *HER* OVER *ME*?!

YOU *BASTARD...* THE OTHER DAY... YOU *PURPOSELY* TRICKED US INTO *OVEREXTENDING* OURSELVES...

KNOCKING YOU CUCKOOS OUT WAS THE *ONLY* WAY TO GET A PSYCHIC SIGNAL TO *CYCLOPS* AND *EMMA* WITHOUT YOU KNOWING ABOUT IT.

I AM THE *BETTER* PSYCHIC, ESME, AND NOW YOU'RE GOING TO TELL ME *EVERYTHING* ABOUT MAGNETO'S PLAN FOR THE *PHOENIX EGG.*

WHETHER YOU WANT TO OR NOT!

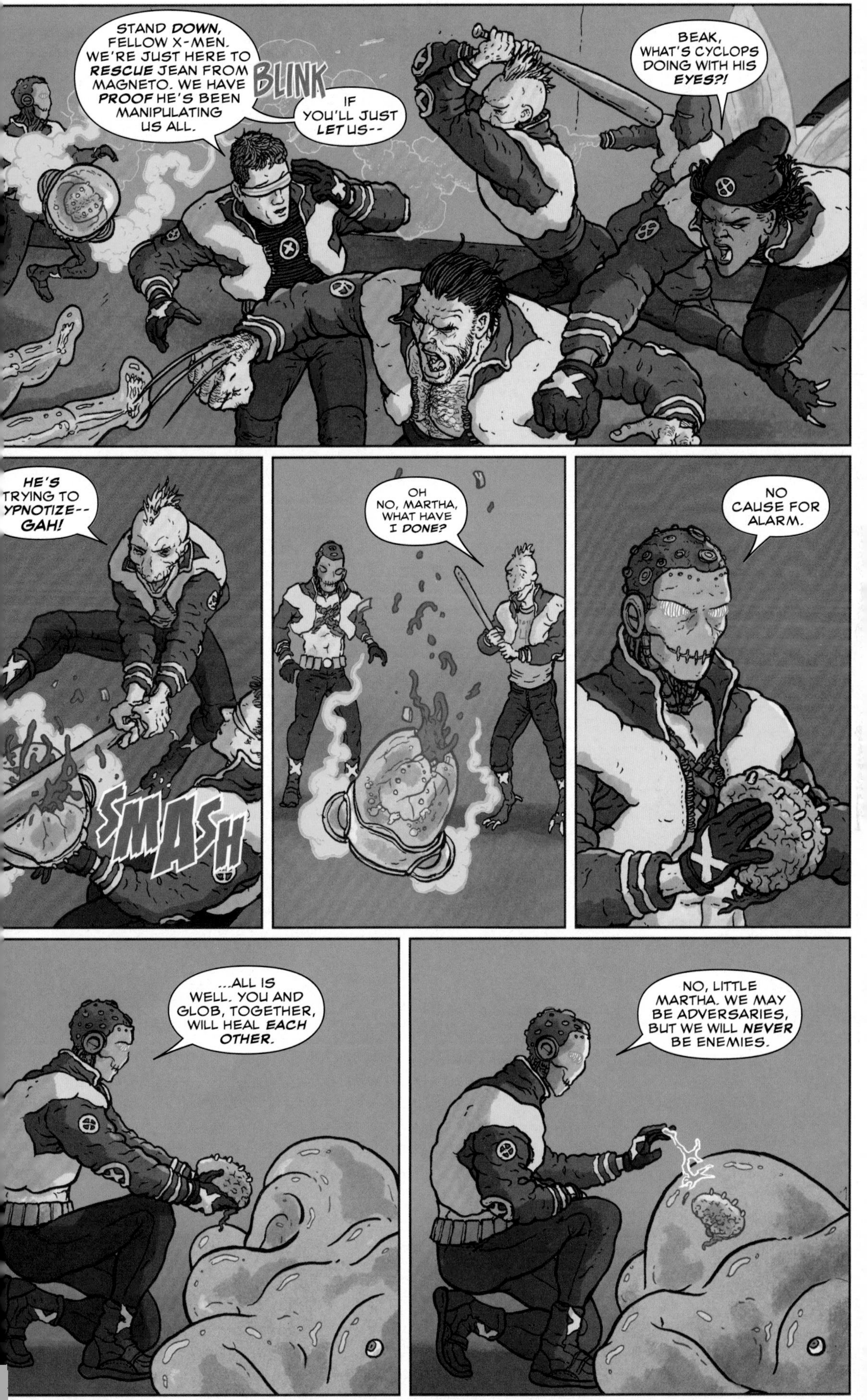

STAND DOWN, FELLOW X-MEN. WE'RE JUST HERE TO RESCUE JEAN FROM MAGNETO. WE HAVE PROOF HE'S BEEN MANIPULATING US ALL.
BLINK
IF YOU'LL JUST LET US--
BEAK, WHAT'S CYCLOPS DOING WITH HIS EYES?!
HE'S TRYING TO YPNOTIZE-- GAH!
SMASH
OH NO, MARTHA, WHAT HAVE I DONE?
NO CAUSE FOR ALARM.
...ALL IS WELL. YOU AND GLOB, TOGETHER, WILL HEAL EACH OTHER.
NO, LITTLE MARTHA. WE MAY BE ADVERSARIES, BUT WE WILL NEVER BE ENEMIES.

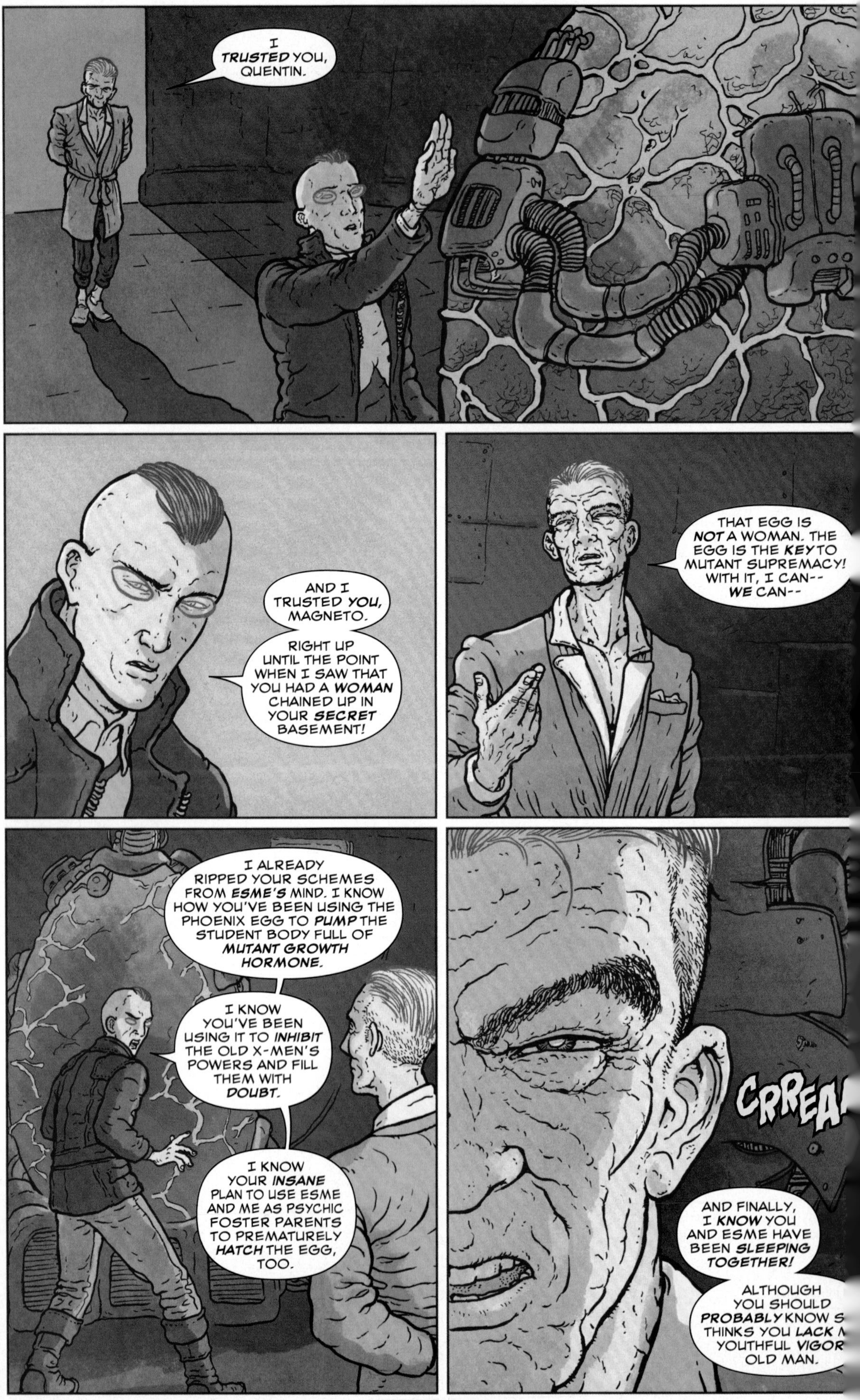

I TRUSTED YOU, QUENTIN.
AND I TRUSTED YOU, MAGNETO.
RIGHT UP UNTIL THE POINT WHEN I SAW THAT YOU HAD A WOMAN CHAINED UP IN YOUR SECRET BASEMENT!
THAT EGG IS NOT A WOMAN. THE EGG IS THE KEY TO MUTANT SUPREMACY! WITH IT, I CAN-- WE CAN--
I ALREADY RIPPED YOUR SCHEMES FROM ESME'S MIND. I KNOW HOW YOU'VE BEEN USING THE PHOENIX EGG TO PUMP THE STUDENT BODY FULL OF MUTANT GROWTH HORMONE.
I KNOW YOU'VE BEEN USING IT TO INHIBIT THE OLD X-MEN'S POWERS AND FILL THEM WITH DOUBT.
I KNOW YOUR INSANE PLAN TO USE ESME AND ME AS PSYCHIC FOSTER PARENTS TO PREMATURELY HATCH THE EGG, TOO.
CRREA
AND FINALLY, I KNOW YOU AND ESME HAVE BEEN SLEEPING TOGETHER!
ALTHOUGH YOU SHOULD PROBABLY KNOW S THINKS YOU LACK M YOUTHFUL VIGOR OLD MAN.

YOU *DARE* SPEAK TO ME AS A *RIVAL?* AN *EQUAL?* YOU THINK YOU COULD EVER OPERATE AT *MY* LEVEL, QUENTIN QUIRE?

I AM *MAGNETO,* MASTER OF MAGNETISM.

SPLOORCH

THE *SUPERIOR* HOMO SUPERIOR!

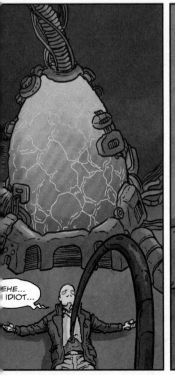

EHE... IDIOT...

...I...ALREADY... BONDED MYSELF...TO THE...EGGGGGG...

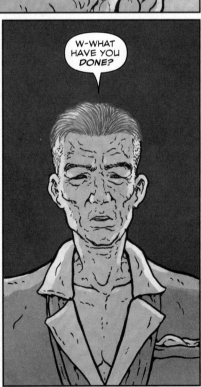

W-WHAT HAVE YOU *DONE?*

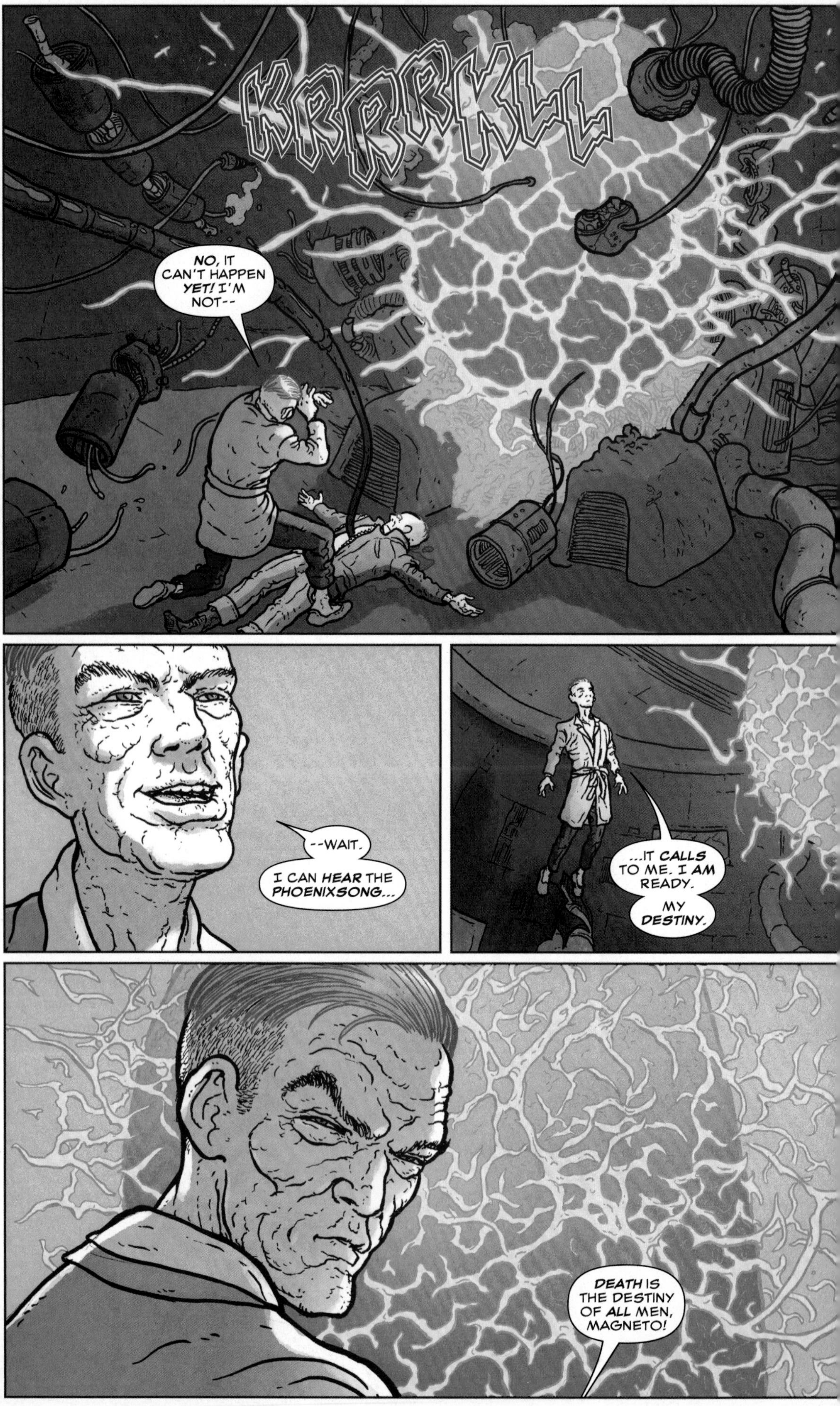
KRRRKLL
NO, IT CAN'T HAPPEN YET! I'M NOT--
--WAIT.
I CAN HEAR THE PHOENIXSONG...
...IT CALLS TO ME. I AM READY.
MY DESTINY.
DEATH IS THE DESTINY OF ALL MEN, MAGNETO!

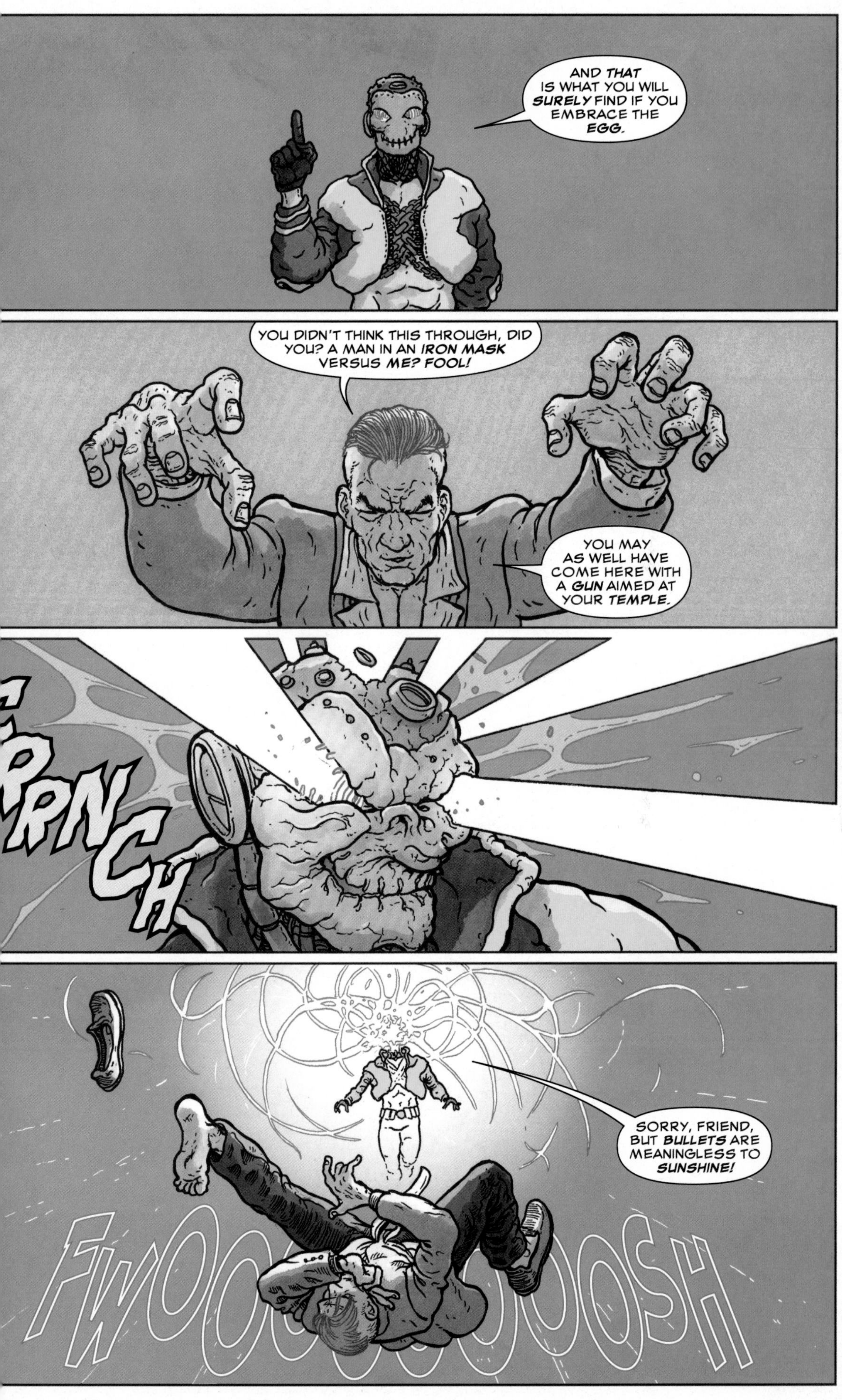
AND THAT IS WHAT YOU WILL SURELY FIND IF YOU EMBRACE THE EGG.
YOU DIDN'T THINK THIS THROUGH, DID YOU? A MAN IN AN IRON MASK VERSUS ME? FOOL!
YOU MAY AS WELL HAVE COME HERE WITH A GUN AIMED AT YOUR TEMPLE.
RRNCH
SORRY, FRIEND, BUT BULLETS ARE MEANINGLESS TO SUNSHINE!
FWOOOOOOOOOOSH

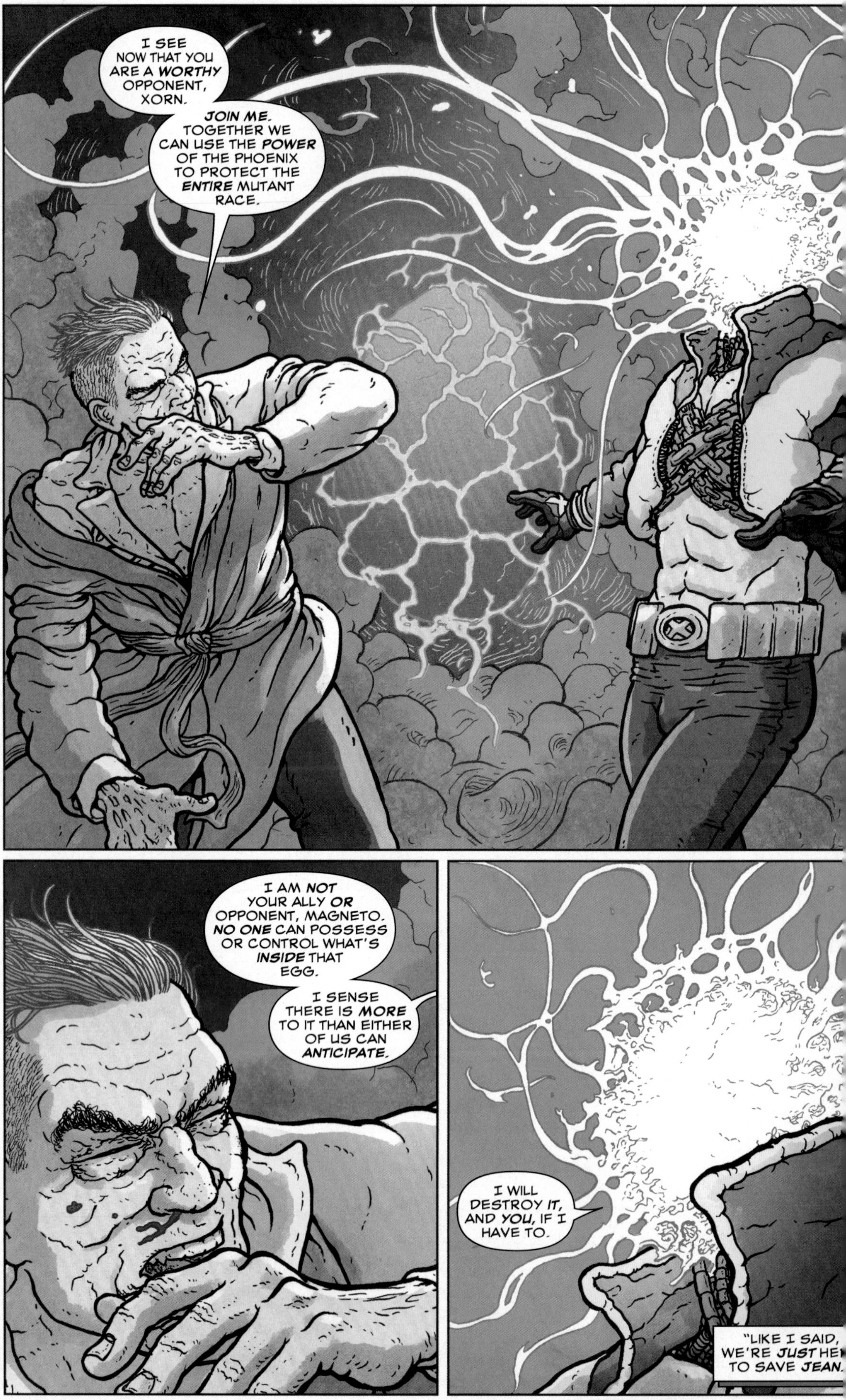
I SEE NOW THAT YOU ARE A *WORTHY* OPPONENT, XORN.
JOIN ME. TOGETHER WE CAN USE THE *POWER* OF THE PHOENIX TO PROTECT THE *ENTIRE* MUTANT RACE.
I AM *NOT* YOUR ALLY *OR* OPPONENT, MAGNETO. *NO ONE* CAN POSSESS OR CONTROL WHAT'S *INSIDE* THAT EGG.
I SENSE THERE IS *MORE* TO IT THAN EITHER OF US CAN *ANTICIPATE.*
I WILL DESTROY *IT,* AND *YOU,* IF I HAVE TO.
"LIKE I SAID, WE'RE *JUST* HE TO SAVE *JEAN.*

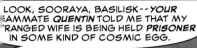

LOOK, SOORAYA, BASILISK--*YOUR* TEAMMATE *QUENTIN* TOLD ME THAT MY *ESTRANGED WIFE* IS BEING HELD *PRISONER* IN SOME KIND OF COSMIC EGG.

MAGNETO HAS *PROBABLY* BEEN USING HER POWER TO PIT US *AGAINST* EACH OTHER FOR *YEARS!*

YOUR *ARGUMENT* WOULD BE *FAR* MORE *COMPELLING* IF YOU WEREN'T JUST CAUGHT TRYING TO *HYPNOTIZE* US INTO BELIEVING WE WERE BEING *MANIPULATED!*

YOU COME INTO *OUR* SCHOOL IN THE MIDDLE OF THE *NIGHT* SHOOTING LASERS--

OPTIC *BLASTS.*

THIS IS WHY YOU *NEVER* ACCOMPLISH *ANYTHING,* SCOTT SUMMERS! WHO EVEN KNOWS IF YOUR WIFE IS *ACTUALLY* HERE?

SOORAYA, HE'S *RIGHT.* MAGNETO *DOES* HAVE JEAN WRAPPED UP IN A PHOENIX EGG.

BUT I'VE GOT FULL *FAITH* IN WHAT ERIK'S DOING WITH IT. HAS HE *EVER* LED *US* ASTRAY BEFORE?

UNLIKE THAT *BALD CRIPPLE* WHO CHOSE *SUICIDE* OVER FACING REALITY.

NOW, YOUNG LADY. YOU'RE *INVALIDATING* YOUR ARGUMENT RIGHT THERE BY RESORTING TO *MEAN-SPIRITED* AD HOMINEM ATTACKS...

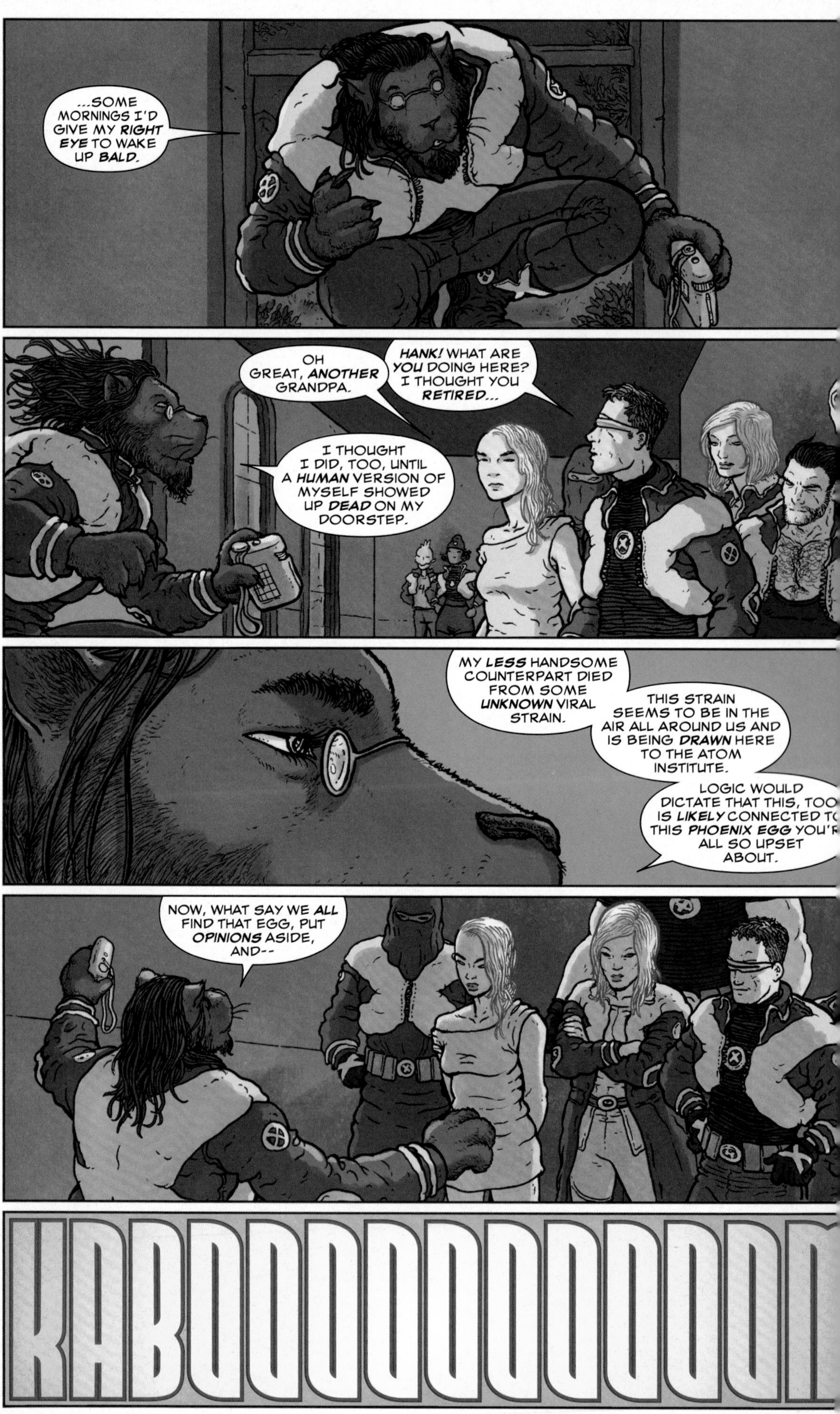
...SOME MORNINGS I'D GIVE MY RIGHT EYE TO WAKE UP BALD.
OH GREAT, ANOTHER GRANDPA.
HANK! WHAT ARE YOU DOING HERE? I THOUGHT YOU RETIRED...
I THOUGHT I DID, TOO, UNTIL A HUMAN VERSION OF MYSELF SHOWED UP DEAD ON MY DOORSTEP.
MY LESS HANDSOME COUNTERPART DIED FROM SOME UNKNOWN VIRAL STRAIN.
THIS STRAIN SEEMS TO BE IN THE AIR ALL AROUND US AND IS BEING DRAWN HERE TO THE ATOM INSTITUTE.
LOGIC WOULD DICTATE THAT THIS, TOO IS LIKELY CONNECTED TO THIS PHOENIX EGG YOU'R ALL SO UPSET ABOUT.
NOW, WHAT SAY WE ALL FIND THAT EGG, PUT OPINIONS ASIDE, AND--
KABOOOOOOOOOOM

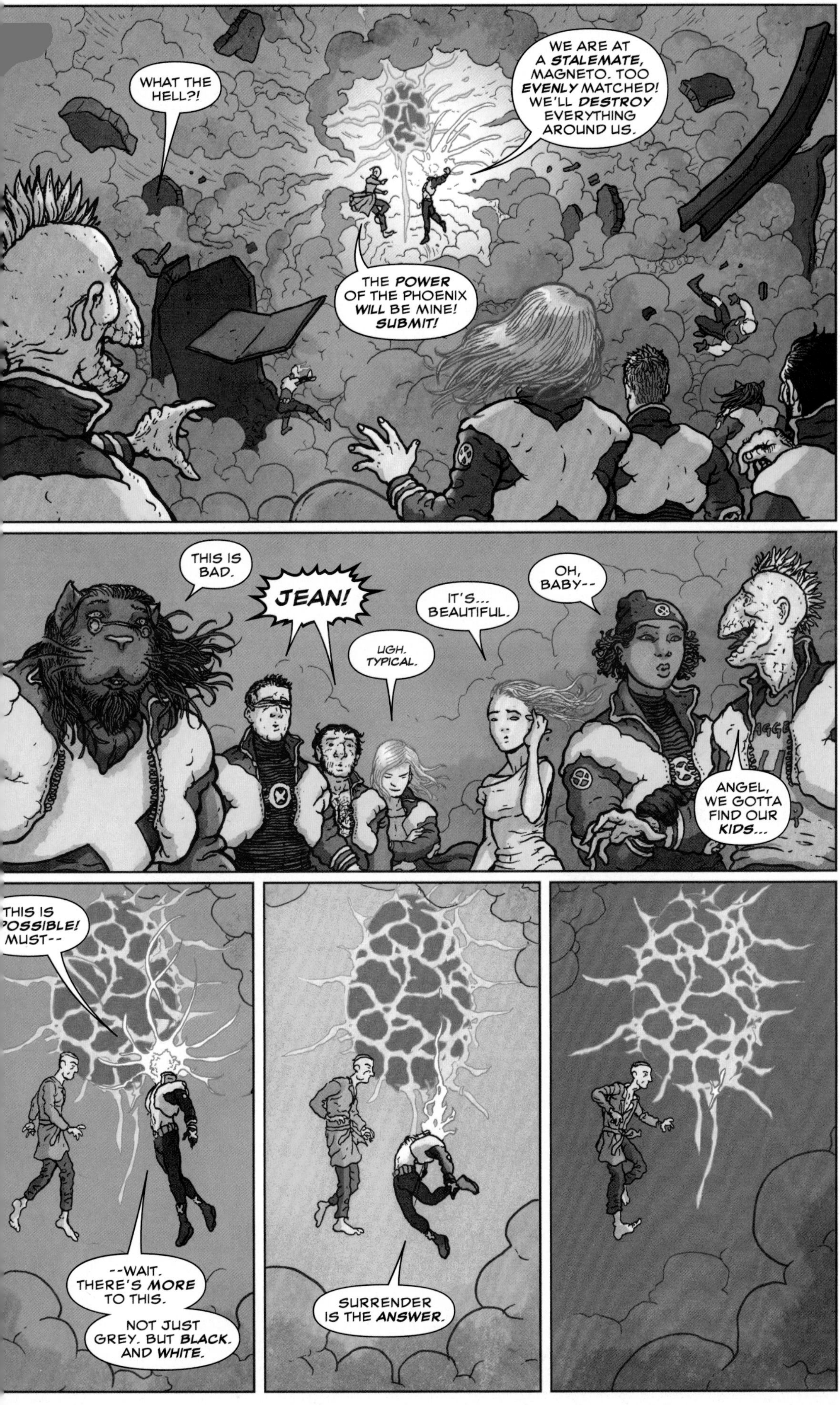
WHAT THE HELL?!
WE ARE AT A STALEMATE, MAGNETO. TOO EVENLY MATCHED! WE'LL DESTROY EVERYTHING AROUND US.
THE POWER OF THE PHOENIX WILL BE MINE! SUBMIT!
THIS IS BAD.
JEAN!
UGH. TYPICAL.
IT'S... BEAUTIFUL.
OH, BABY--
ANGEL, WE GOTTA FIND OUR KIDS...
THIS IS POSSIBLE! MUST--
--WAIT. THERE'S MORE TO THIS.
NOT JUST GREY. BUT BLACK. AND WHITE.
SURRENDER IS THE ANSWER.

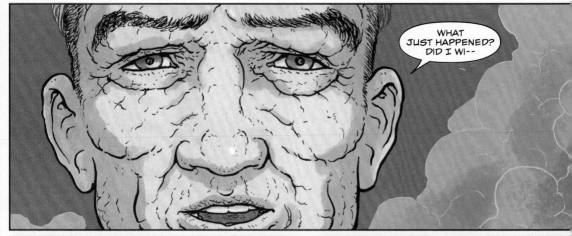

WHAT JUST HAPPENED? DID I WI--

SPLACK

THUMP

:GASP:

OH, ERIK.

LOOKS LIKE THE EGG HAS GONE *DORMANT.* THERE IS *NO* GREAT POWER TO BE DERIVED FROM THIS.

LOOKS LIK MAGNETO W *WRONG* AFT ALL.

NO, MY *HANDSOM* FRIEND--

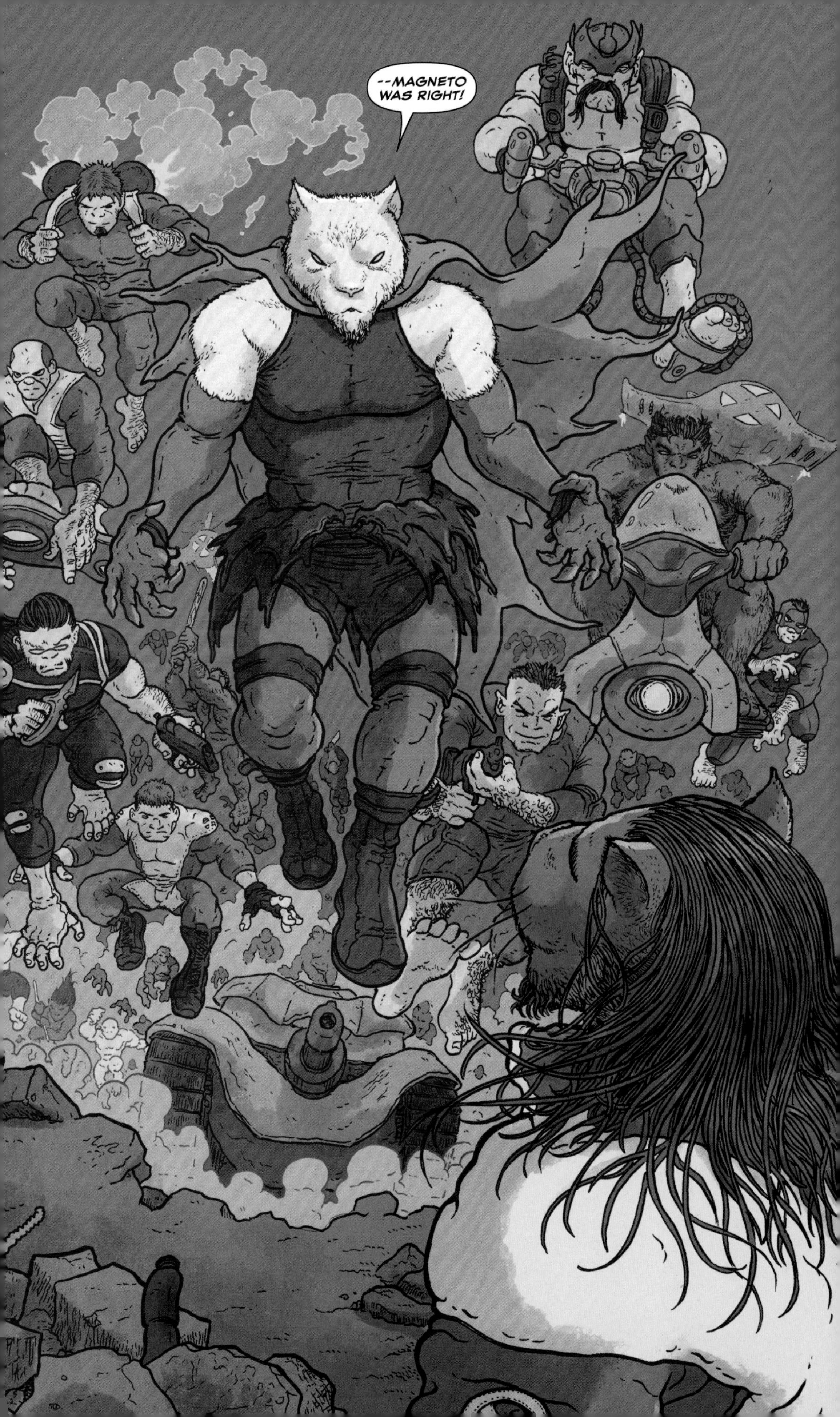
--MAGNETO WAS RIGHT!

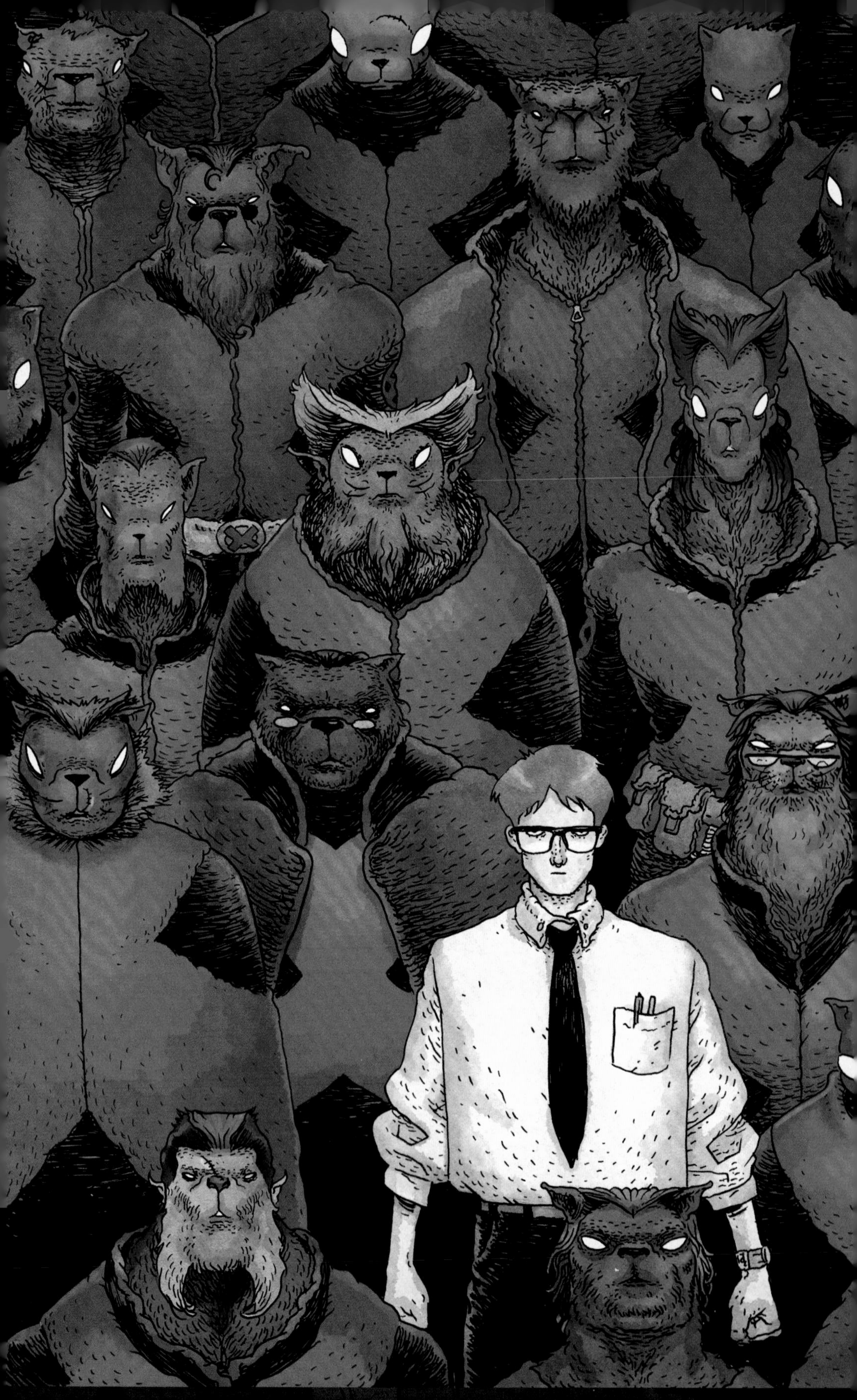

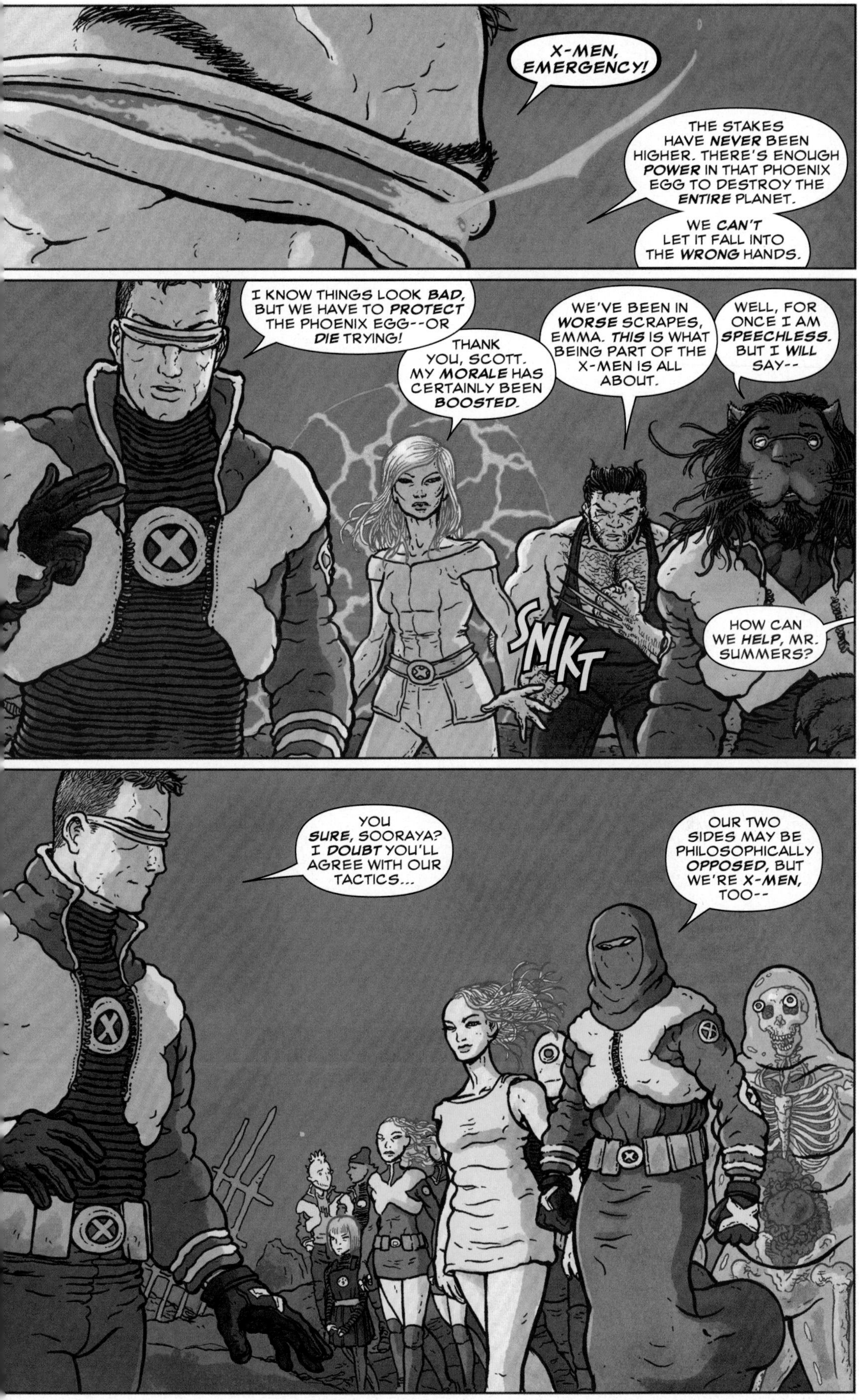
X-MEN, EMERGENCY!
THE STAKES HAVE NEVER BEEN HIGHER. THERE'S ENOUGH POWER IN THAT PHOENIX EGG TO DESTROY THE ENTIRE PLANET.
WE CAN'T LET IT FALL INTO THE WRONG HANDS.
I KNOW THINGS LOOK BAD, BUT WE HAVE TO PROTECT THE PHOENIX EGG--OR DIE TRYING!
THANK YOU, SCOTT. MY MORALE HAS CERTAINLY BEEN BOOSTED.
WE'VE BEEN IN WORSE SCRAPES, EMMA. THIS IS WHAT BEING PART OF THE X-MEN IS ALL ABOUT.
WELL, FOR ONCE I AM SPEECHLESS. BUT I WILL SAY--
SNIKT
HOW CAN WE HELP, MR. SUMMERS?
YOU SURE, SOORAYA? I DOUBT YOU'LL AGREE WITH OUR TACTICS...
OUR TWO SIDES MAY BE PHILOSOPHICALLY OPPOSED, BUT WE'RE X-MEN, TOO--

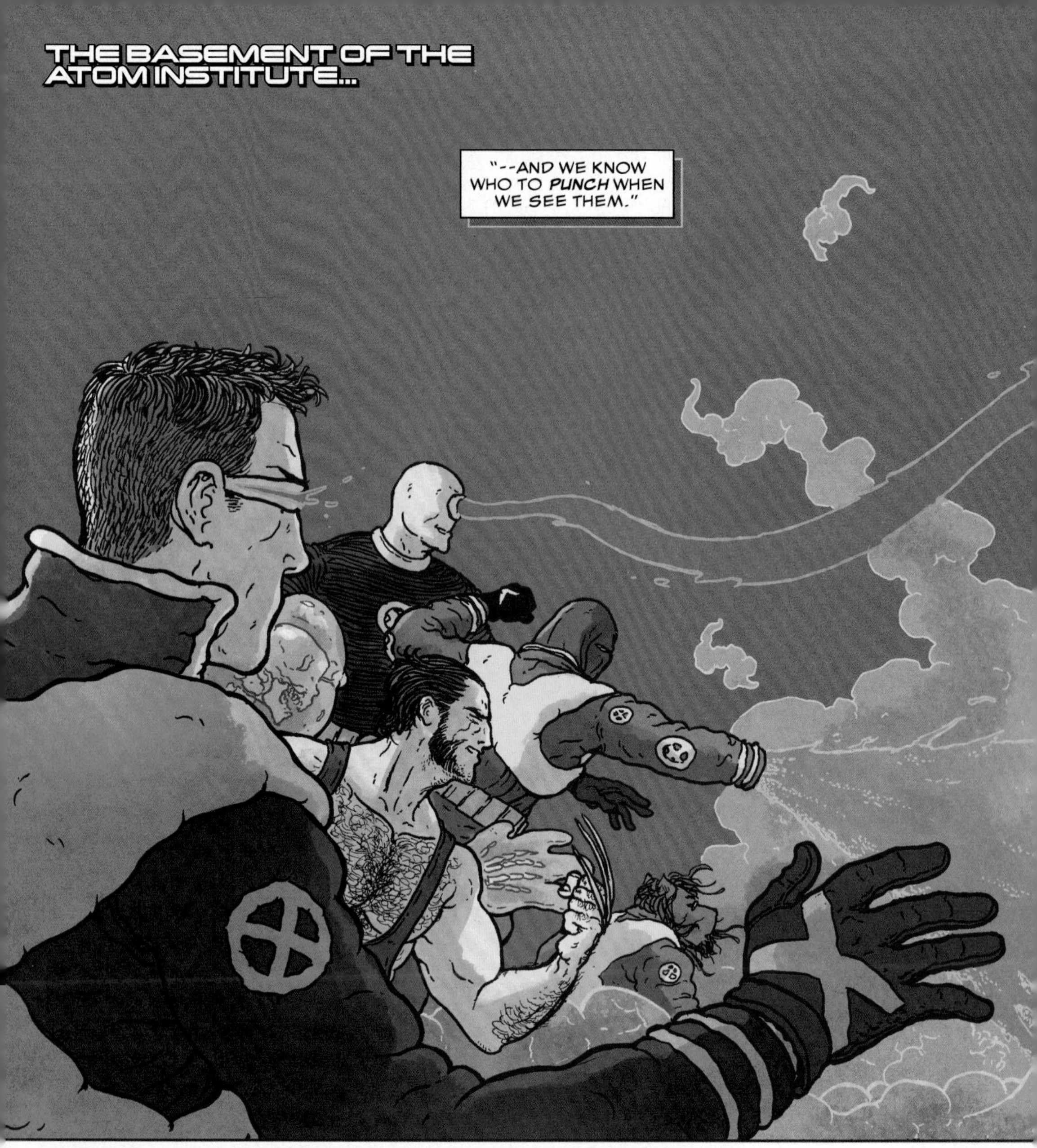
THE BASEMENT OF THE ATOM INSTITUTE...
"--AND WE KNOW WHO TO PUNCH WHEN WE SEE THEM."

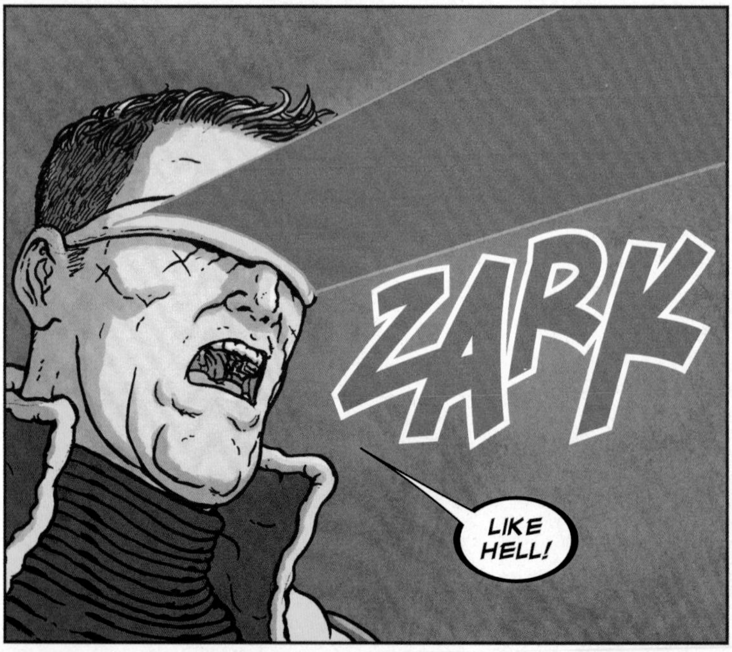
ZARK
LIKE HELL!

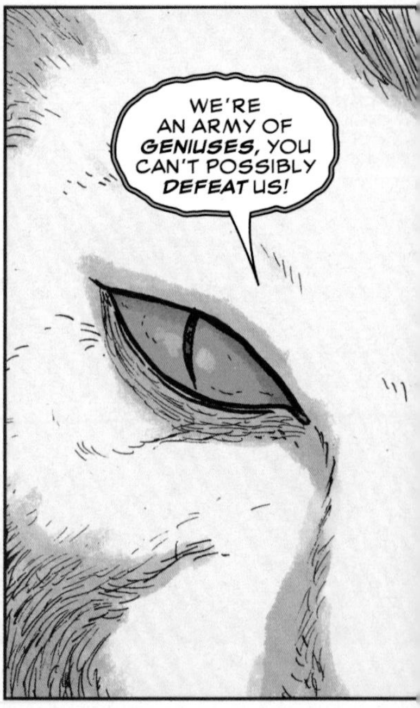
WE'RE AN ARMY OF GENIUSES, YOU CAN'T POSSIBLY DEFEAT US!

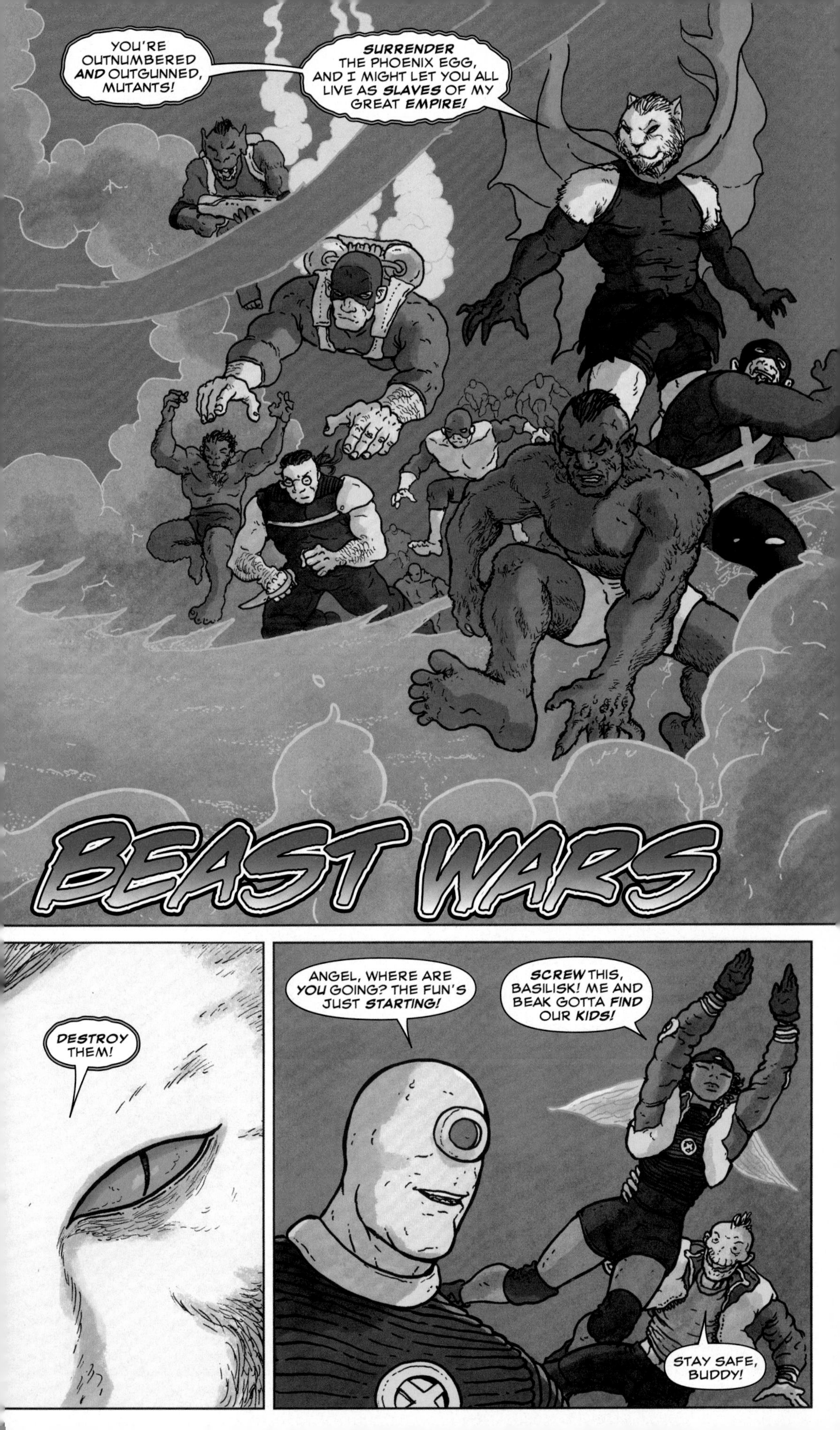
YOU'RE OUTNUMBERED AND OUTGUNNED, MUTANTS!
SURRENDER THE PHOENIX EGG, AND I MIGHT LET YOU ALL LIVE AS SLAVES OF MY GREAT EMPIRE!
BEAST WARS
DESTROY THEM!
ANGEL, WHERE ARE YOU GOING? THE FUN'S JUST STARTING!
SCREW THIS, BASILISK! ME AND BEAK GOTTA FIND OUR KIDS!
STAY SAFE, BUDDY!

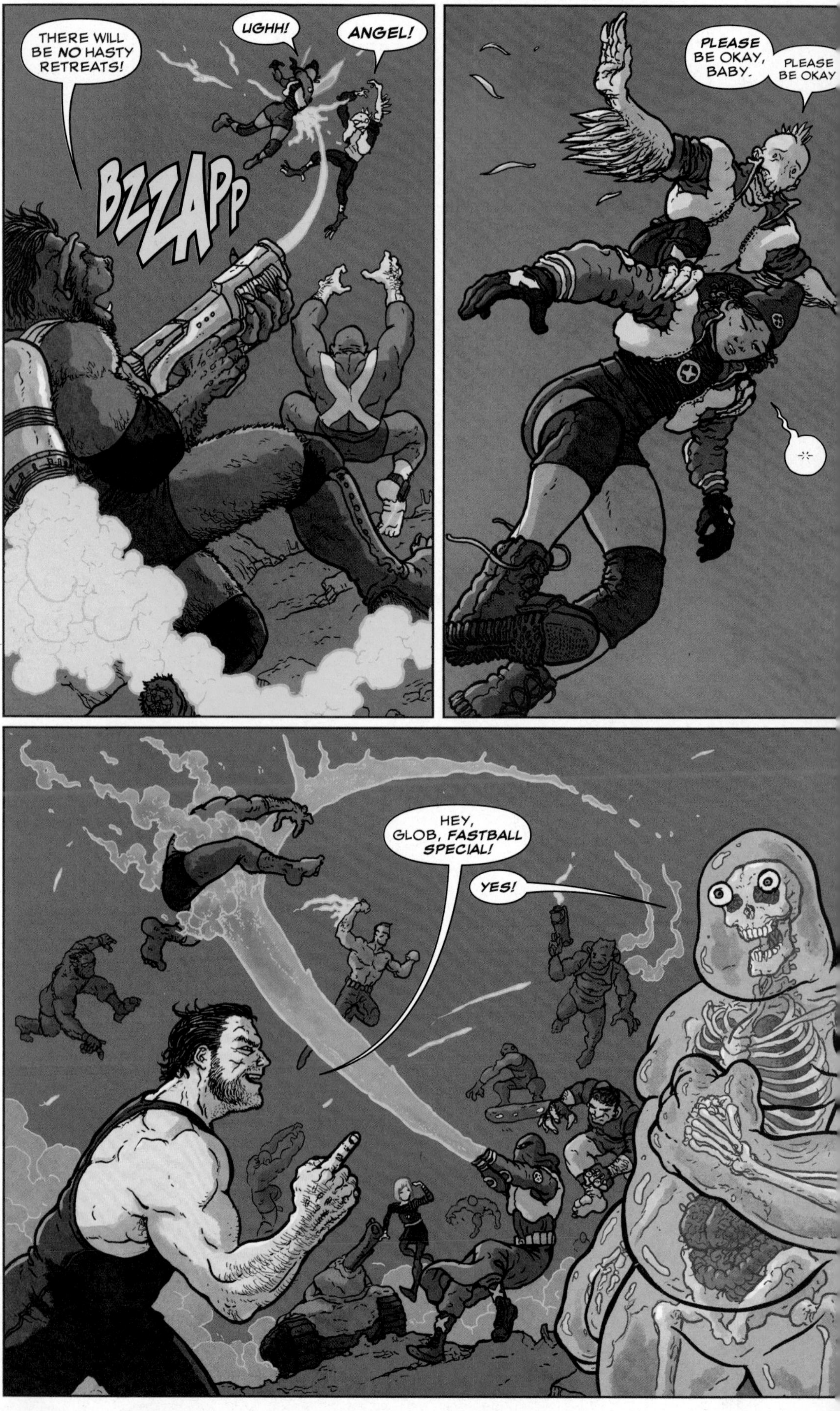
THERE WILL BE NO HASTY RETREATS!
UGHH!
ANGEL!
BZZAPP
PLEASE BE OKAY, BABY.
PLEASE BE OKAY
HEY, GLOB, FASTBALL SPECIAL!
YES!

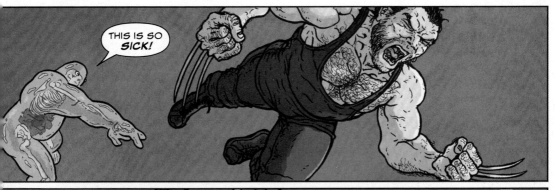

THIS IS SO *SICK!*

OH, MY STARS AND-- *GURK!*

SHUT UP! SHUT UP! SHUT UP!

GOOD JOB, *WOLVERINE!* KEEP AS MANY AS YOU CAN BLINDED, *DUST,* WHILE I PICK THEM OFF. *ERNST,* UH... DO YOUR THING!

MR. SUMMERS, THEY MUST HAVE *PSYCHIC DAMPENERS!* WE CUCKOOS CAN'T--

ESME, GIRLS, I *MIGHT* HAVE A PLAN BUT I NEED YOUR HELP.

SCOTT, BASILISK, CAN YOU TWO *COVER* US FOR A COUPLE OF MINUTES?

HYUK!

I'VE HAD *DREAMS* LIKE THIS...

COME ON, BABY, *HOLD* ON...

S'OKAY...JUST *FIND* OUR KIDS... KEEP THEM... *SAFE.*

DON'T WORRY, MOMMA--

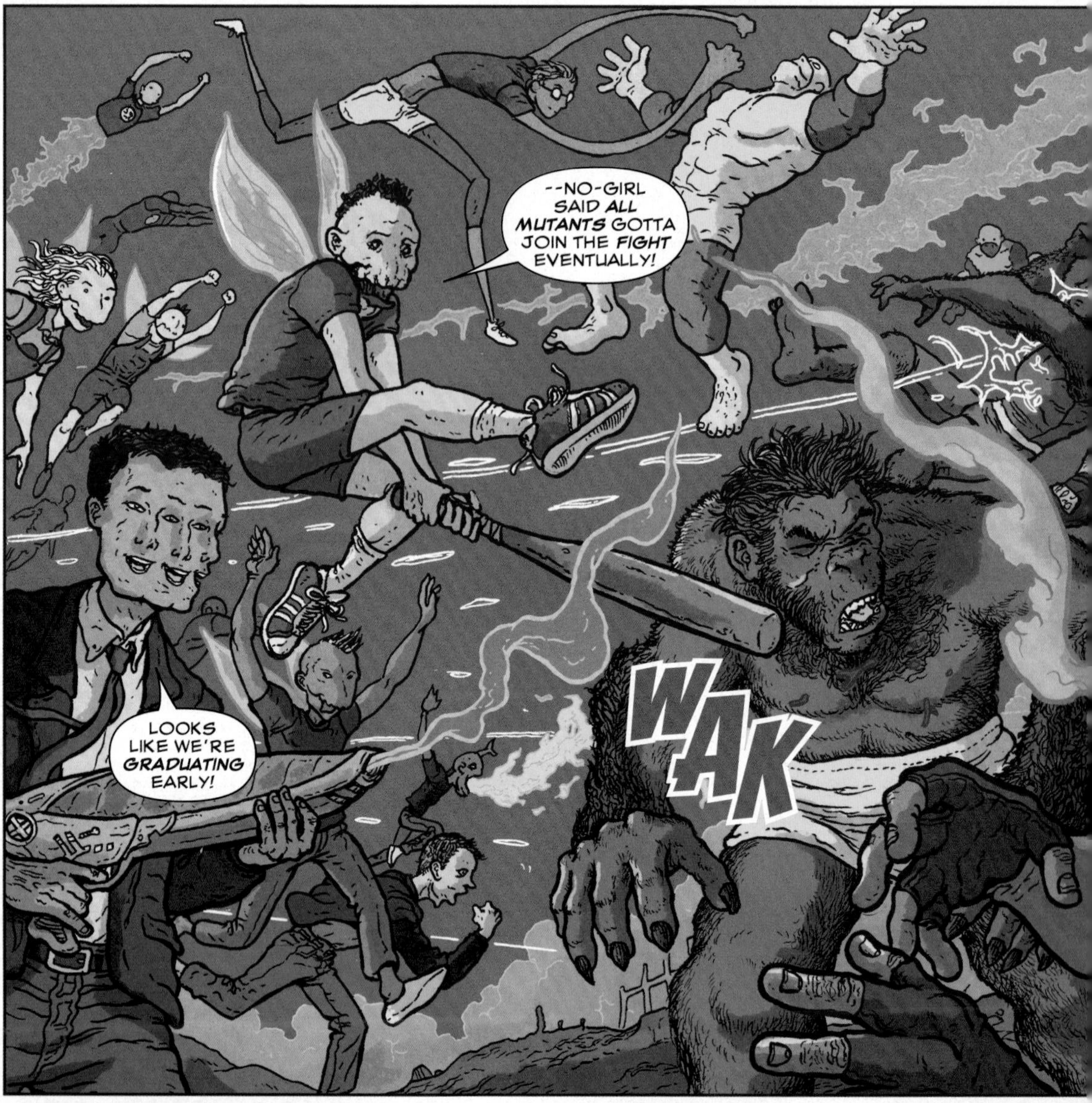
--NO-GIRL SAID *ALL* *MUTANTS* GOTTA JOIN THE *FIGHT* EVENTUALLY!
LOOKS LIKE WE'RE *GRADUATING* EARLY!
WAK

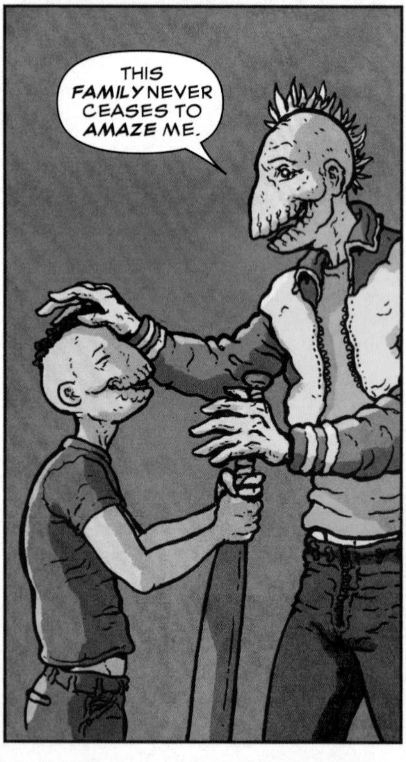
THIS *FAMILY* NEVER CEASES TO *AMAZE* ME.

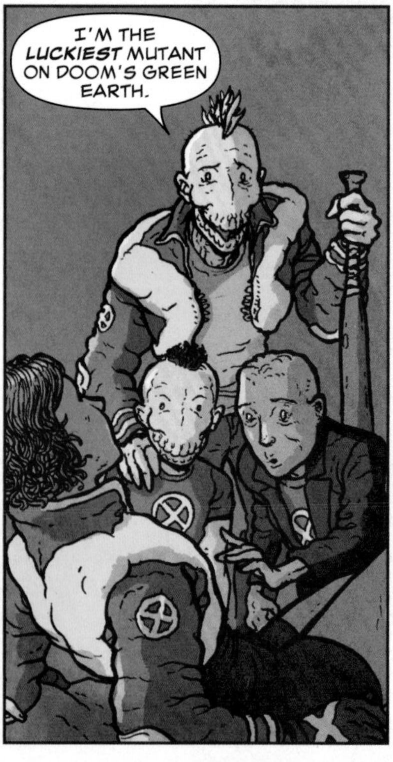
I'M THE *LUCKIEST* MUTANT ON DOOM'S GREEN EARTH.

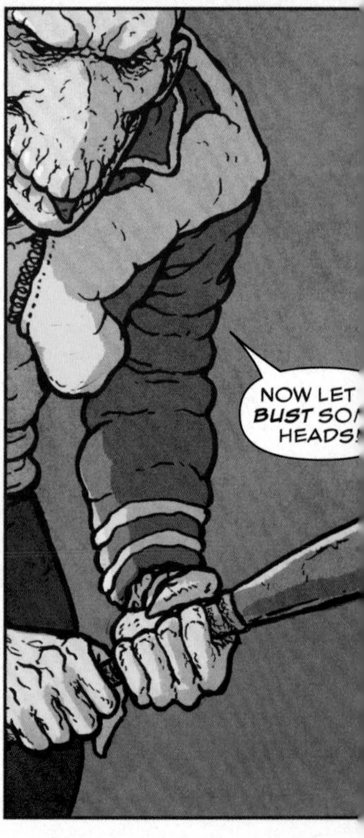
NOW LET
BUST SO
HEADS!

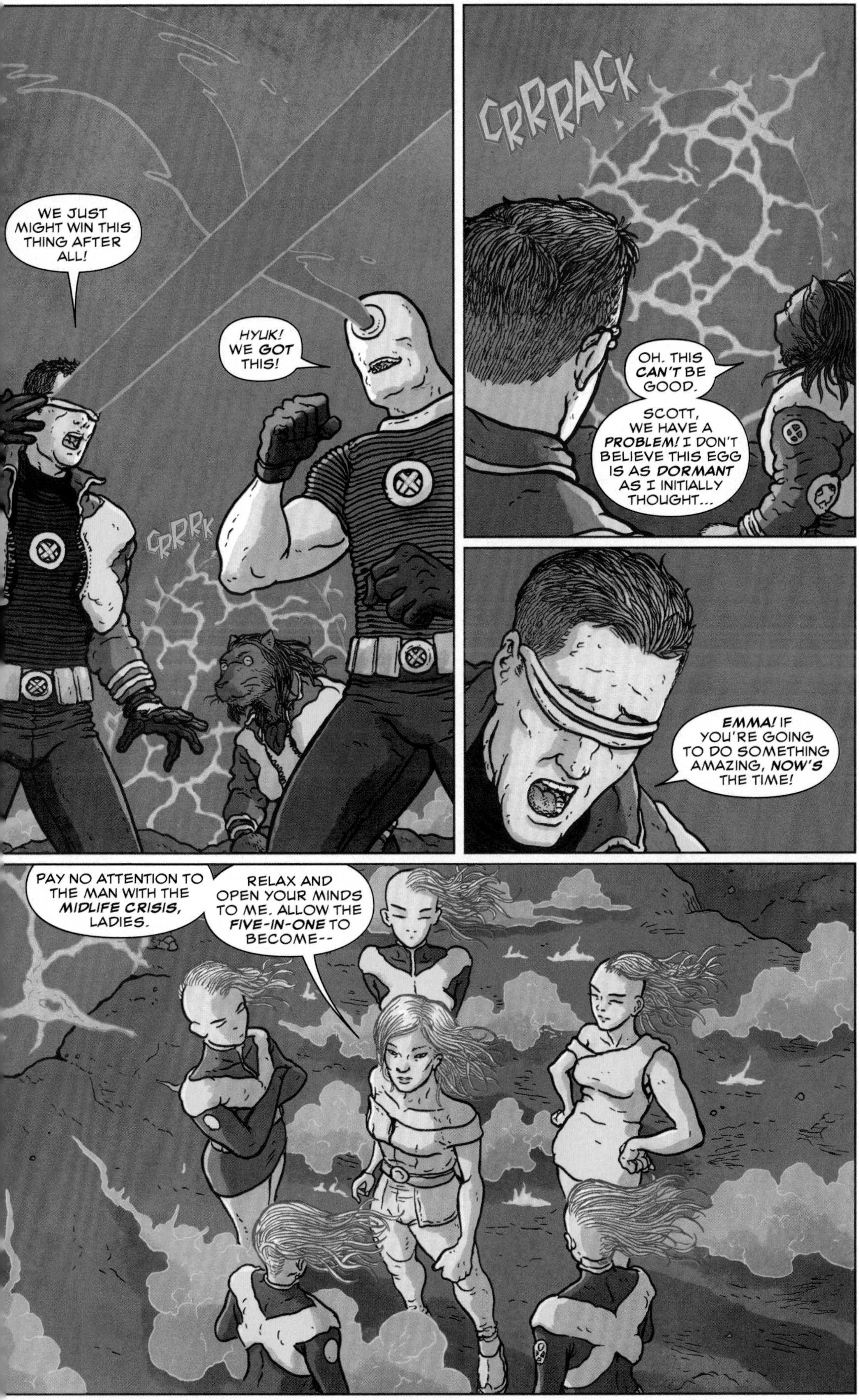
WE JUST MIGHT WIN THIS THING AFTER ALL!
HYUK! WE GOT THIS!
CRRRK
CRRRACK
OH. THIS CAN'T BE GOOD.
SCOTT, WE HAVE A PROBLEM! I DON'T BELIEVE THIS EGG IS AS DORMANT AS I INITIALLY THOUGHT...
EMMA! IF YOU'RE GOING TO DO SOMETHING AMAZING, NOW'S THE TIME!
PAY NO ATTENTION TO THE MAN WITH THE MIDLIFE CRISIS, LADIES.
RELAX AND OPEN YOUR MINDS TO ME. ALLOW THE FIVE-IN-ONE TO BECOME--

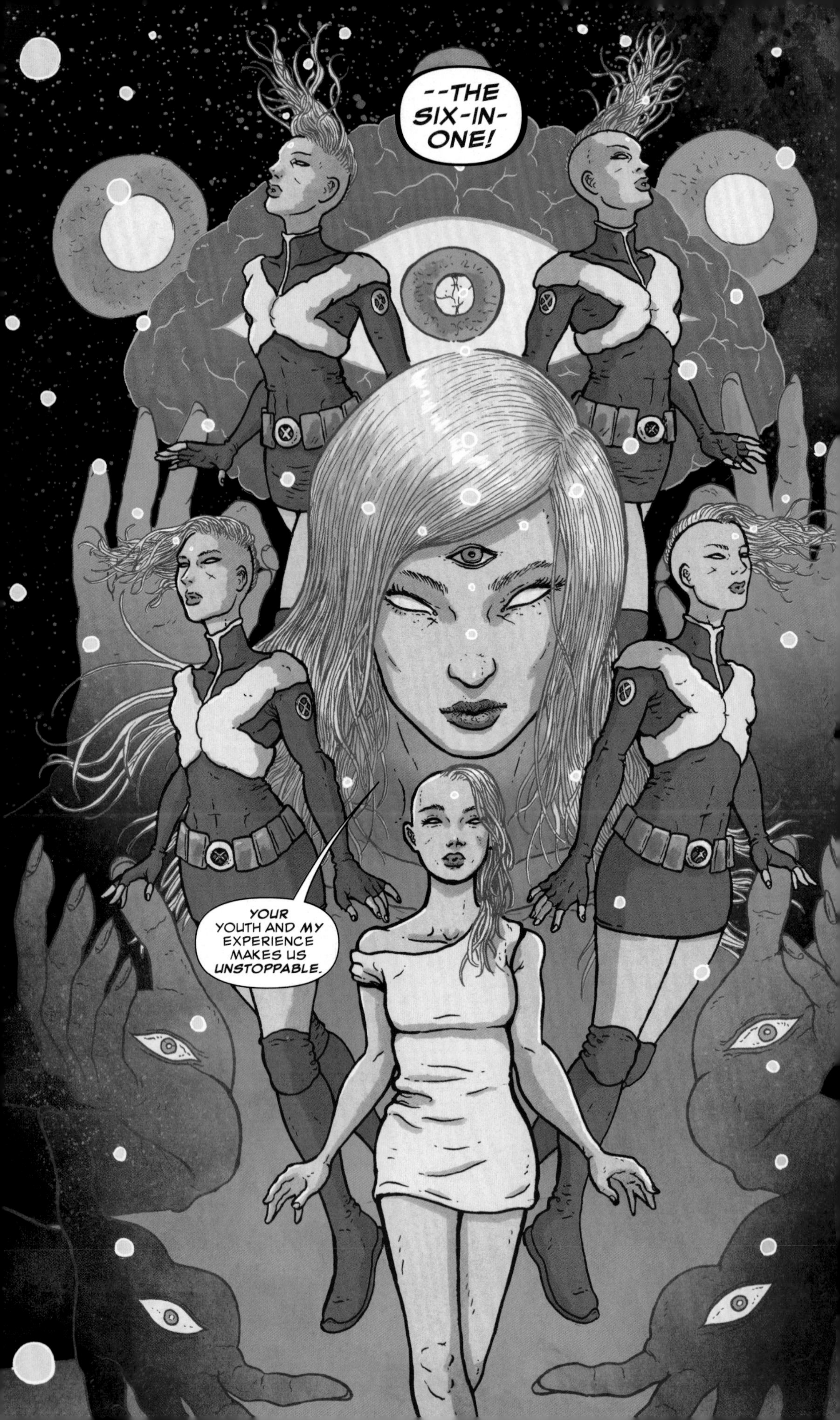
--THE SIX-IN-ONE!
YOUR YOUTH AND MY EXPERIENCE MAKES US UNSTOPPABLE.

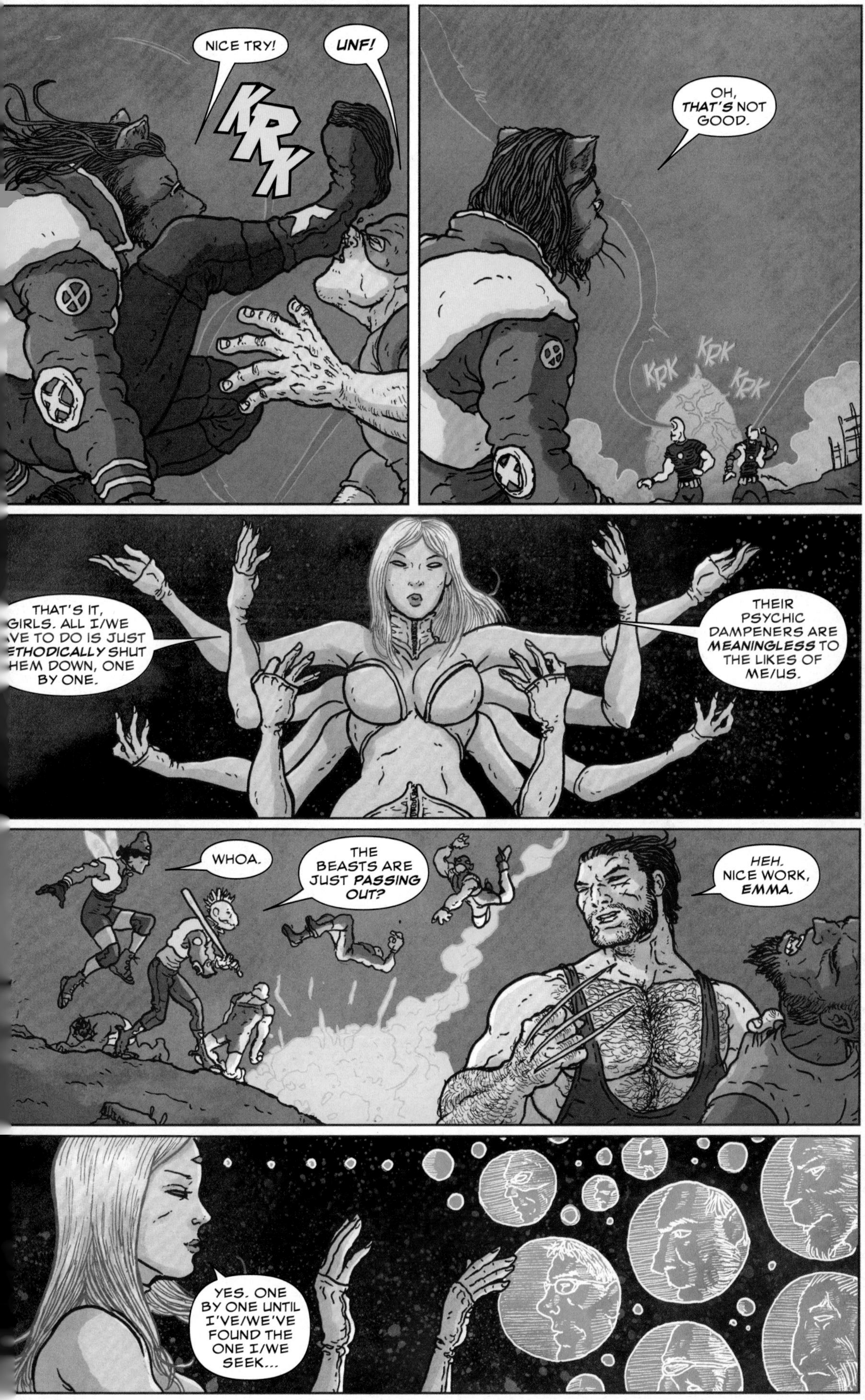
NICE TRY!
UNF!
KRK
OH, THAT'S NOT GOOD.
KRK KRK KRK
THAT'S IT, GIRLS. ALL I/WE ...VE TO DO IS JUST ...ETHODICALLY SHUT ...HEM DOWN, ONE BY ONE.
THEIR PSYCHIC DAMPENERS ARE MEANINGLESS TO THE LIKES OF ME/US.
WHOA.
THE BEASTS ARE JUST PASSING OUT?
HEH. NICE WORK, EMMA.
YES. ONE BY ONE UNTIL I'VE/WE'VE FOUND THE ONE I/WE SEEK...

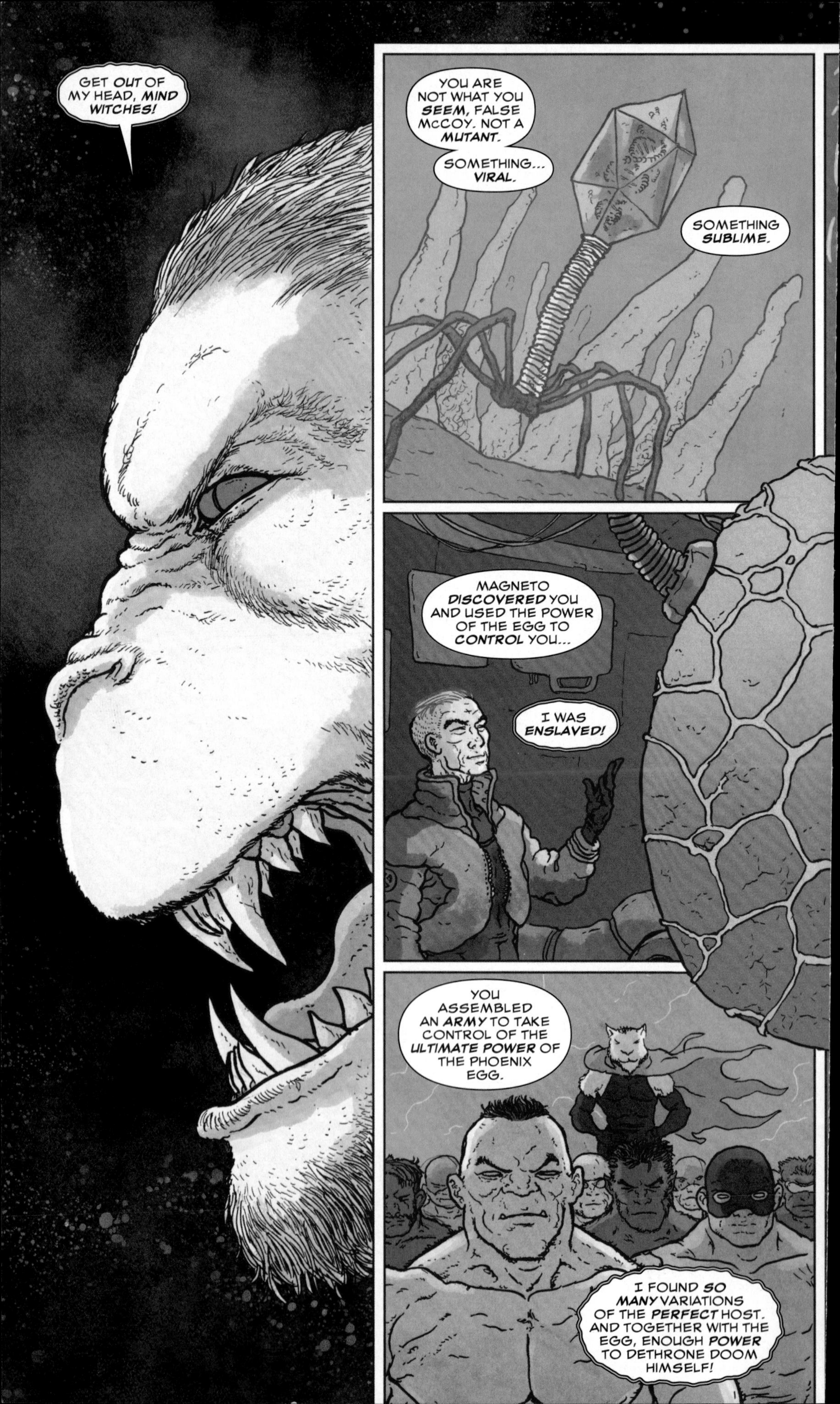

GET OUT OF MY HEAD, MIND WITCHES!
YOU ARE NOT WHAT YOU SEEM, FALSE McCOY. NOT A MUTANT.
SOMETHING... VIRAL.
SOMETHING SUBLIME.
MAGNETO DISCOVERED YOU AND USED THE POWER OF THE EGG TO CONTROL YOU...
I WAS ENSLAVED!
YOU ASSEMBLED AN ARMY TO TAKE CONTROL OF THE ULTIMATE POWER OF THE PHOENIX EGG.
I FOUND SO MANY VARIATIONS OF THE PERFECT HOST. AND TOGETHER WITH THE EGG, ENOUGH POWER TO DETHRONE DOOM HIMSELF!

USING THE PHOENIX EGG, MAGNETO AMPLIFIED HIS POWERS WITH *MUTANT GROWTH HORMONE* WHERE YOUR VIRAL FORM LAY HIDDEN...

I WAS PATIENT. I PLAYED THE *LONG GAME*. I WAS *INEVITABLE* UNTIL--

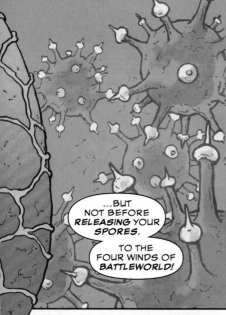

...BUT NOT BEFORE *RELEASING* YOUR *SPORES*.

TO THE *FOUR WINDS* OF *BATTLEWORLD!*

BUT *YOU* OVERLOOKED SOMETHING *IMPORTANT*, EMMA FROST...

WHAT? OUR HANK? HOW COULD I... WE MISS THAT?

ESME!

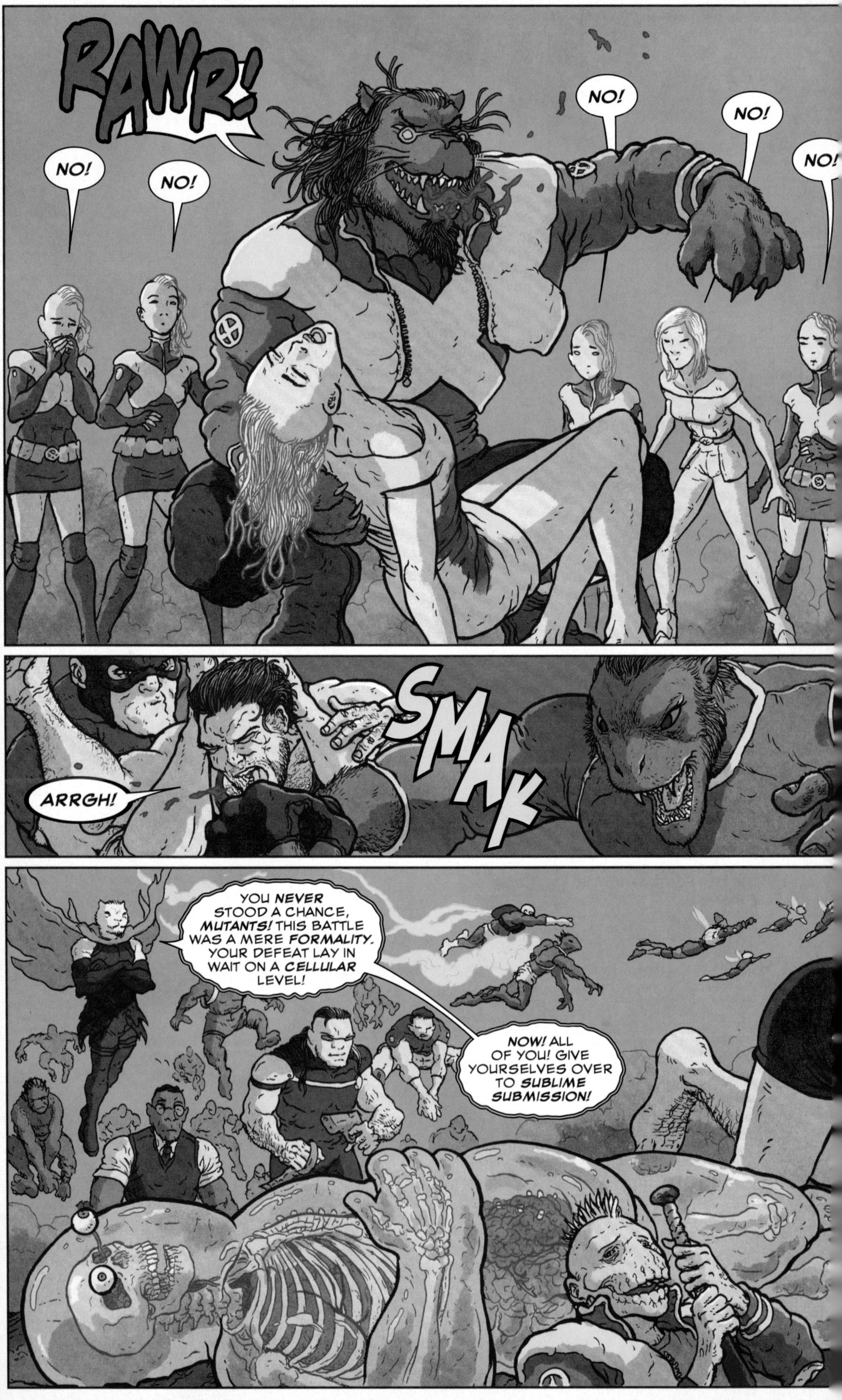
RAWR!
NO!
NO!
NO!
NO!
NO!
SMAK
ARRGH!
YOU NEVER STOOD A CHANCE, MUTANTS! THIS BATTLE WAS A MERE FORMALITY. YOUR DEFEAT LAY IN WAIT ON A CELLULAR LEVEL!
NOW! ALL OF YOU! GIVE YOURSELVES OVER TO SUBLIME SUBMISSION!

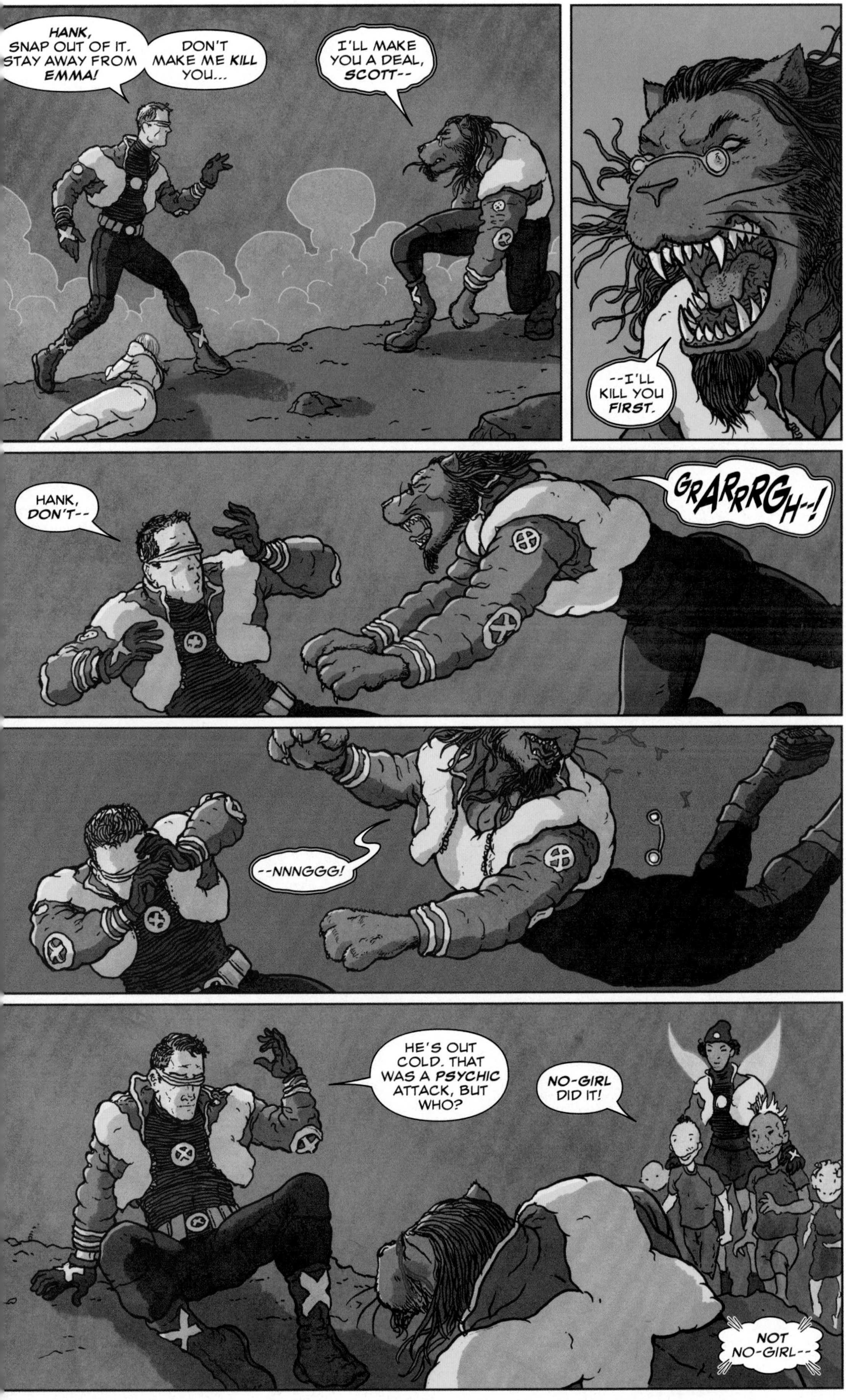
HANK, SNAP OUT OF IT. STAY AWAY FROM EMMA!
DON'T MAKE ME KILL YOU...
I'LL MAKE YOU A DEAL, SCOTT--
--I'LL KILL YOU FIRST.
HANK, DON'T--
GRARRRGH--!
--NNNGGG!
HE'S OUT COLD. THAT WAS A PSYCHIC ATTACK, BUT WHO?
NO-GIRL DID IT!
NOT NO-GIRL--

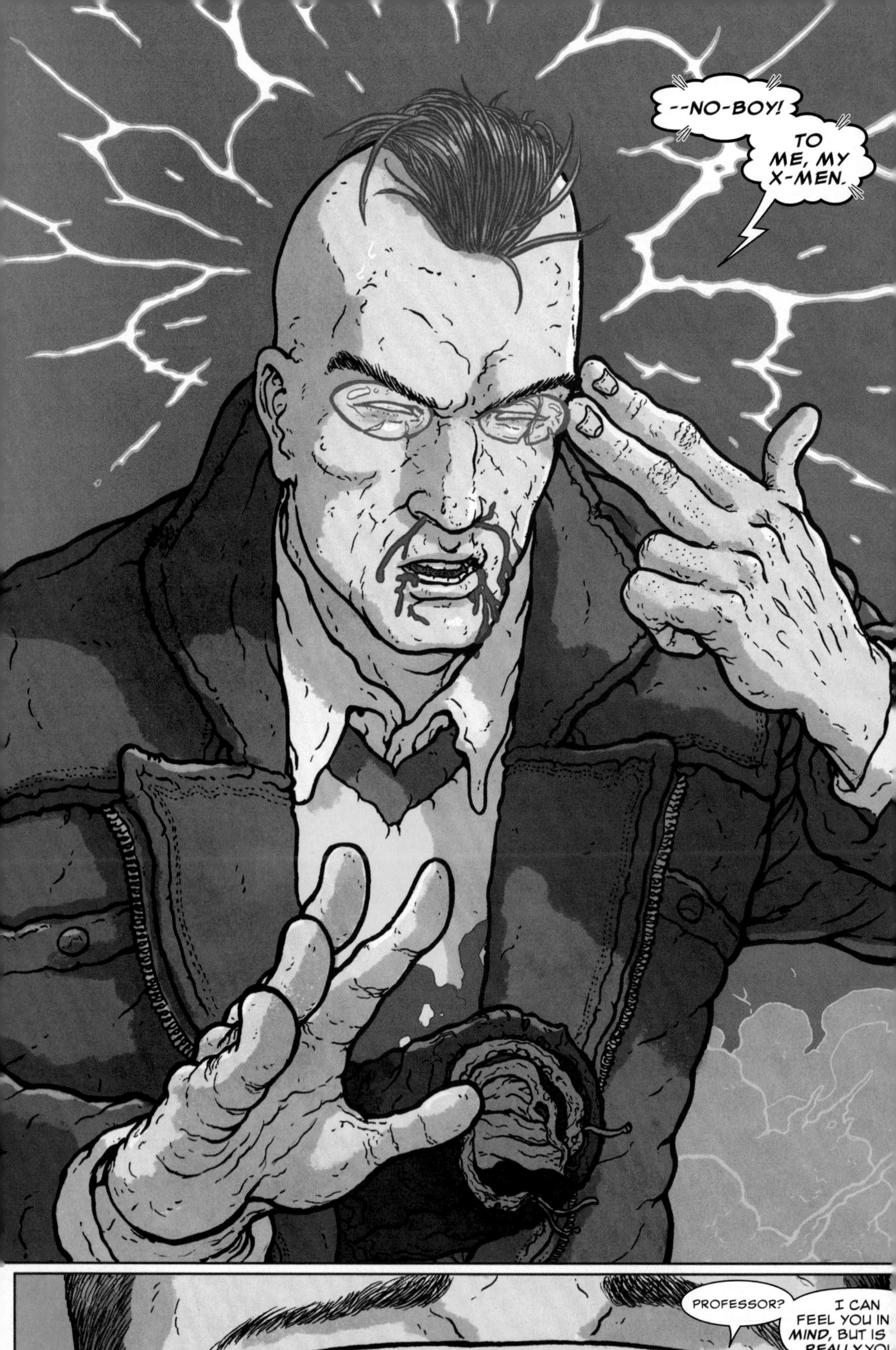
--NO-BOY!
TO ME, MY X-MEN.
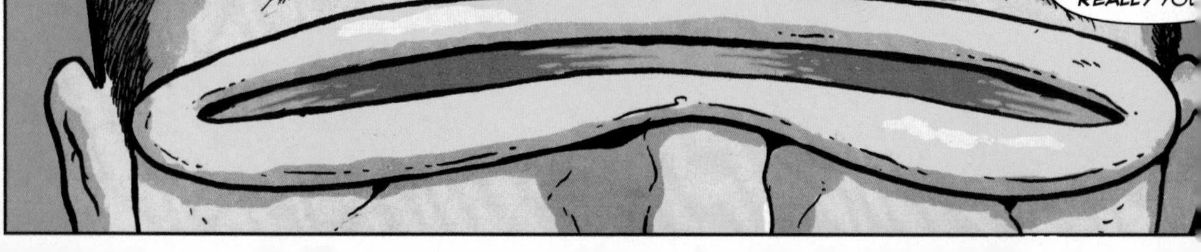
PROFESSOR?
I CAN FEEL YOU IN MIND, BUT IS REALLY YOU

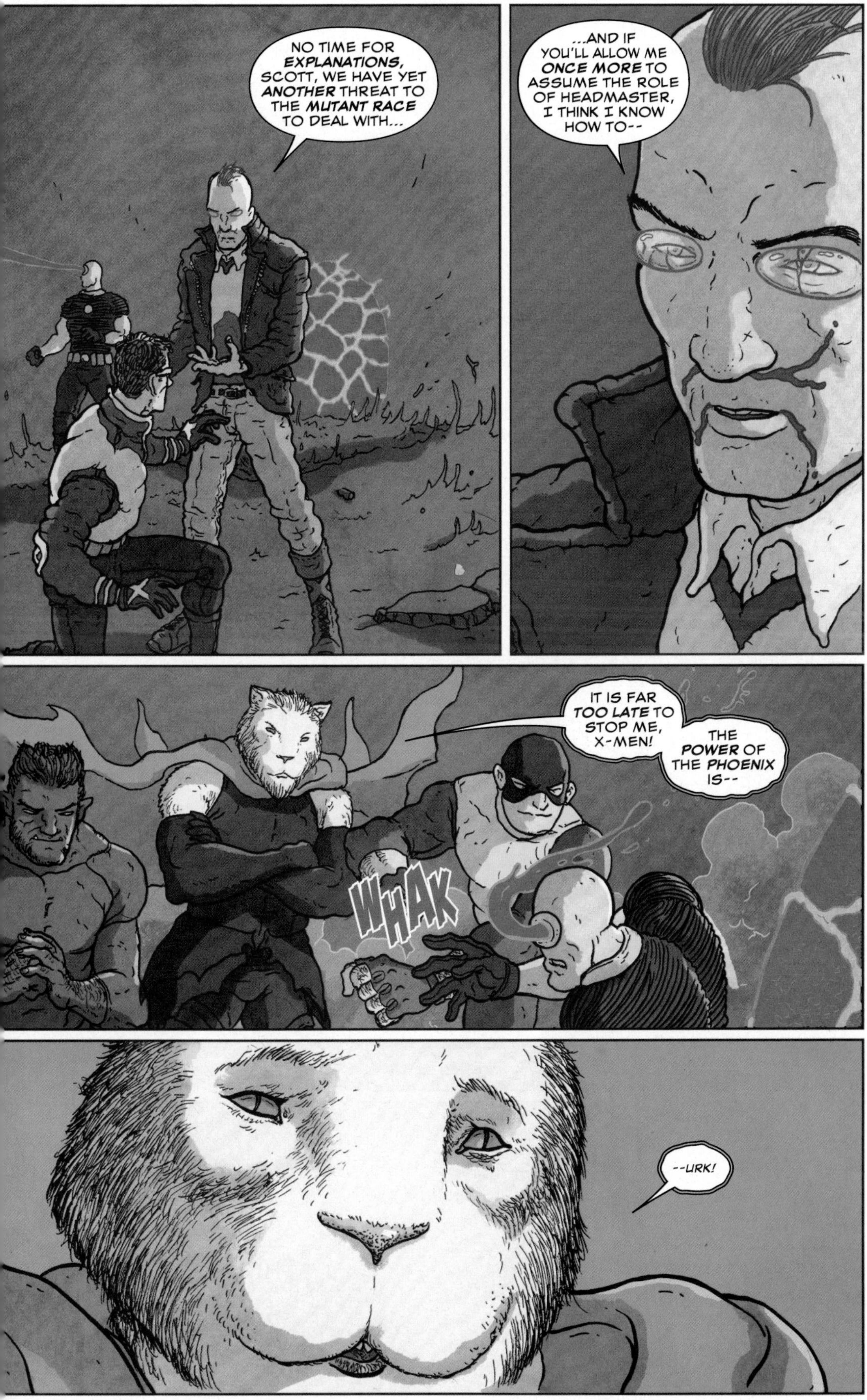
NO TIME FOR EXPLANATIONS, SCOTT, WE HAVE YET ANOTHER THREAT TO THE MUTANT RACE TO DEAL WITH...
...AND IF YOU'LL ALLOW ME ONCE MORE TO ASSUME THE ROLE OF HEADMASTER, I THINK I KNOW HOW TO--
IT IS FAR TOO LATE TO STOP ME, X-MEN!
THE POWER OF THE PHOENIX IS--
WHAK
--URK!

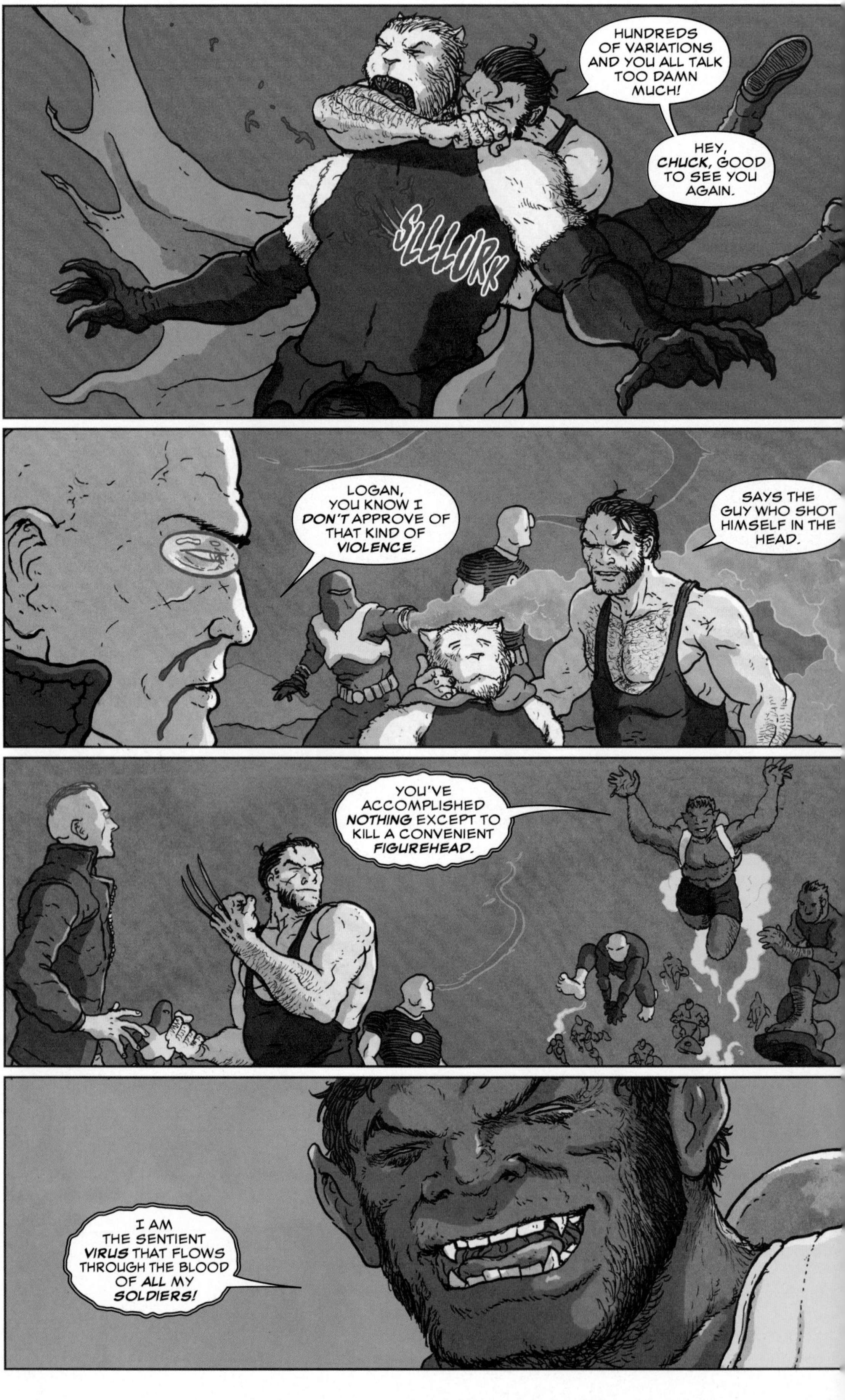
HUNDREDS OF VARIATIONS AND YOU ALL TALK TOO DAMN MUCH!
HEY, CHUCK, GOOD TO SEE YOU AGAIN.
SLLLURK
LOGAN, YOU KNOW I DON'T APPROVE OF THAT KIND OF VIOLENCE.
SAYS THE GUY WHO SHOT HIMSELF IN THE HEAD.
YOU'VE ACCOMPLISHED NOTHING EXCEPT TO KILL A CONVENIENT FIGUREHEAD.
I AM THE SENTIENT VIRUS THAT FLOWS THROUGH THE BLOOD OF ALL MY SOLDIERS!

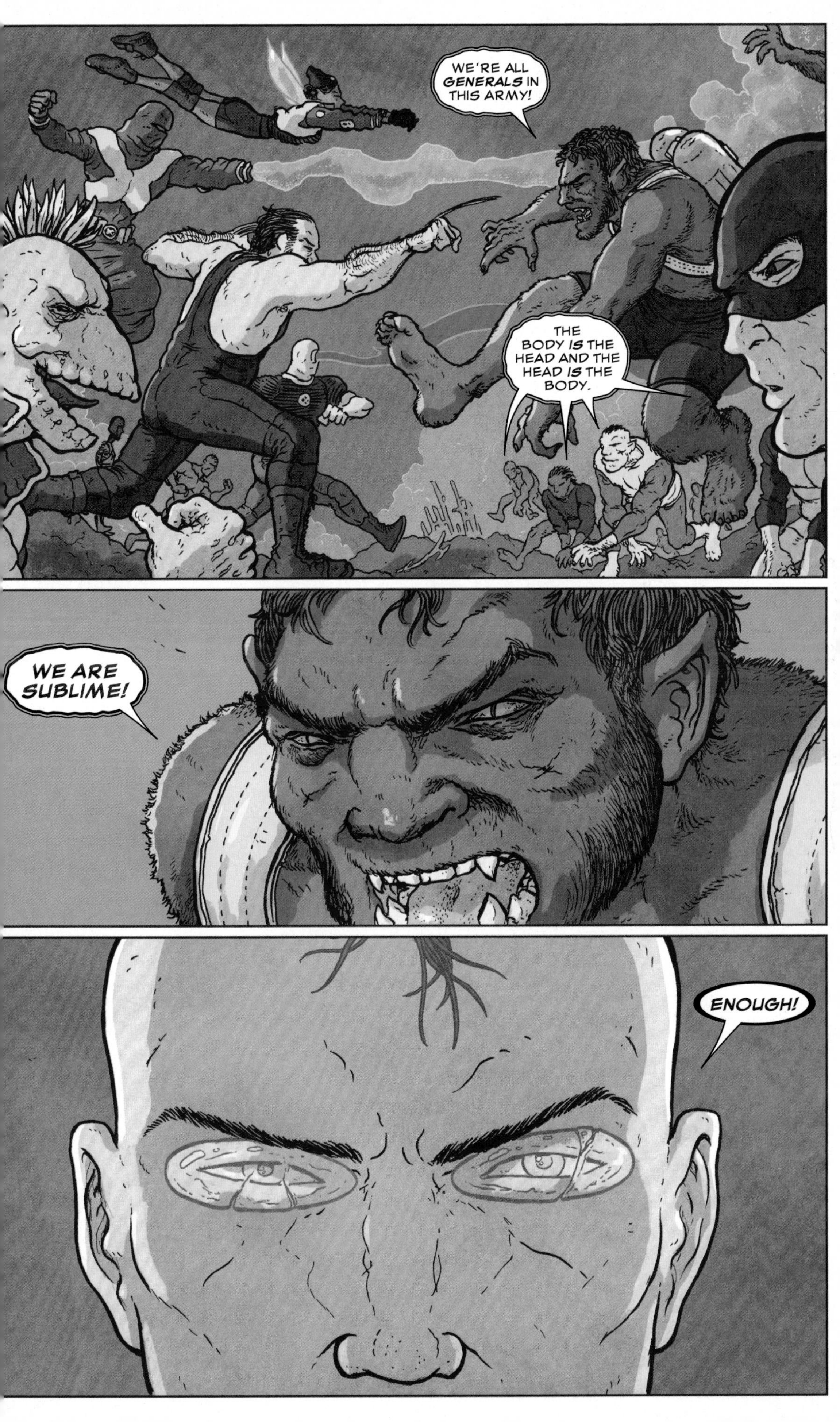
WE'RE ALL GENERALS IN THIS ARMY!
THE BODY IS THE HEAD AND THE HEAD IS THE BODY.
WE ARE SUBLIME!
ENOUGH!

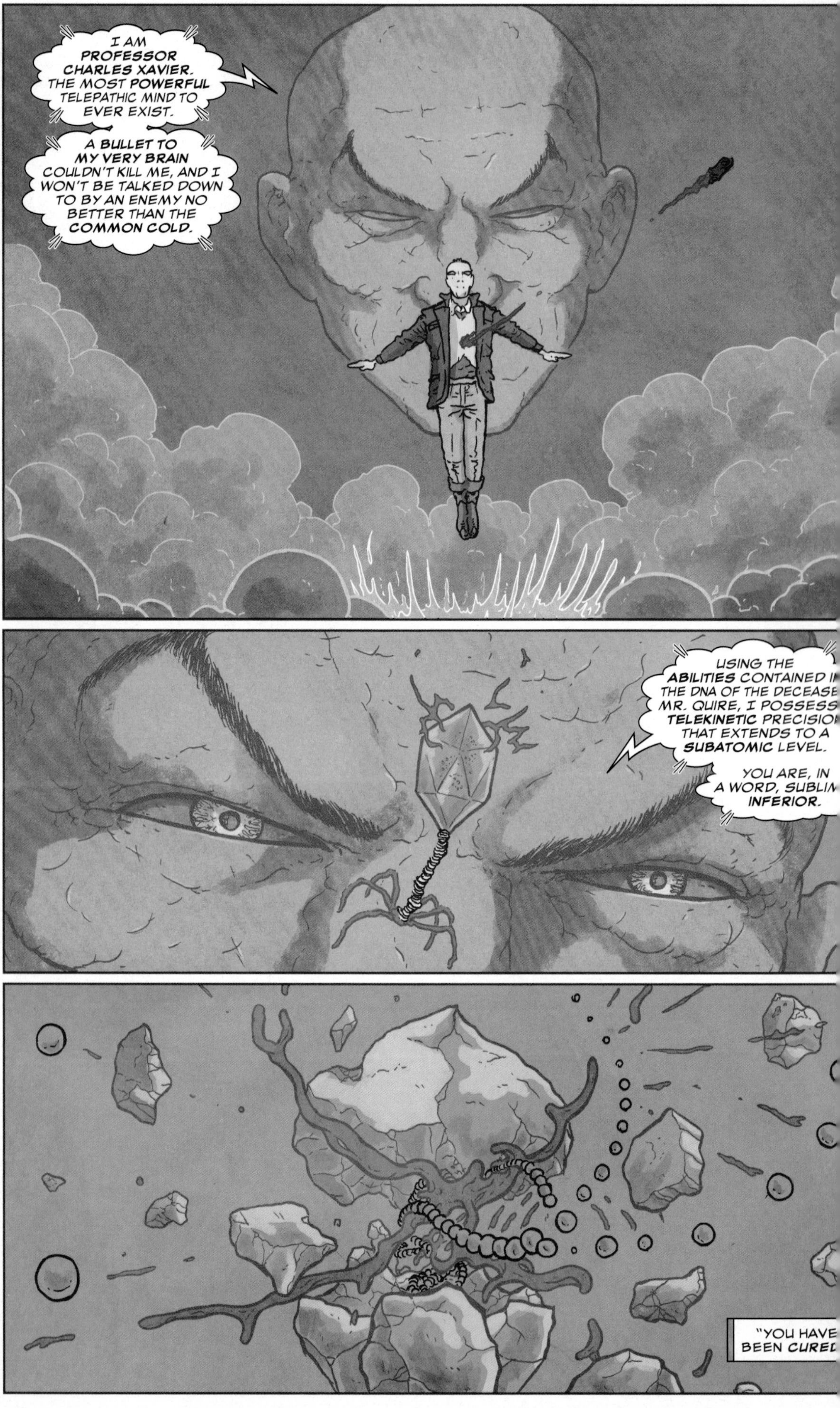
I AM PROFESSOR CHARLES XAVIER. THE MOST POWERFUL TELEPATHIC MIND TO EVER EXIST.
A BULLET TO MY VERY BRAIN COULDN'T KILL ME, AND I WON'T BE TALKED DOWN TO BY AN ENEMY NO BETTER THAN THE COMMON COLD.
USING THE ABILITIES CONTAINED I THE DNA OF THE DECEASE MR. QUIRE, I POSSESS TELEKINETIC PRECISIO THAT EXTENDS TO A SUBATOMIC LEVEL.
YOU ARE, IN A WORD, SUBLIM INFERIOR.
"YOU HAVE BEEN CURED

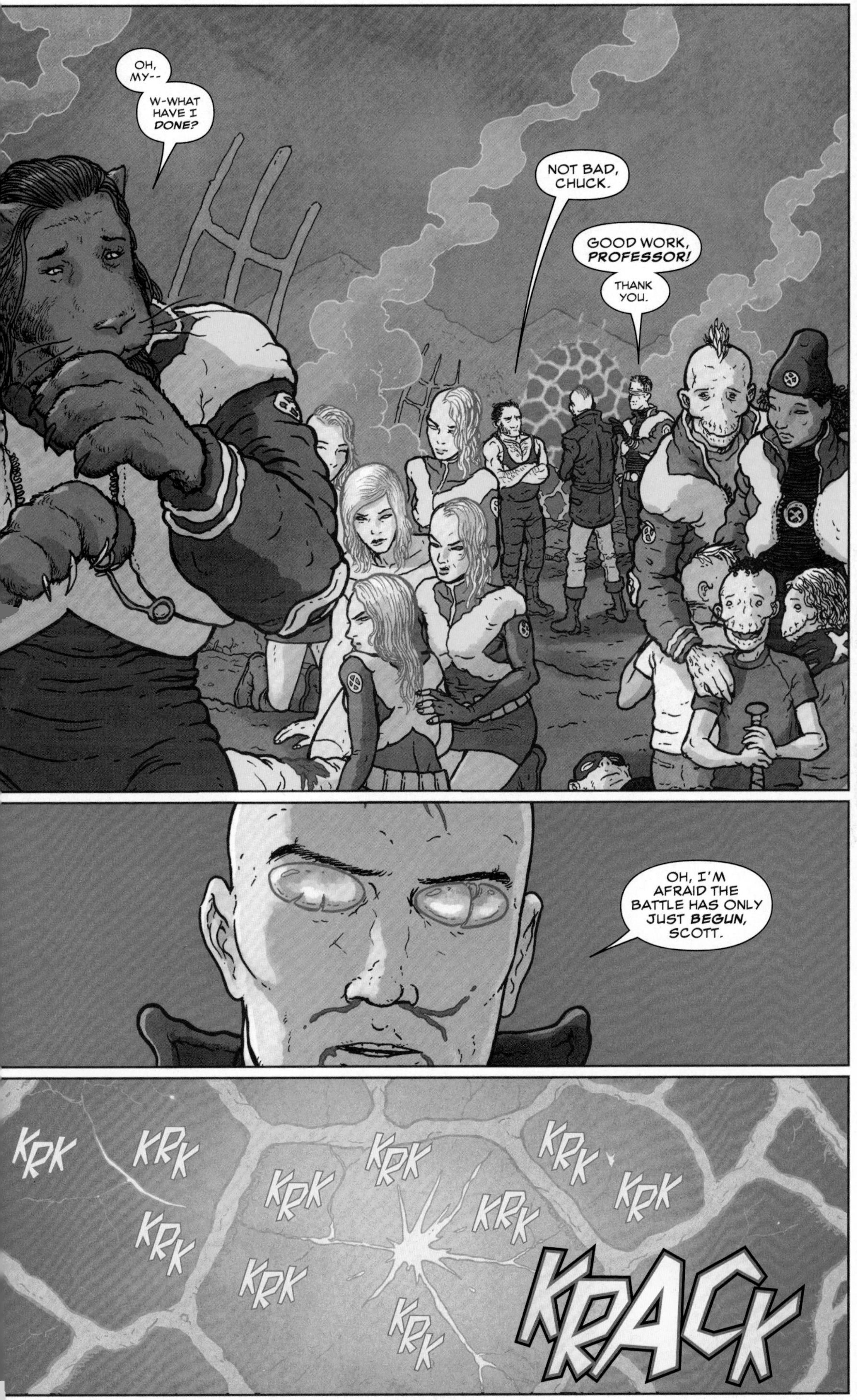
OH, MY--
W-WHAT HAVE I DONE?
NOT BAD, CHUCK.
GOOD WORK, PROFESSOR!
THANK YOU.
OH, I'M AFRAID THE BATTLE HAS ONLY JUST BEGUN, SCOTT.
KRK KRK KRK KRK KRK KRK KRK KRK KRK KRK
KRACK

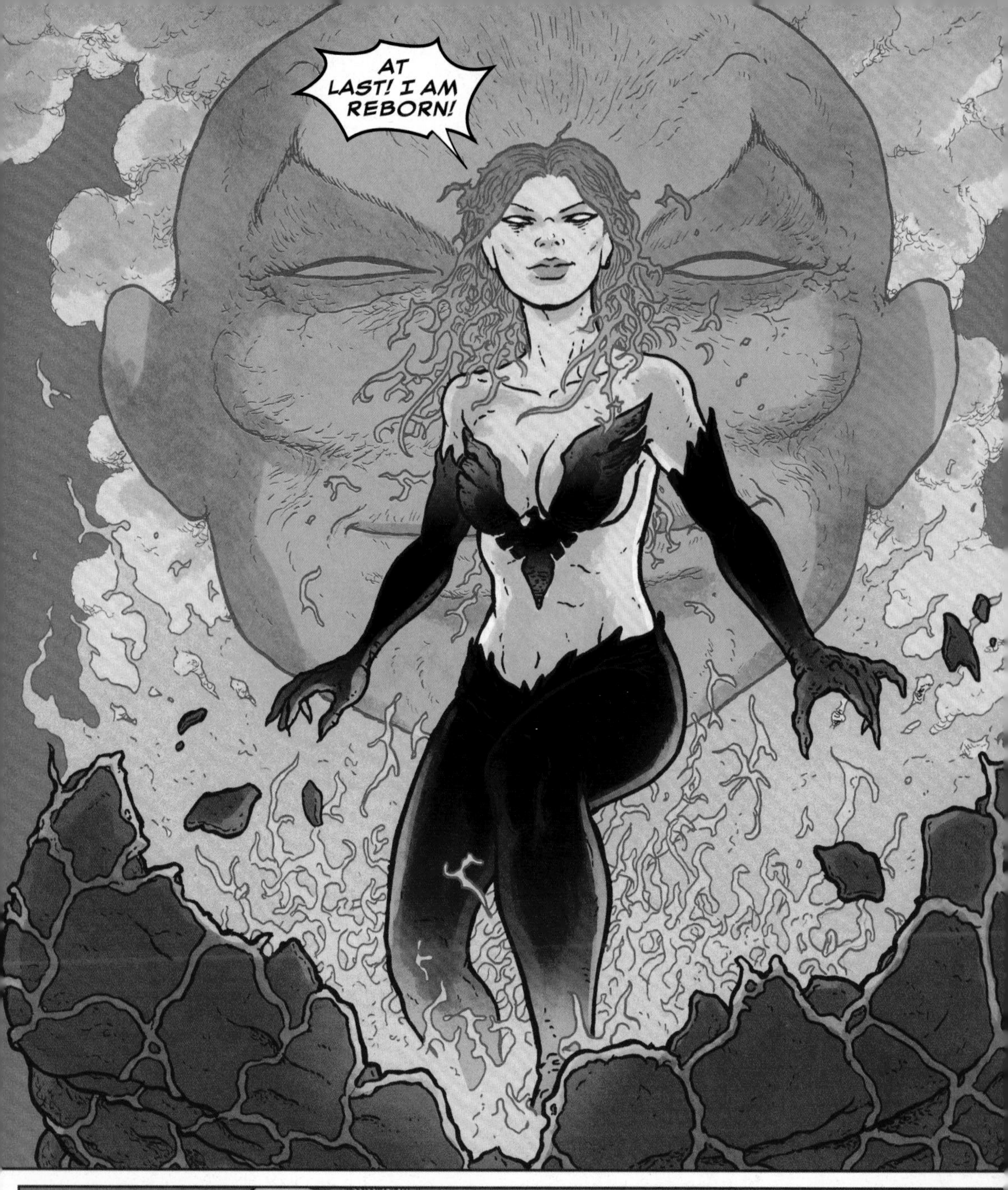
AT LAST! I AM REBORN!

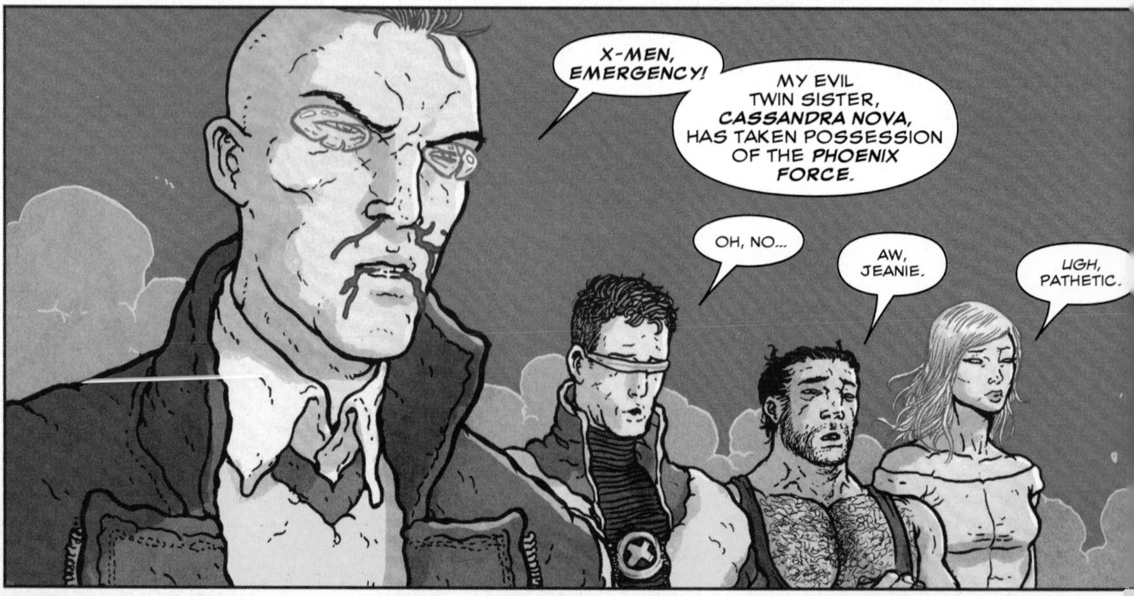
X-MEN, EMERGENCY!
MY EVIL TWIN SISTER, CASSANDRA NOVA, HAS TAKEN POSSESSION OF THE PHOENIX FORCE.
OH, NO...
AW, JEANIE.
UGH, PATHETIC.

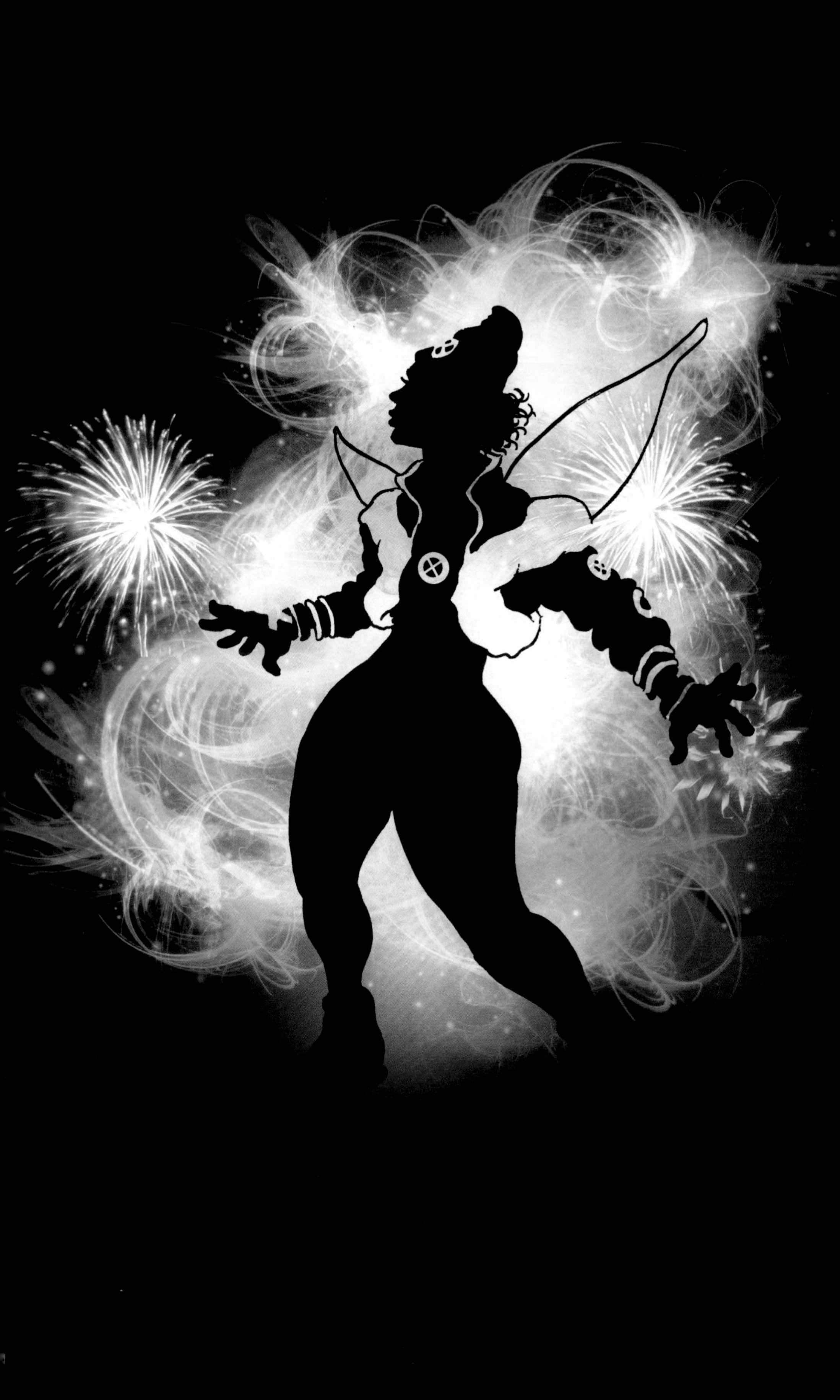

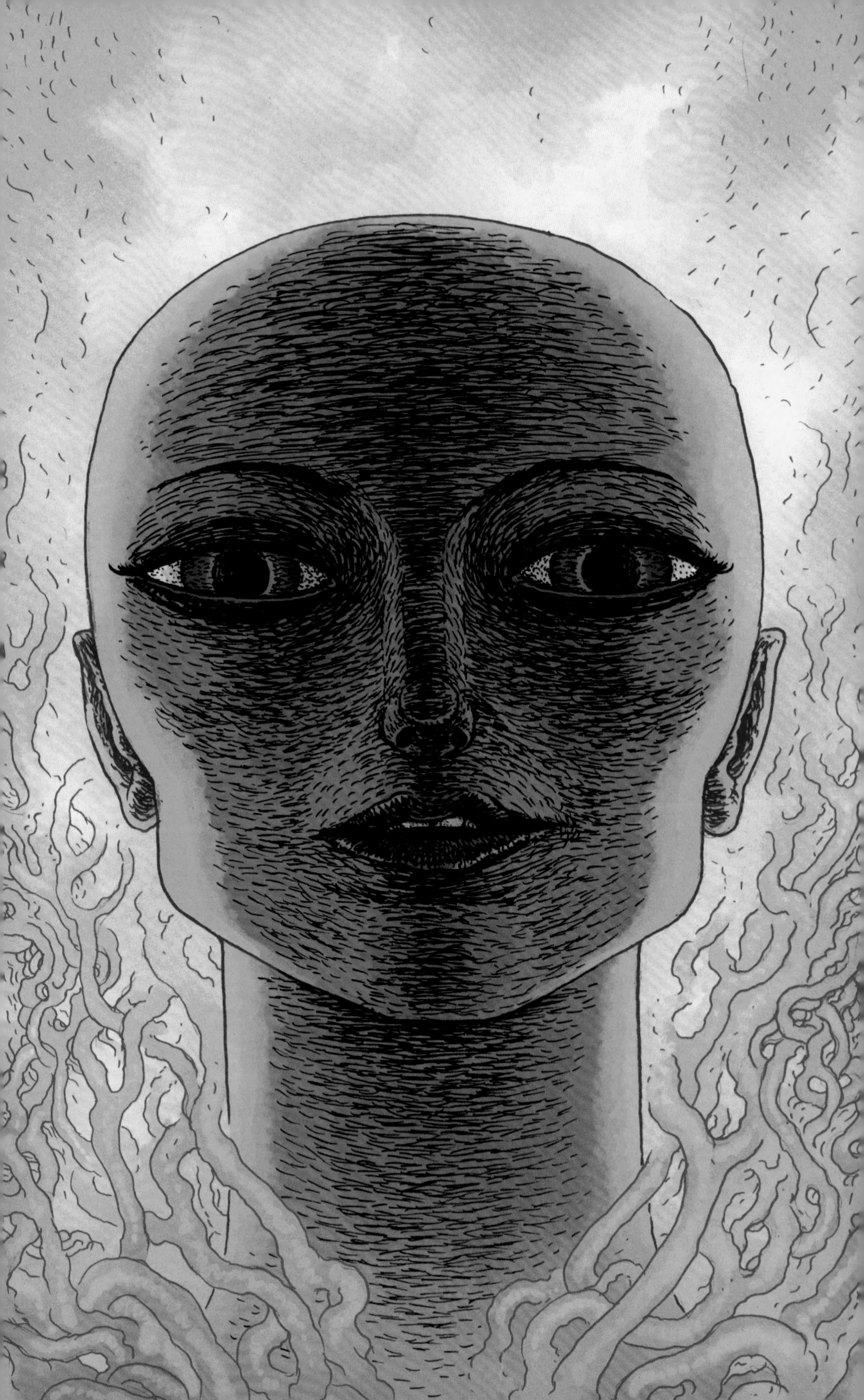

ARE THESE WORDS FROM THE PAST?

THIS IS ONLY HOW IT STARTED...

ARE YOU OKAY, JEAN?

I'M FINE, HANK. MY ALARM *DIDN'T* GO OFF THIS MORNING. THE WHOLE DAY HAS FELT... OFF.

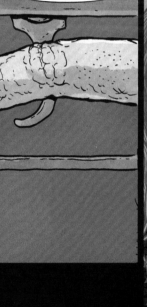

CASSANDRA, GET OUT OF MY HEAD OR I FIRE.

PROFESSOR?

CLK

JEAN! GET OUT OF MY MIND!

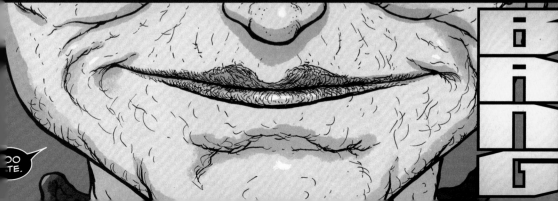

BANG

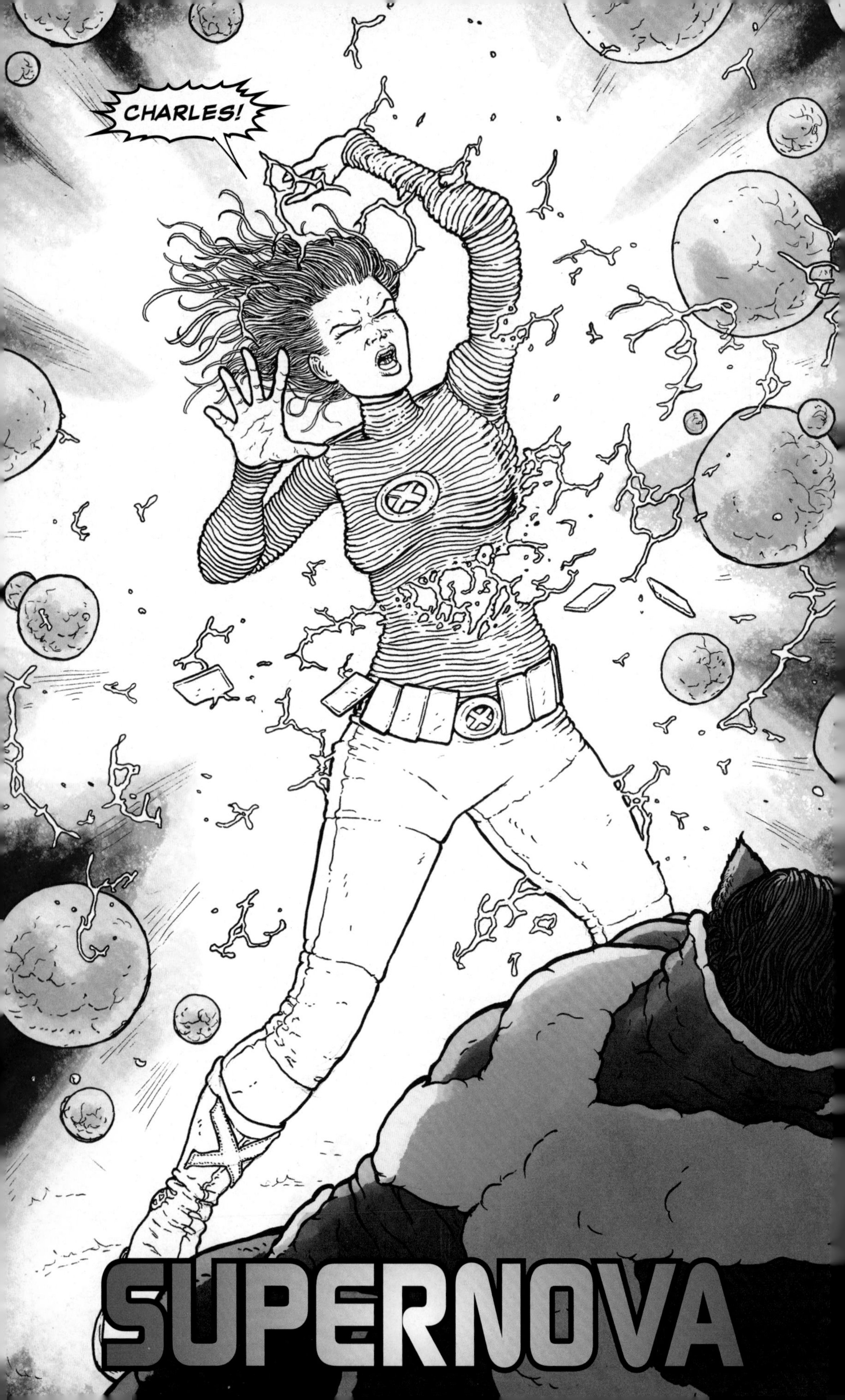
CHARLES!
SUPERNOVA

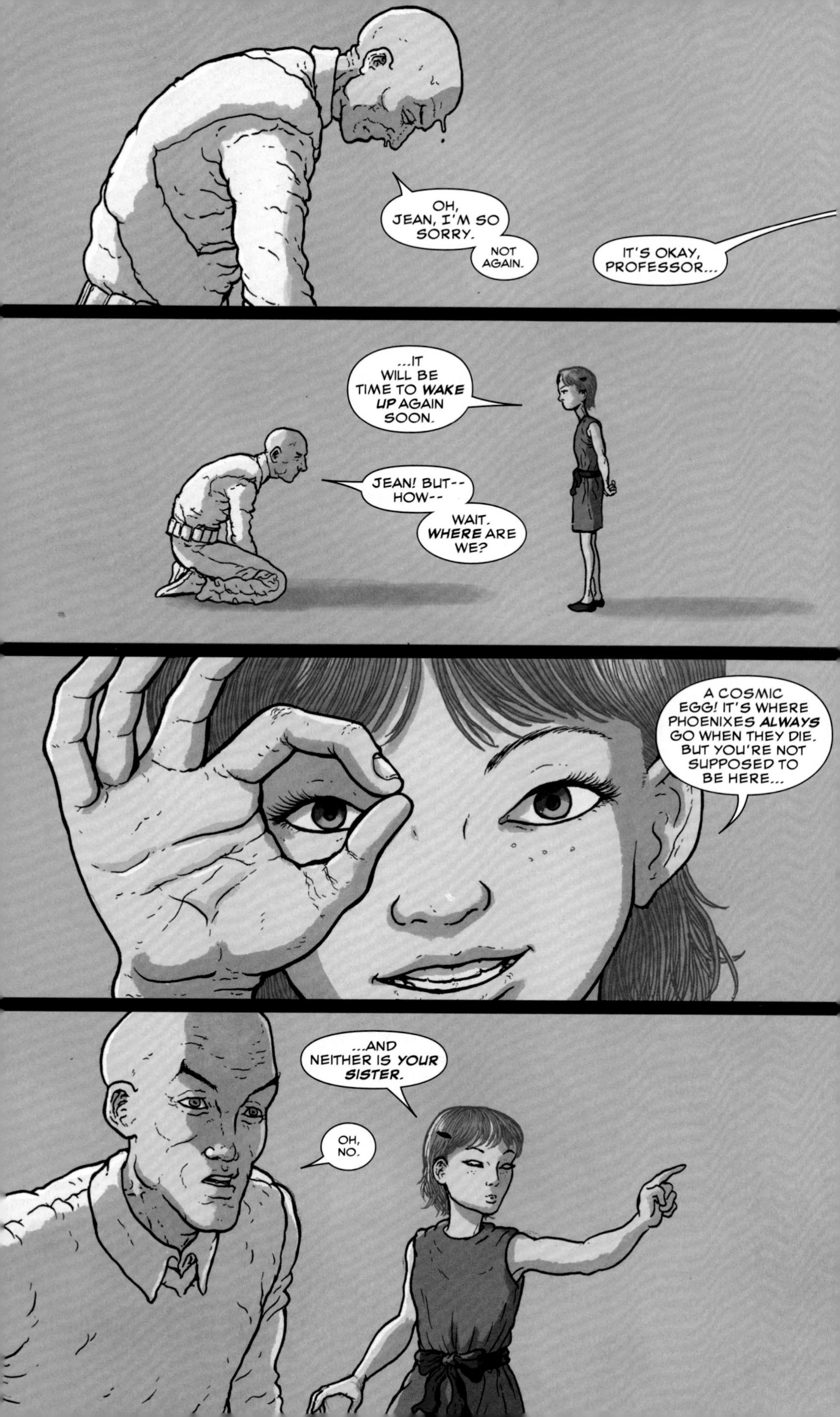
OH, JEAN, I'M SO SORRY.
NOT AGAIN.
IT'S OKAY, PROFESSOR...
...IT WILL BE TIME TO *WAKE UP* AGAIN SOON.
JEAN! BUT-- HOW--
WAIT. *WHERE* ARE WE?
A COSMIC EGG! IT'S WHERE PHOENIXES *ALWAYS* GO WHEN THEY DIE. BUT YOU'RE NOT SUPPOSED TO BE HERE...
...AND NEITHER IS *YOUR SISTER.*
OH, NO.

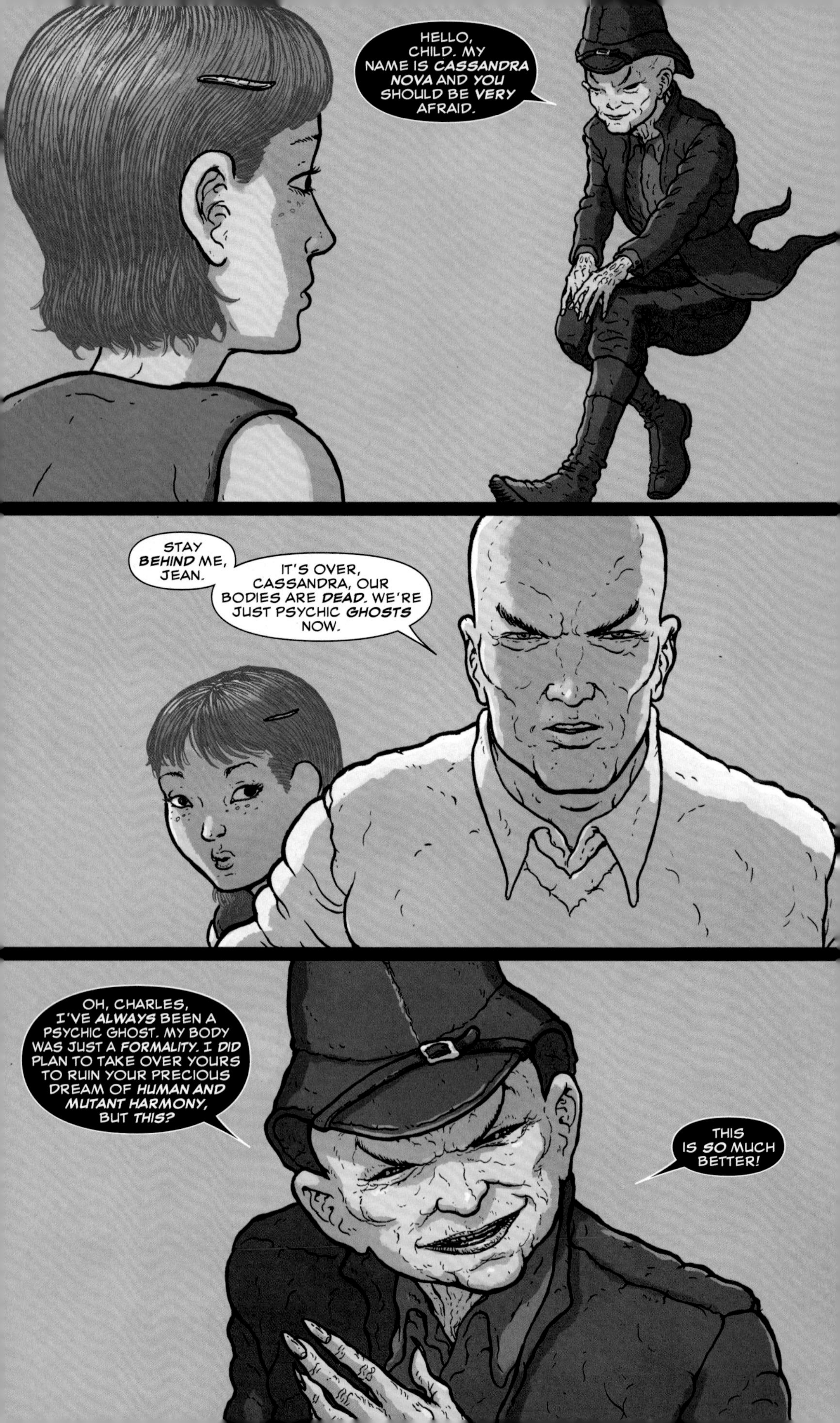
HELLO, CHILD. MY NAME IS CASSANDRA NOVA AND YOU SHOULD BE VERY AFRAID.
STAY BEHIND ME, JEAN.
IT'S OVER, CASSANDRA, OUR BODIES ARE DEAD. WE'RE JUST PSYCHIC GHOSTS NOW.
OH, CHARLES, I'VE ALWAYS BEEN A PSYCHIC GHOST. MY BODY WAS JUST A FORMALITY. I DID PLAN TO TAKE OVER YOURS TO RUIN YOUR PRECIOUS DREAM OF HUMAN AND MUTANT HARMONY, BUT THIS?
THIS IS SO MUCH BETTER!

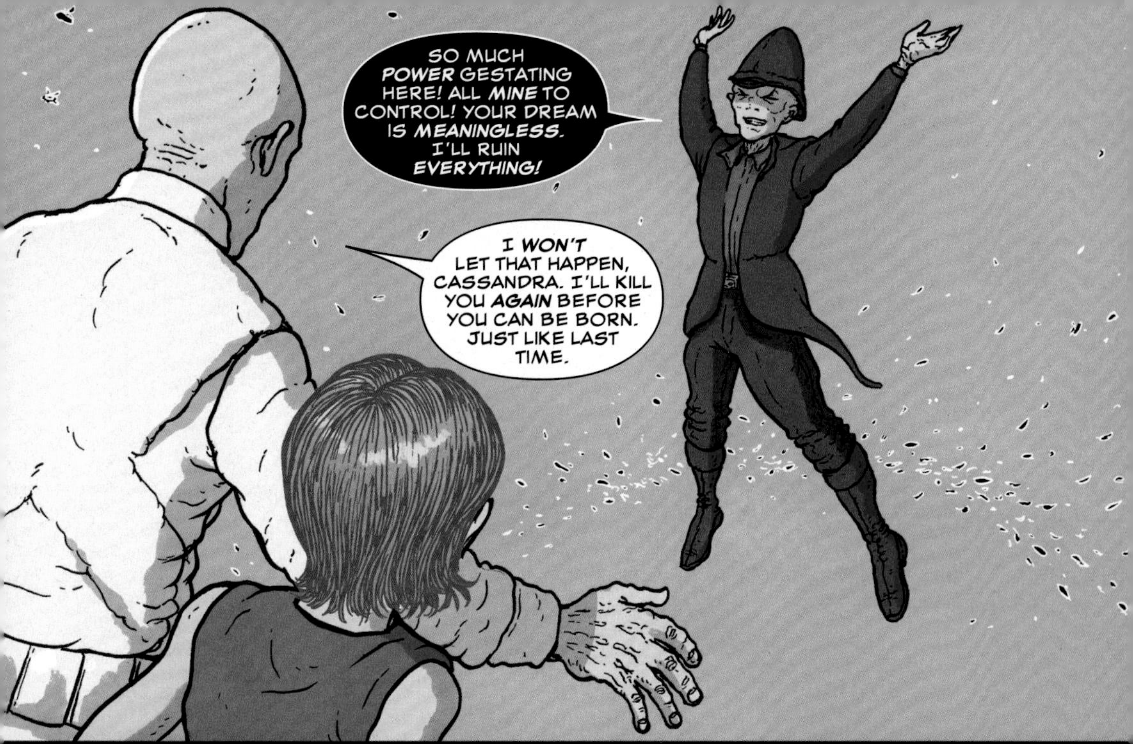
SO MUCH POWER GESTATING HERE! ALL MINE TO CONTROL! YOUR DREAM IS MEANINGLESS. I'LL RUIN EVERYTHING!
I WON'T LET THAT HAPPEN, CASSANDRA. I'LL KILL YOU AGAIN BEFORE YOU CAN BE BORN. JUST LIKE LAST TIME.

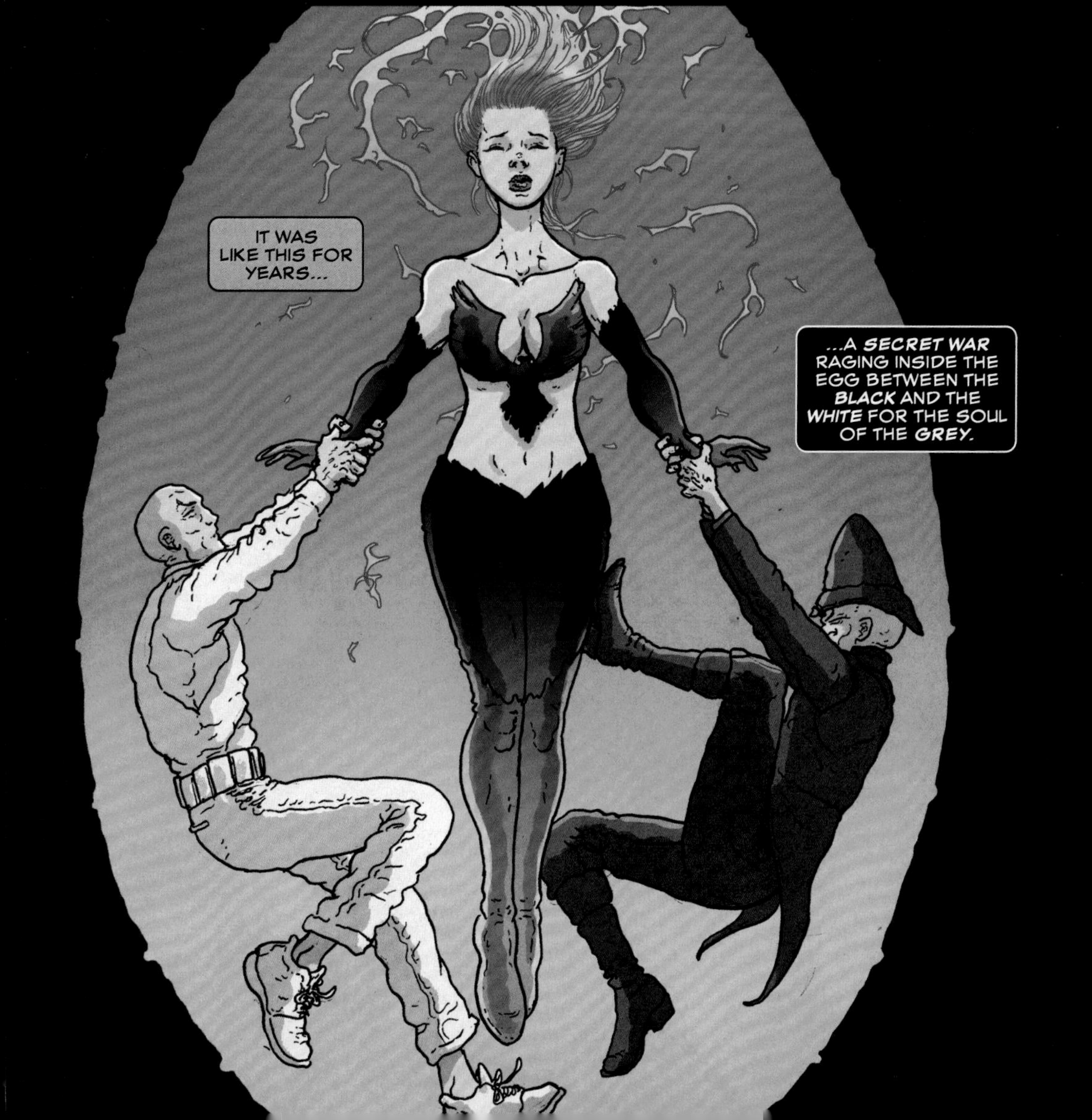
IT WAS LIKE THIS FOR YEARS...
...A SECRET WAR RAGING INSIDE THE EGG BETWEEN THE BLACK AND THE WHITE FOR THE SOUL OF THE GREY.

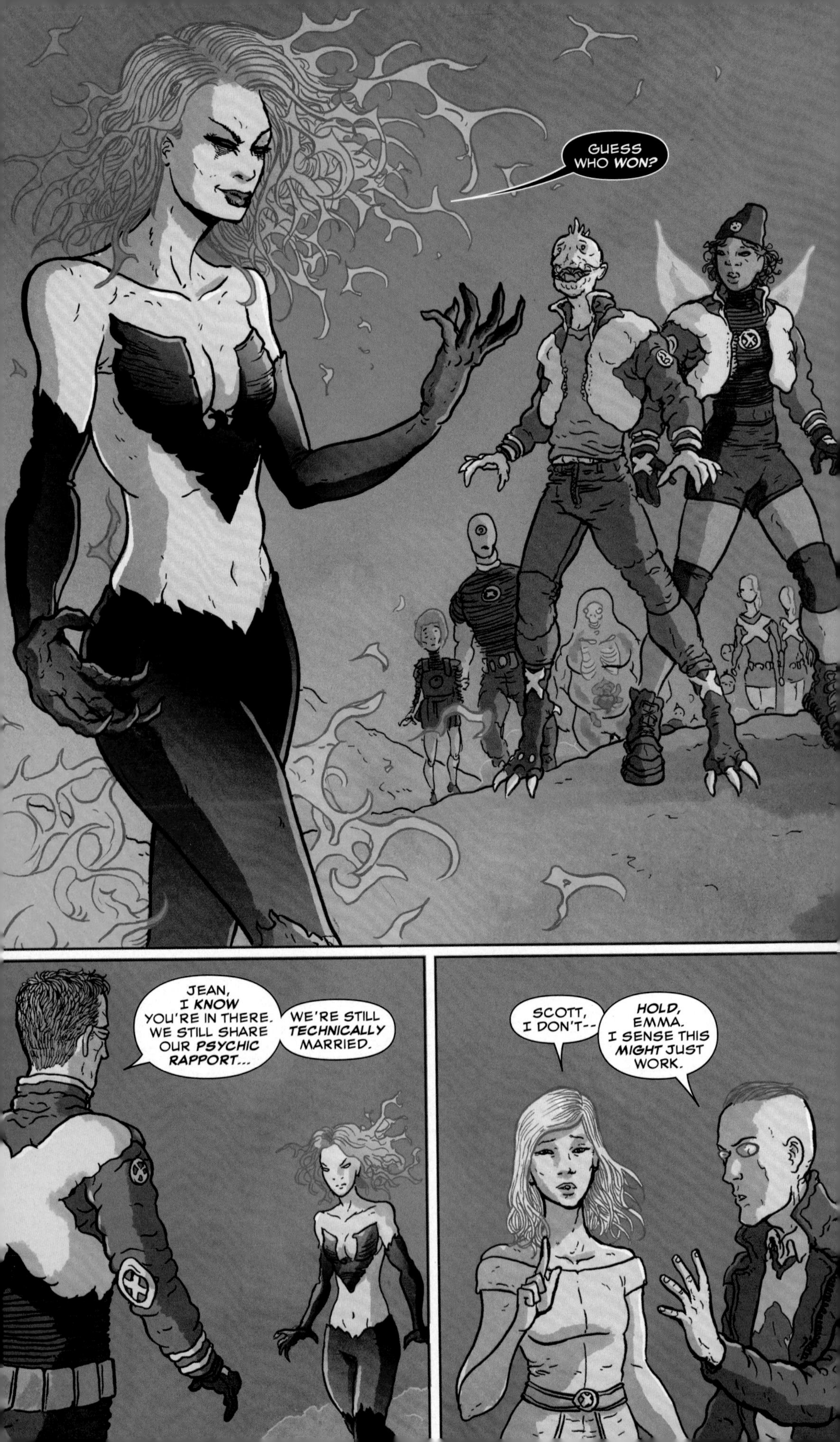
GUESS WHO WON?
JEAN, I KNOW YOU'RE IN THERE. WE STILL SHARE OUR PSYCHIC RAPPORT...
WE'RE STILL TECHNICALLY MARRIED.
SCOTT, I DON'T--
HOLD, EMMA. I SENSE THIS MIGHT JUST WORK.

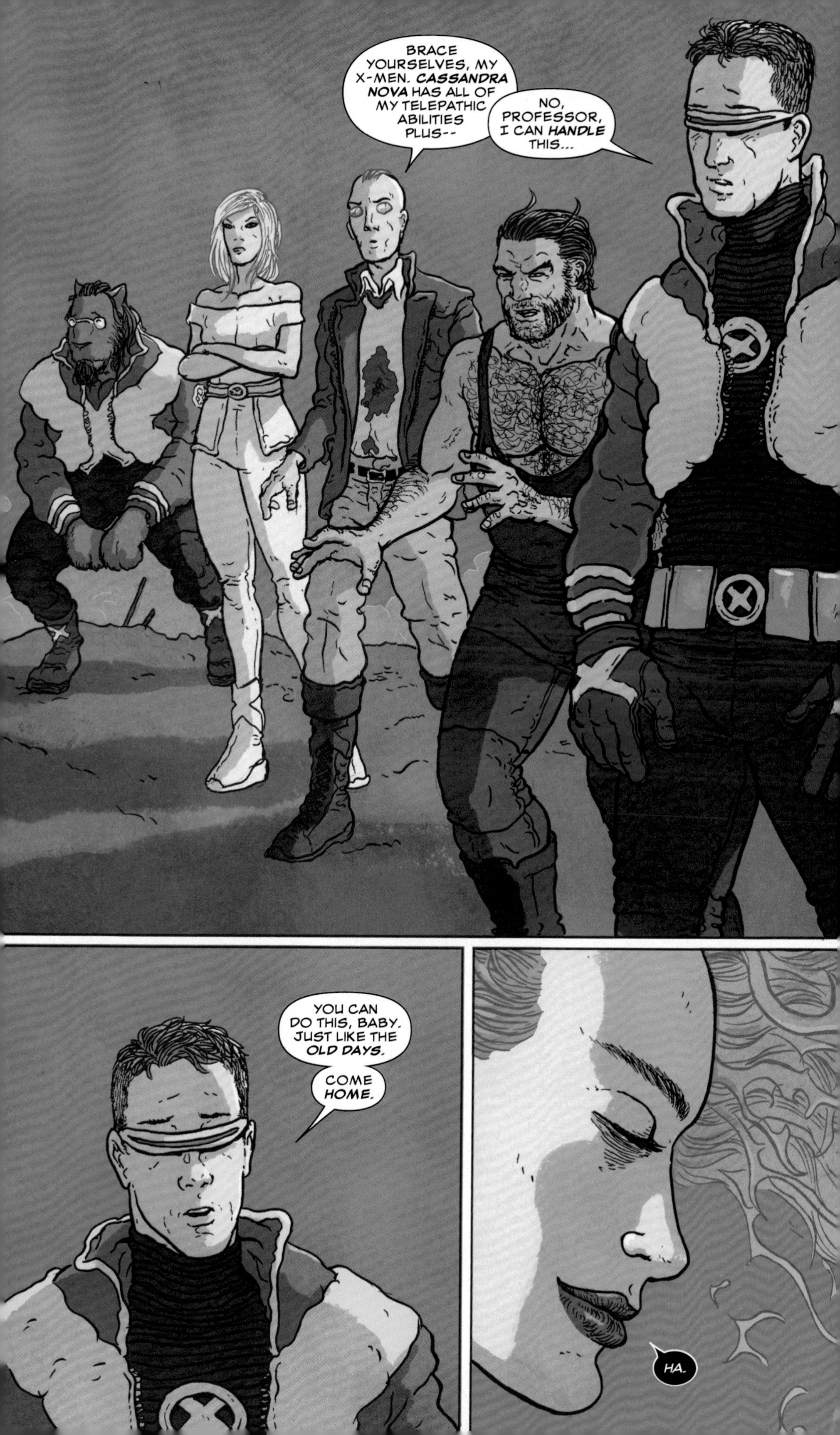
BRACE YOURSELVES, MY X-MEN. CASSANDRA NOVA HAS ALL OF MY TELEPATHIC ABILITIES PLUS--
NO, PROFESSOR, I CAN HANDLE THIS...
YOU CAN DO THIS, BABY. JUST LIKE THE OLD DAYS.
COME HOME.
HA.

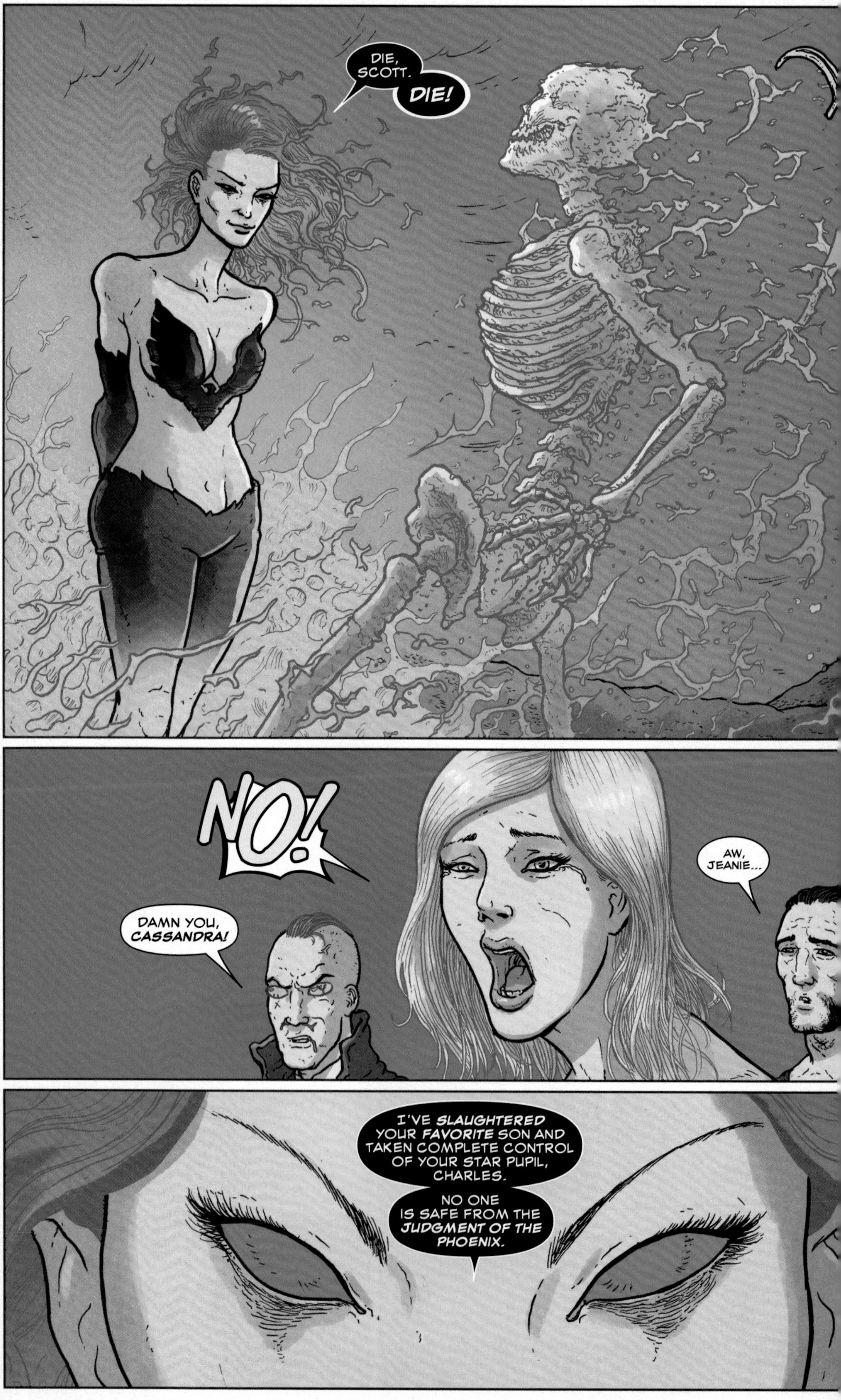

DIE, SCOTT. DIE!
NO!
AW, JEANIE...
DAMN YOU, CASSANDRA!
I'VE SLAUGHTERED YOUR FAVORITE SON AND TAKEN COMPLETE CONTROL OF YOUR STAR PUPIL, CHARLES.
NO ONE IS SAFE FROM THE JUDGMENT OF THE PHOENIX.

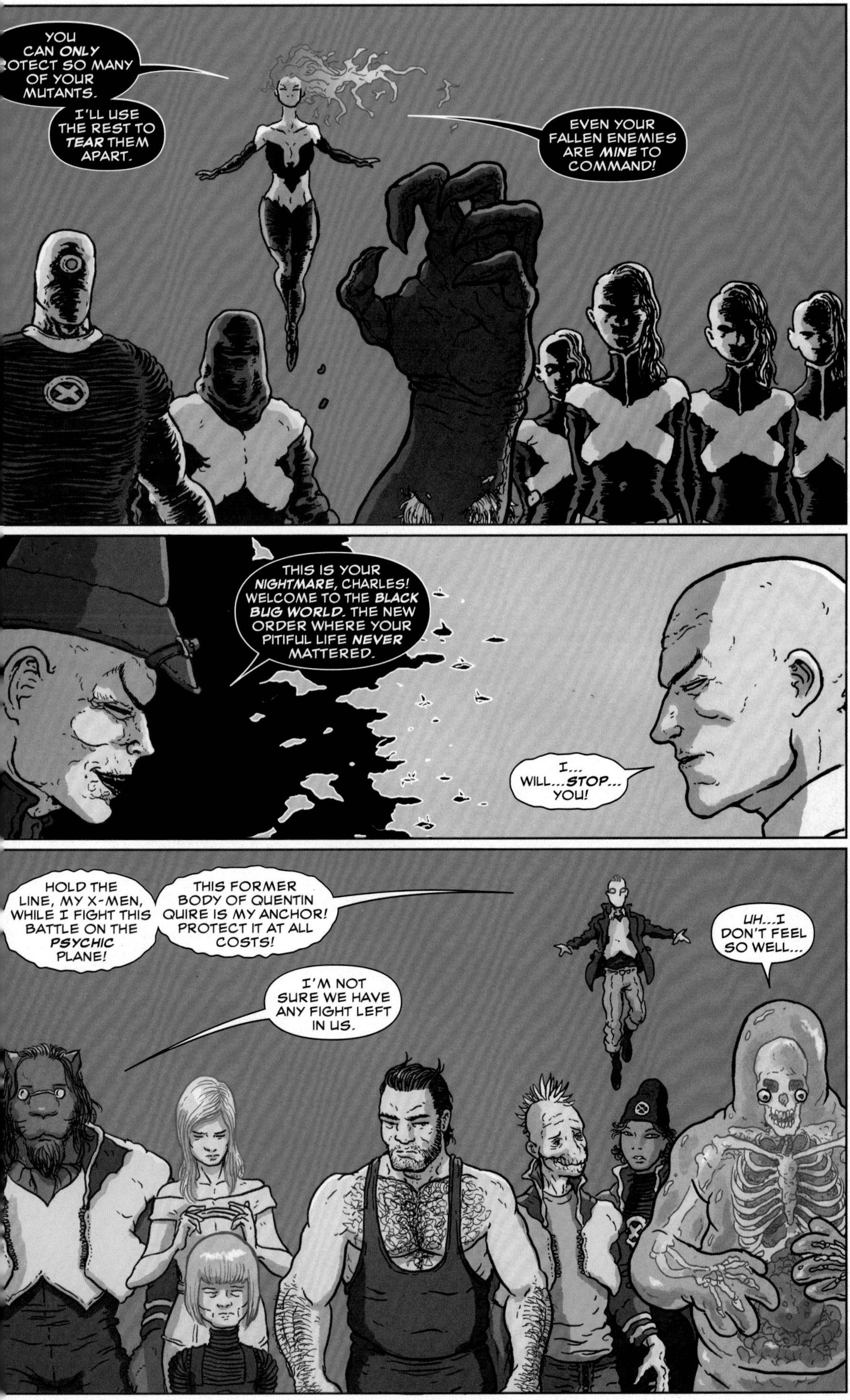
YOU CAN ONLY PROTECT SO MANY OF YOUR MUTANTS.
I'LL USE THE REST TO TEAR THEM APART.
EVEN YOUR FALLEN ENEMIES ARE MINE TO COMMAND!
THIS IS YOUR NIGHTMARE, CHARLES! WELCOME TO THE BLACK BUG WORLD. THE NEW ORDER WHERE YOUR PITIFUL LIFE NEVER MATTERED.
I... WILL...STOP... YOU!
HOLD THE LINE, MY X-MEN, WHILE I FIGHT THIS BATTLE ON THE PSYCHIC PLANE!
THIS FORMER BODY OF QUENTIN QUIRE IS MY ANCHOR! PROTECT IT AT ALL COSTS!
UH...I DON'T FEEL SO WELL...
I'M NOT SURE WE HAVE ANY FIGHT LEFT IN US.

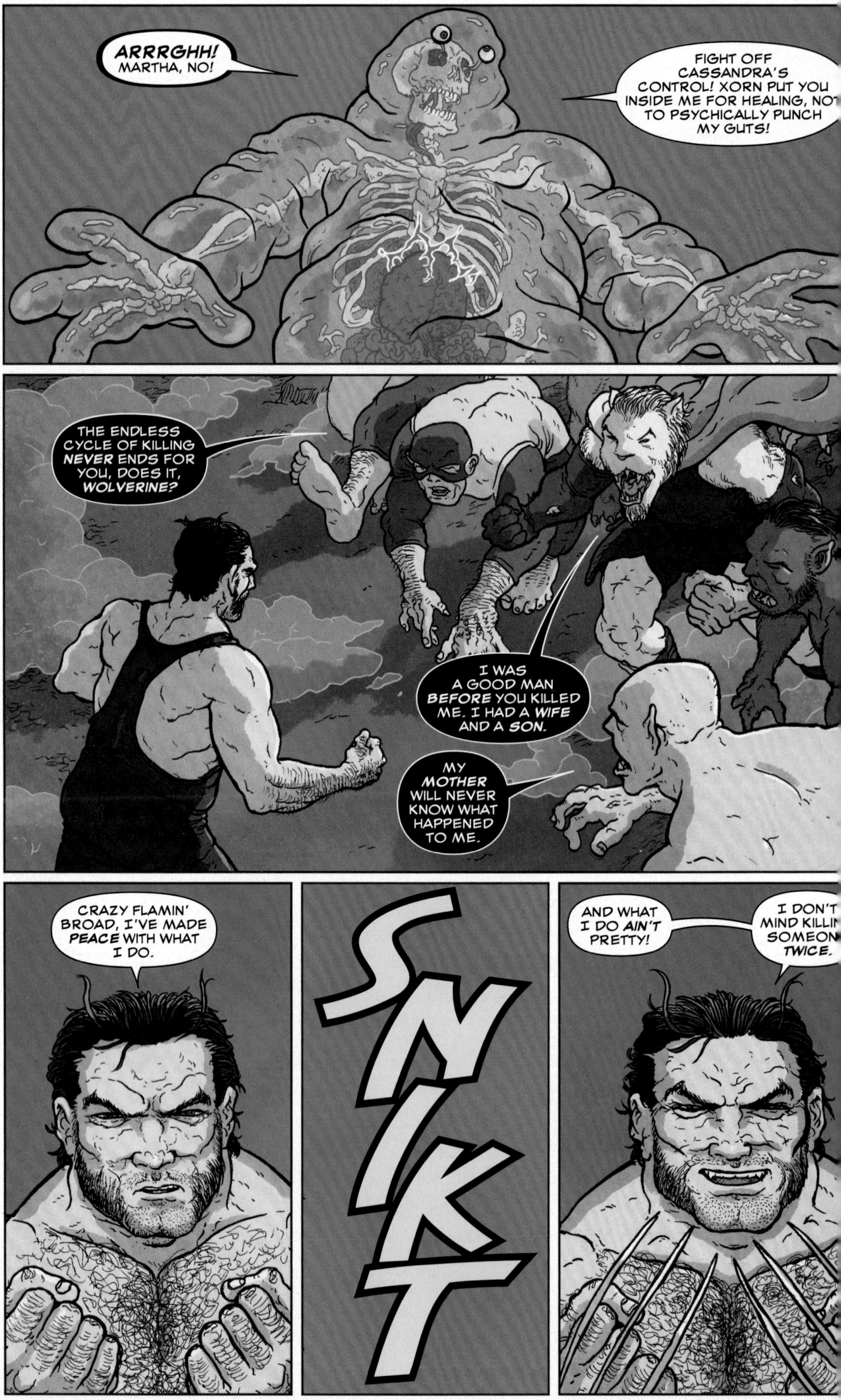

ARRRGHH! MARTHA, NO!
FIGHT OFF CASSANDRA'S CONTROL! XORN PUT YOU INSIDE ME FOR HEALING, NOT TO PSYCHICALLY PUNCH MY GUTS!
THE ENDLESS CYCLE OF KILLING NEVER ENDS FOR YOU, DOES IT, WOLVERINE?
I WAS A GOOD MAN BEFORE YOU KILLED ME. I HAD A WIFE AND A SON.
MY MOTHER WILL NEVER KNOW WHAT HAPPENED TO ME.
CRAZY FLAMIN' BROAD, I'VE MADE PEACE WITH WHAT I DO.
SNIKT
AND WHAT I DO AIN'T PRETTY!
I DON'T MIND KILLIN' SOMEONE TWICE.

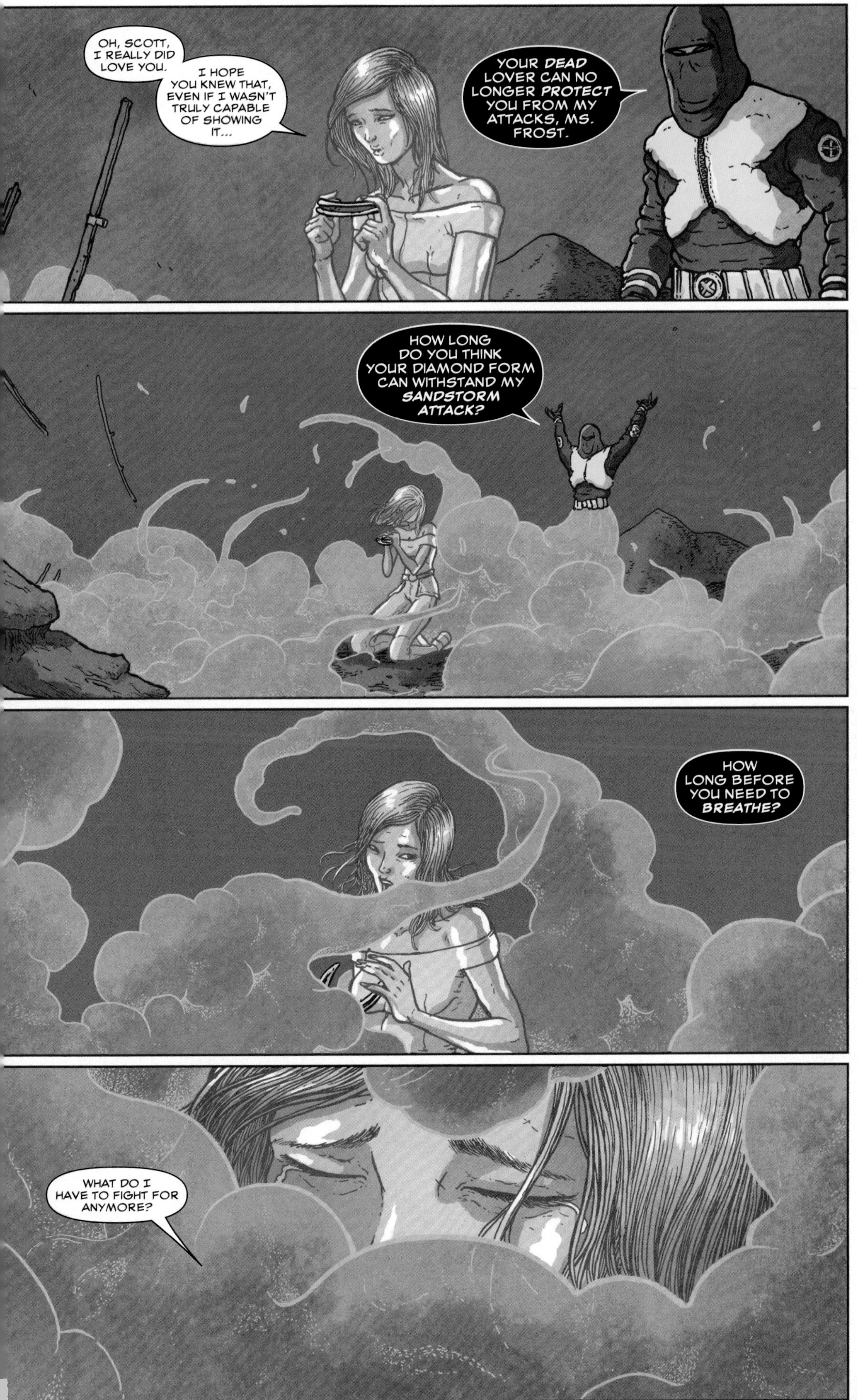
OH, SCOTT, I REALLY DID LOVE YOU.
I HOPE YOU KNEW THAT, EVEN IF I WASN'T TRULY CAPABLE OF SHOWING IT...
YOUR DEAD LOVER CAN NO LONGER PROTECT YOU FROM MY ATTACKS, MS. FROST.
HOW LONG DO YOU THINK YOUR DIAMOND FORM CAN WITHSTAND MY SANDSTORM ATTACK?
HOW LONG BEFORE YOU NEED TO BREATHE?
WHAT DO I HAVE TO FIGHT FOR ANYMORE?

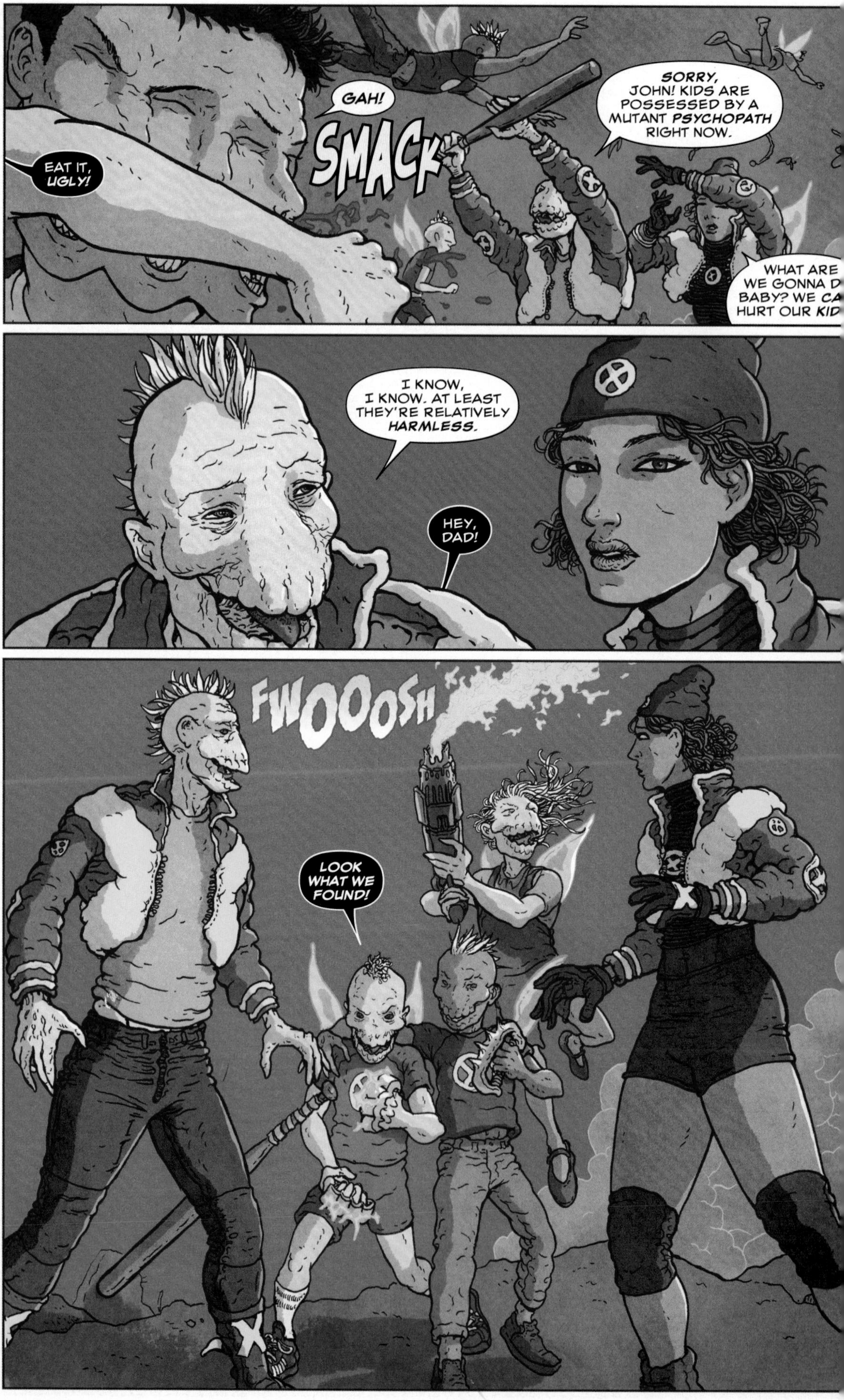

GAH!
SMACK
EAT IT, UGLY!
SORRY, JOHN! KIDS ARE POSSESSED BY A MUTANT PSYCHOPATH RIGHT NOW.
WHAT ARE WE GONNA D BABY? WE CA HURT OUR KID
I KNOW, I KNOW. AT LEAST THEY'RE RELATIVELY HARMLESS.
HEY, DAD!
FWOOOSH
LOOK WHAT WE FOUND!

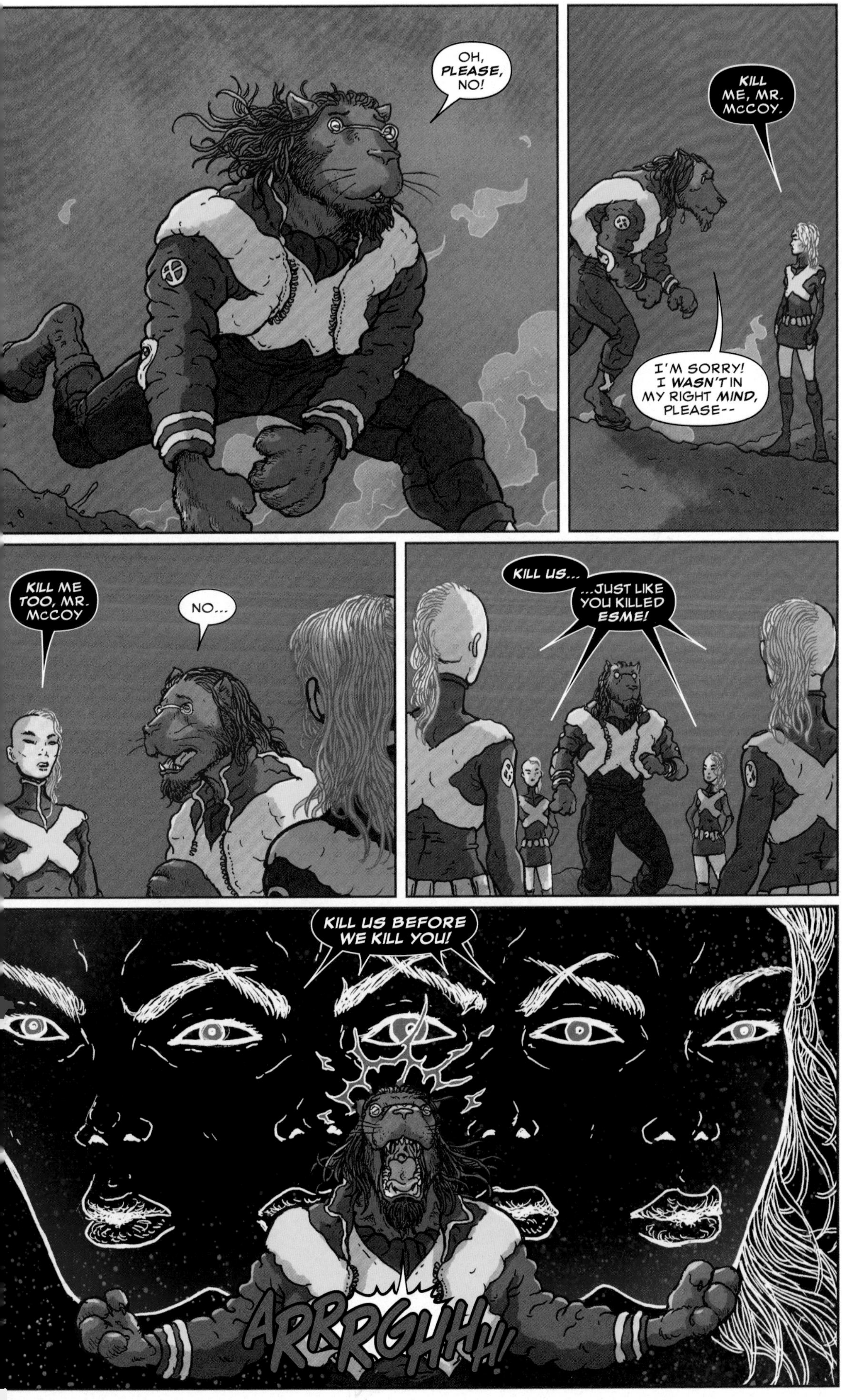
OH, PLEASE, NO!
KILL ME, MR. McCOY.
I'M SORRY! I WASN'T IN MY RIGHT MIND, PLEASE--
KILL ME TOO, MR. McCOY
NO...
KILL US...
...JUST LIKE YOU KILLED ESME!
KILL US BEFORE WE KILL YOU!
ARRRGHHH!

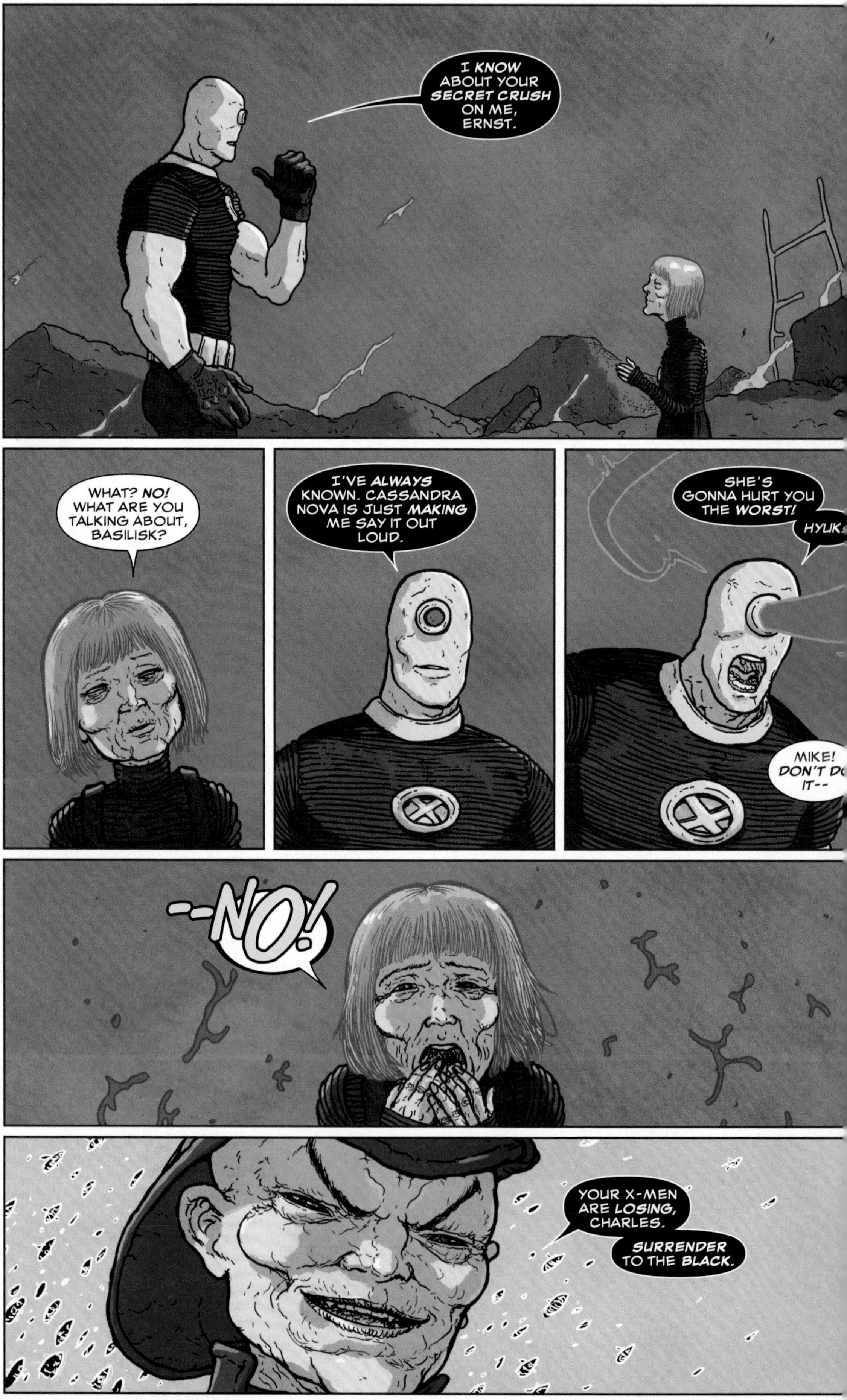
I KNOW ABOUT YOUR SECRET CRUSH ON ME, ERNST.
WHAT? NO! WHAT ARE YOU TALKING ABOUT, BASILISK?
I'VE ALWAYS KNOWN. CASSANDRA NOVA IS JUST MAKING ME SAY IT OUT LOUD.
SHE'S GONNA HURT YOU THE WORST!
HYUK.
MIKE! DON'T DO IT--
--NO!
YOUR X-MEN ARE LOSING, CHARLES.
SURRENDER TO THE BLACK.

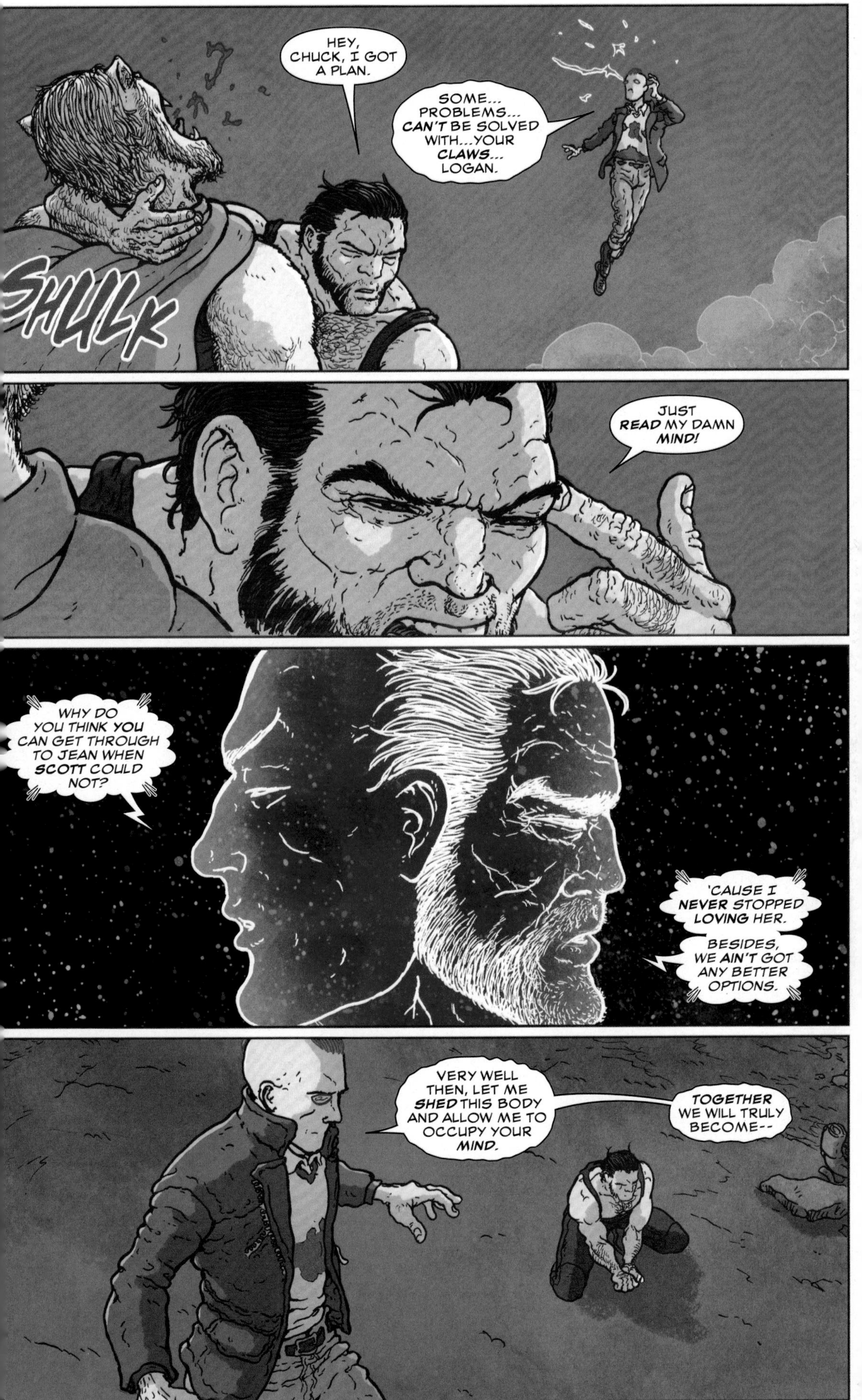
SHULK
HEY, CHUCK, I GOT A PLAN.
SOME... PROBLEMS... CAN'T BE SOLVED WITH... YOUR CLAWS... LOGAN.
JUST READ MY DAMN MIND!
WHY DO YOU THINK YOU CAN GET THROUGH TO JEAN WHEN SCOTT COULD NOT?
'CAUSE I NEVER STOPPED LOVING HER.
BESIDES, WE AIN'T GOT ANY BETTER OPTIONS.
VERY WELL THEN, LET ME SHED THIS BODY AND ALLOW ME TO OCCUPY YOUR MIND.
TOGETHER WE WILL TRULY BECOME--

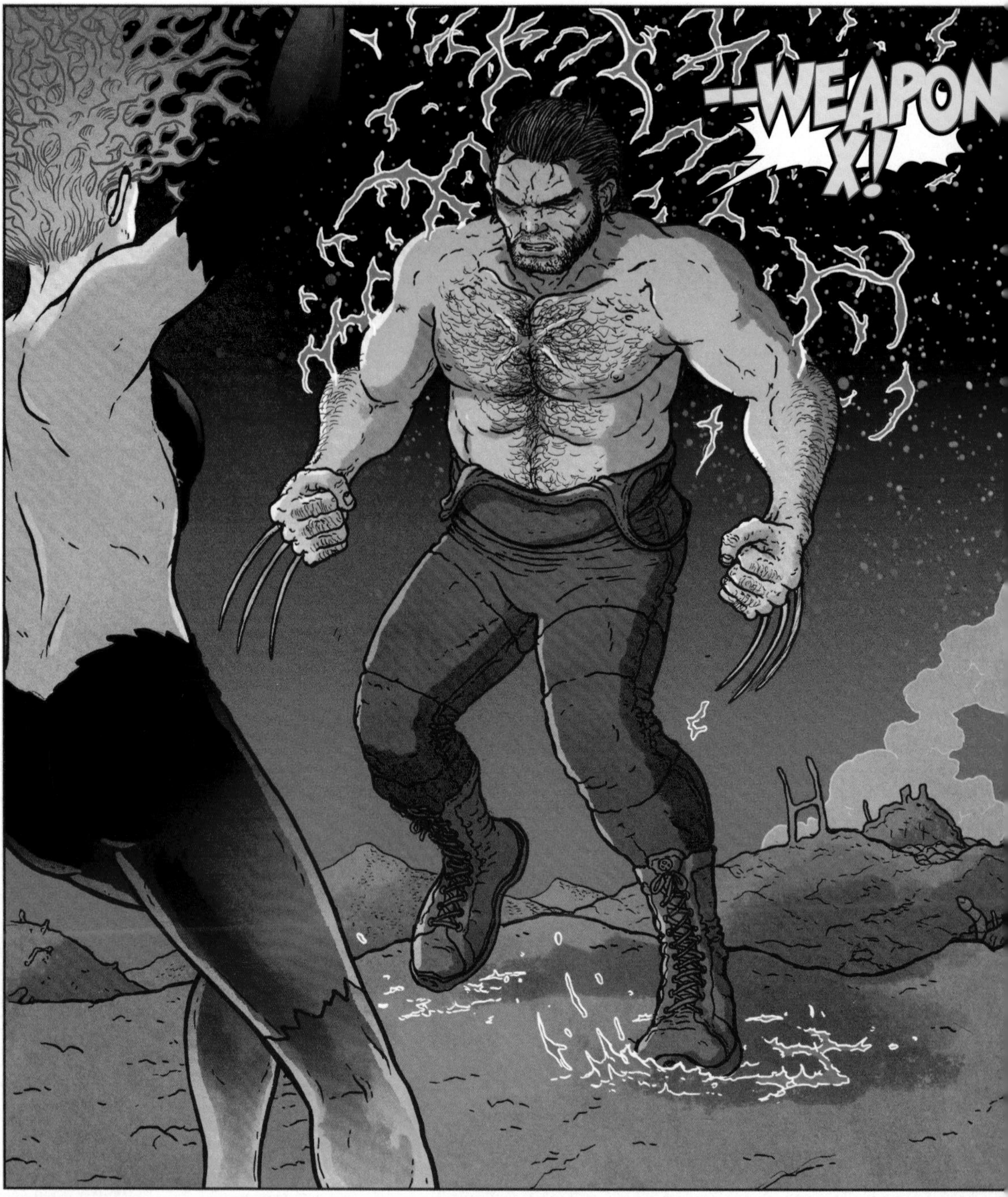
--WEAPON X!

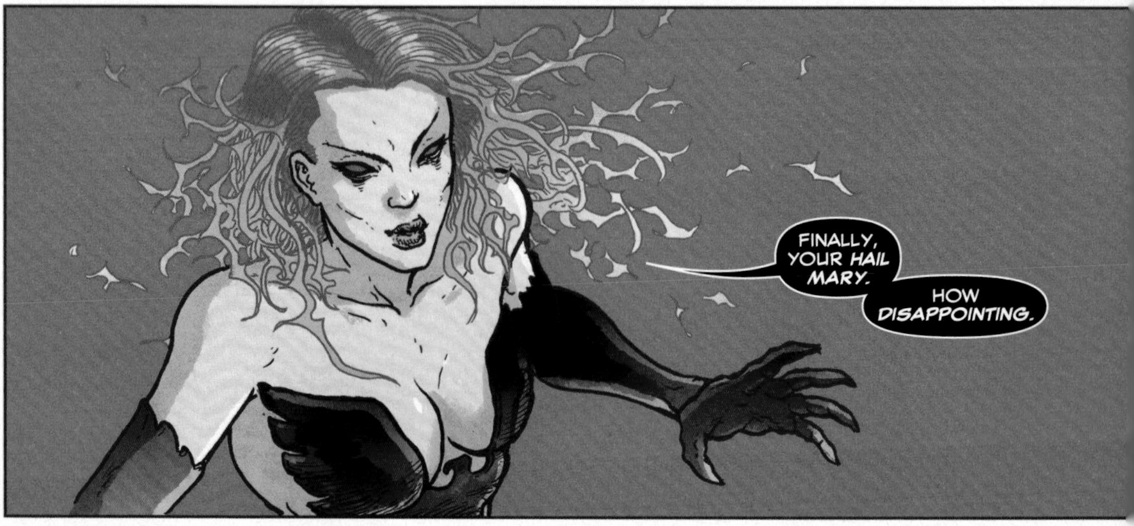
FINALLY, YOUR HAIL MARY.
HOW DISAPPOINTING.

I AM MUMMUDRAI! I AM PHOENIX!

I AM THE *DEATH* OF *ALL THINGS!* THERE IS NO POSSIBLE *ATTACK* THAT COULD STOP ME, YOU *FOOLS!*

THIS *ISN'T* AN ATTACK, DARLIN'.

L-LOGAN?

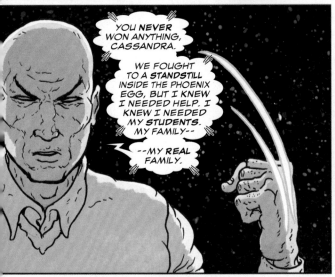

YOU *NEVER* WON ANYTHING, CASSANDRA.

WE FOUGHT TO A *STANDSTILL* INSIDE THE PHOENIX EGG, BUT I KNEW I NEEDED HELP. I KNEW I NEEDED MY *STUDENTS.* MY FAMILY--

--MY *REAL* FAMILY.

LOGAN, WHAT'S--

NO TIME, JEANIE. READ MY MIND.

ONLY ONE THING LEFT TO DO...

SNIKT

I LOVE YOU, TOO.

SNIKT.

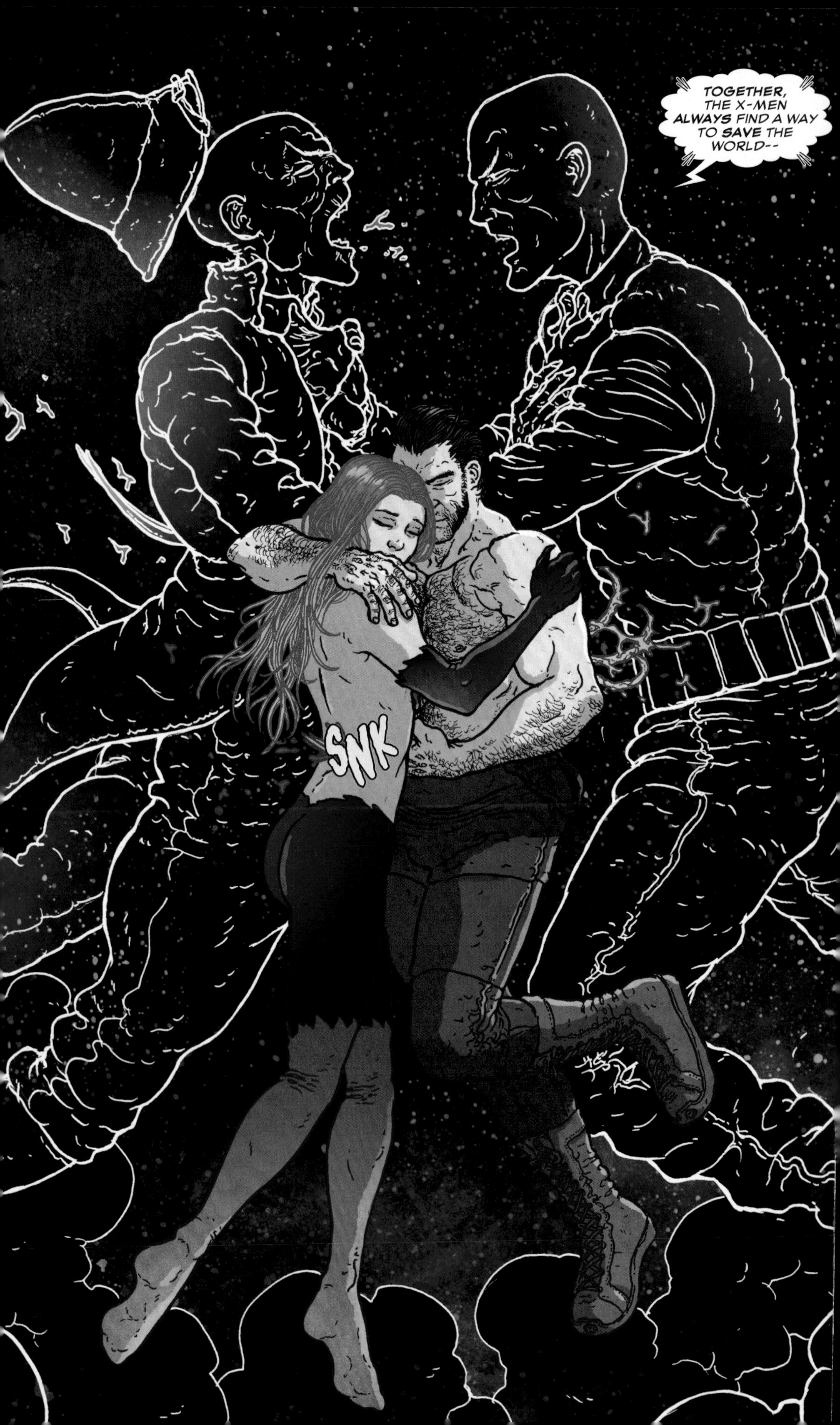
TOGETHER, THE X-MEN ALWAYS FIND A WAY TO SAVE THE WORLD--
SNK

NO MATTER WHAT THE SACRIFICE.

HONEY! WE'VE COME BACK *POSITIVE!*

IF DR. McCOY IS ALL HE CLAIMS TO BE, THEN WE'RE GOING TO BE THE PROUD *PARENTS* OF A BEAUTIFUL *MUTANT--*

--HONEY? WHAT'S WRONG?

IT'S NOTHING. JUST SOME FIREWORKS OUTSIDE THE CITY, IS ALL.

WE SHOULD NAME THE BABY *JAMES* IF IT'S A BOY...

WHAT IF WE HAVE A *GIRL?*

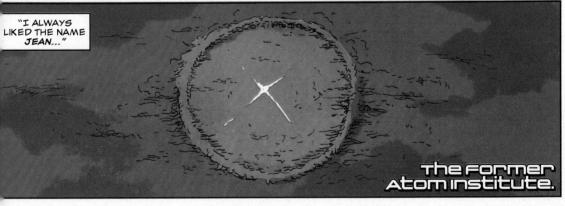

"I ALWAYS LIKED THE NAME *JEAN...*"

THE FORMER ATOM INSTITUTE.

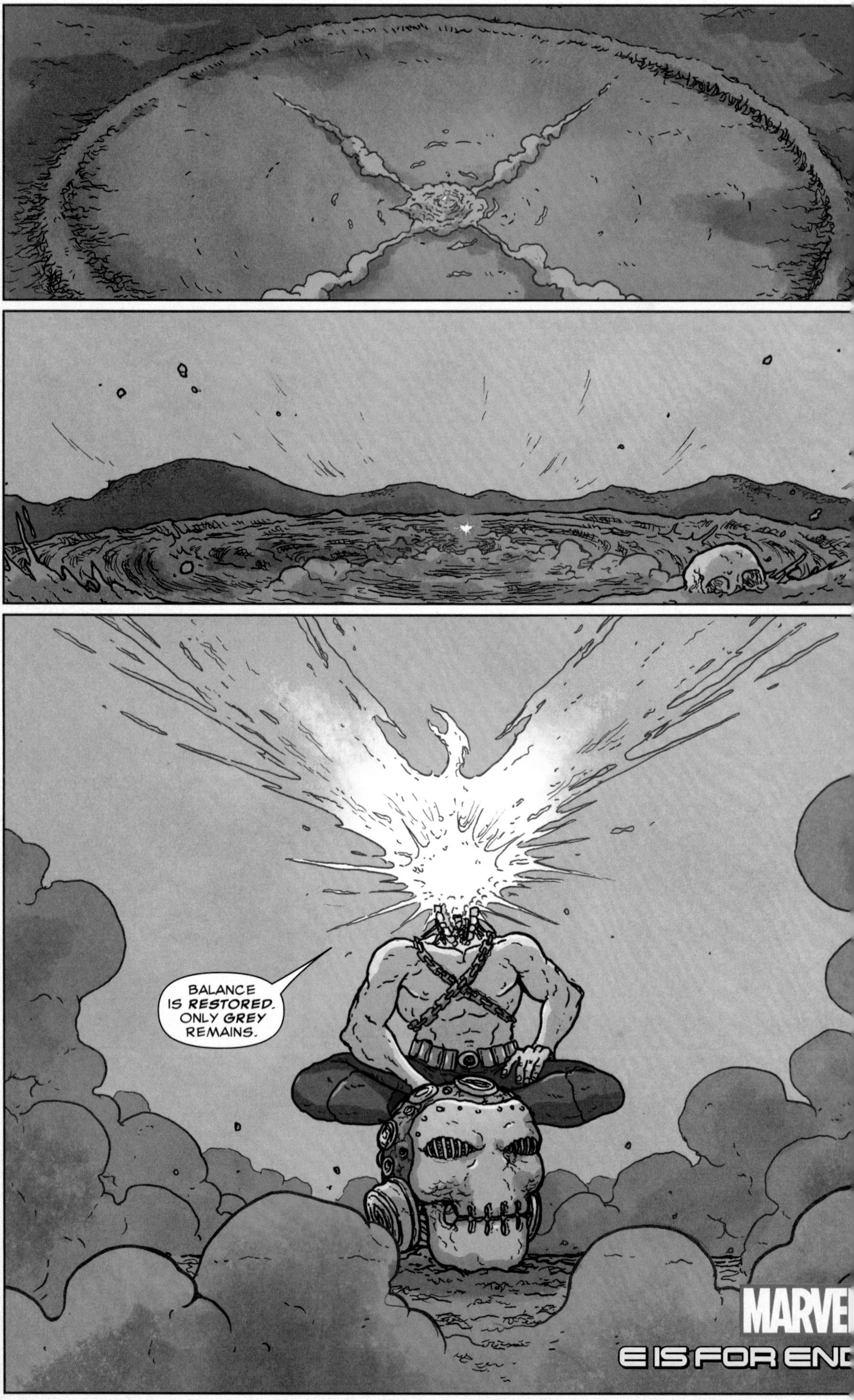
BALANCE IS RESTORED. ONLY GREY REMAINS.
MARVEL
E IS FOR END

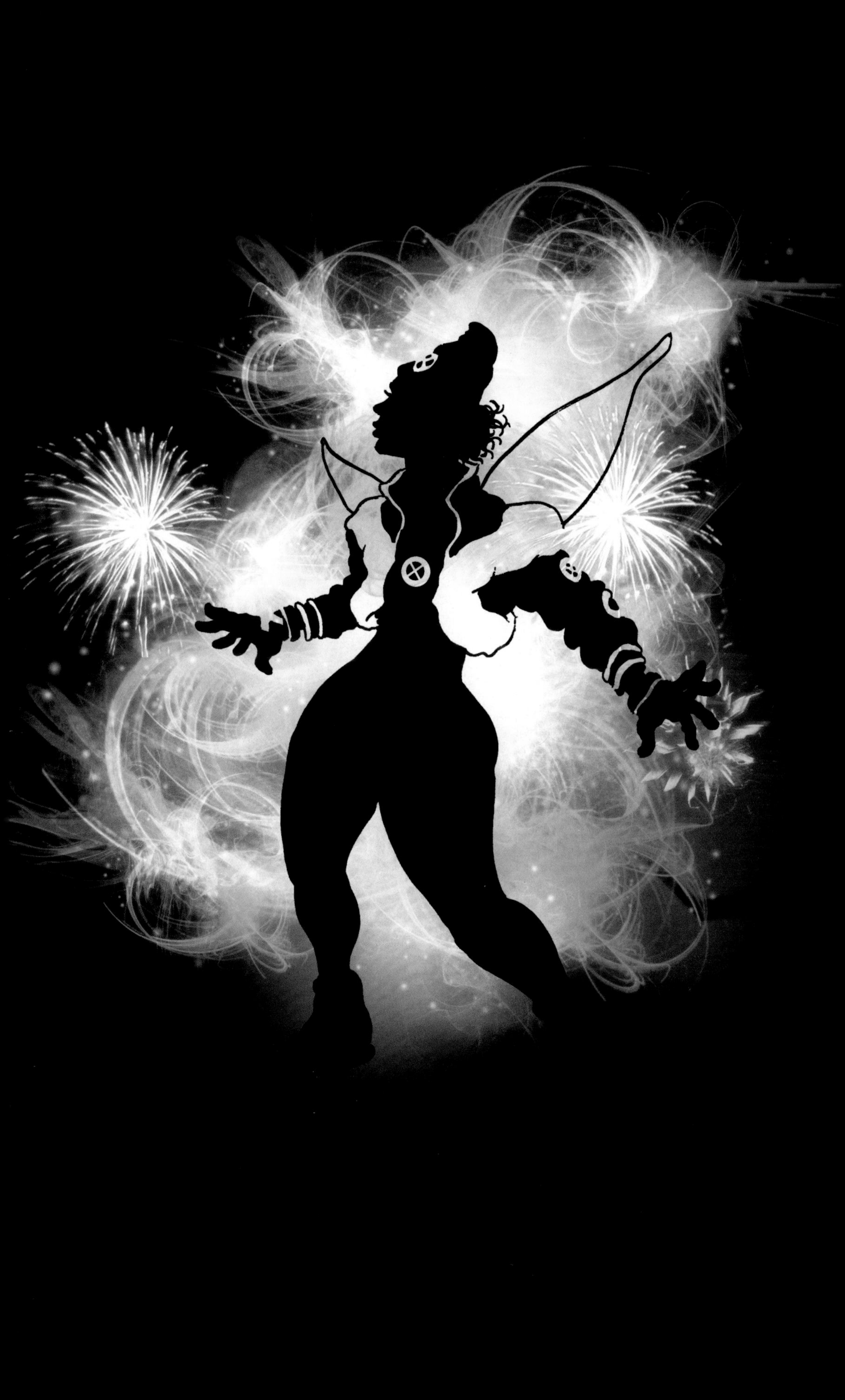

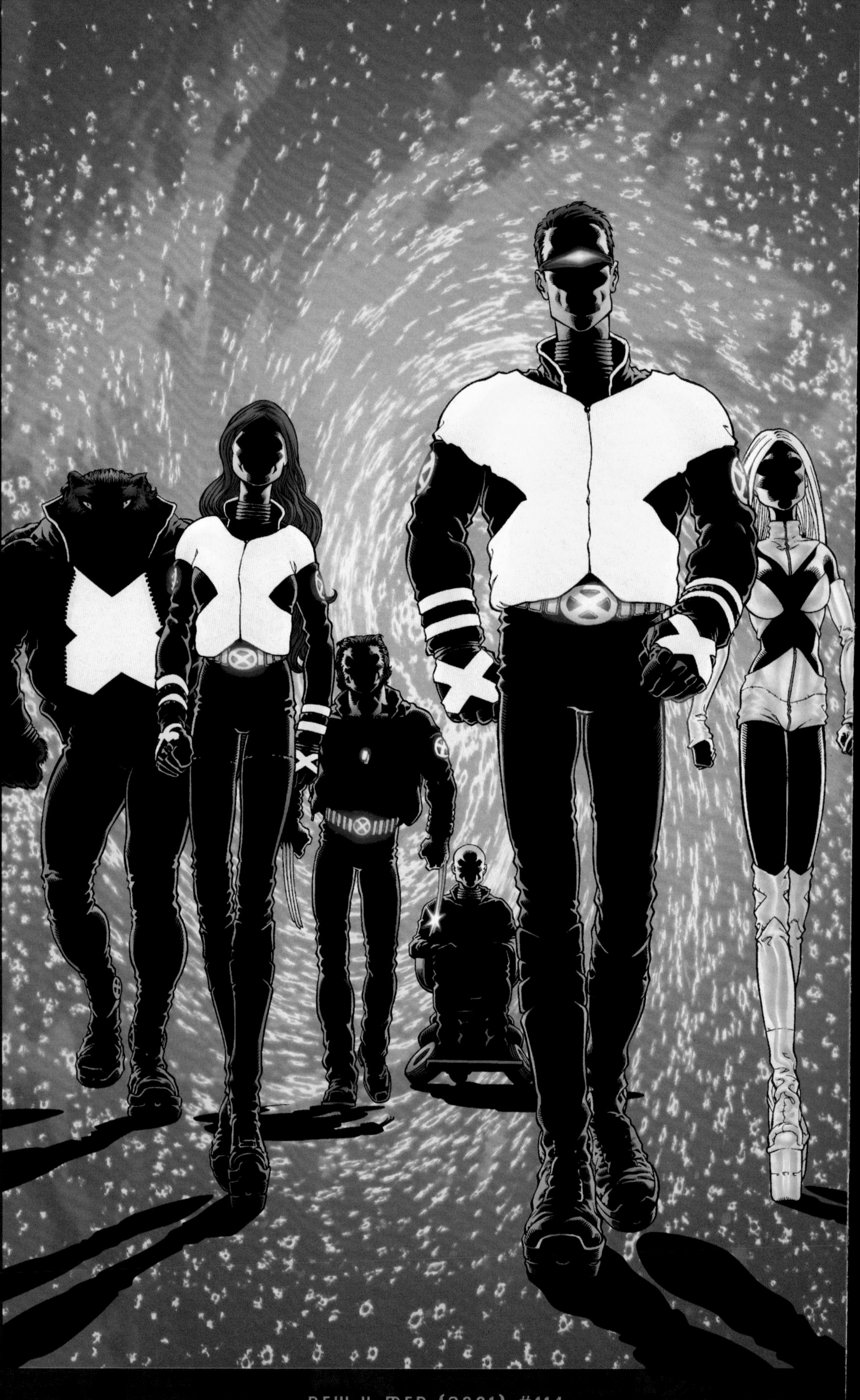

NEW X-MEN (2001) #114

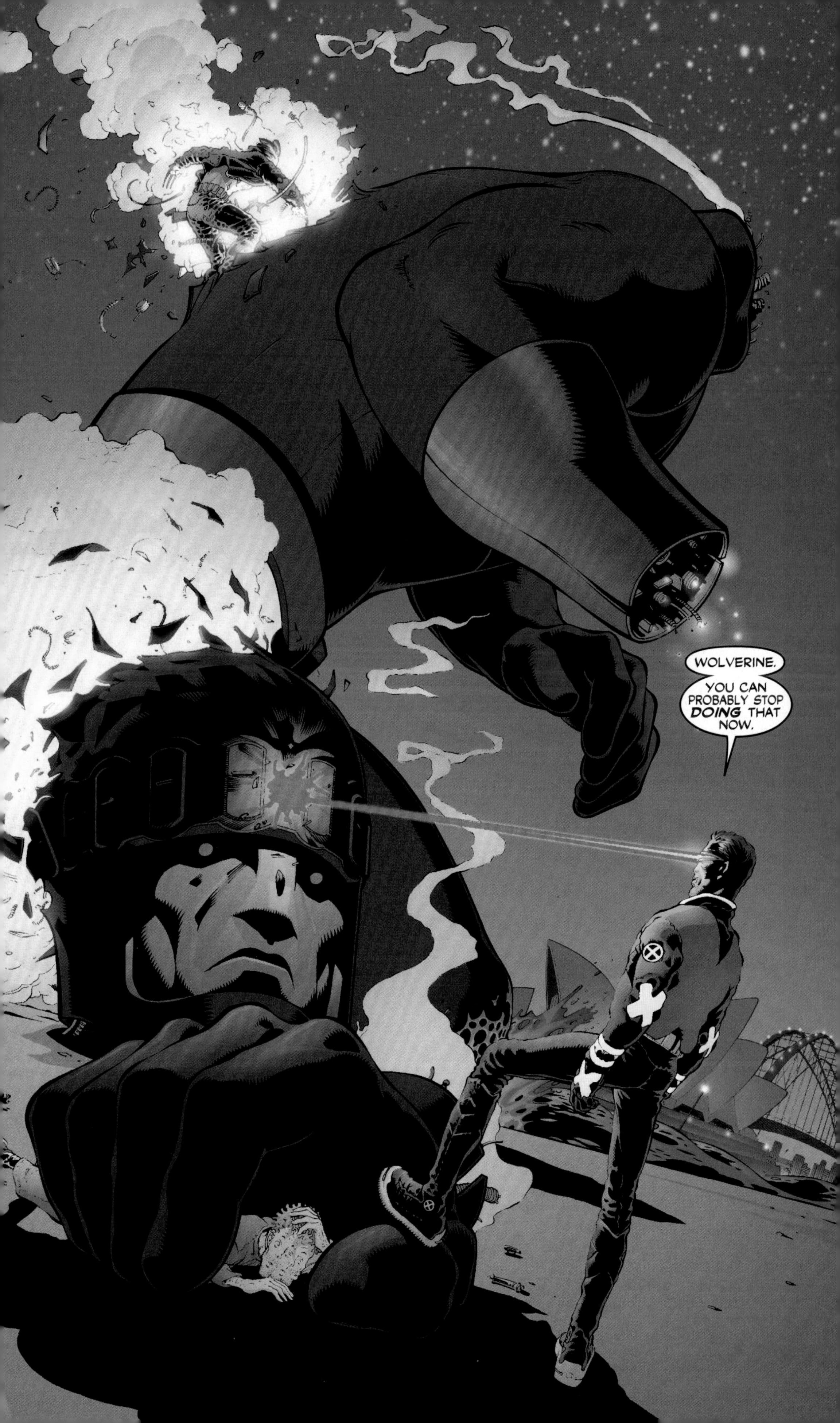
WOLVERINE.
YOU CAN PROBABLY STOP DOING THAT NOW.

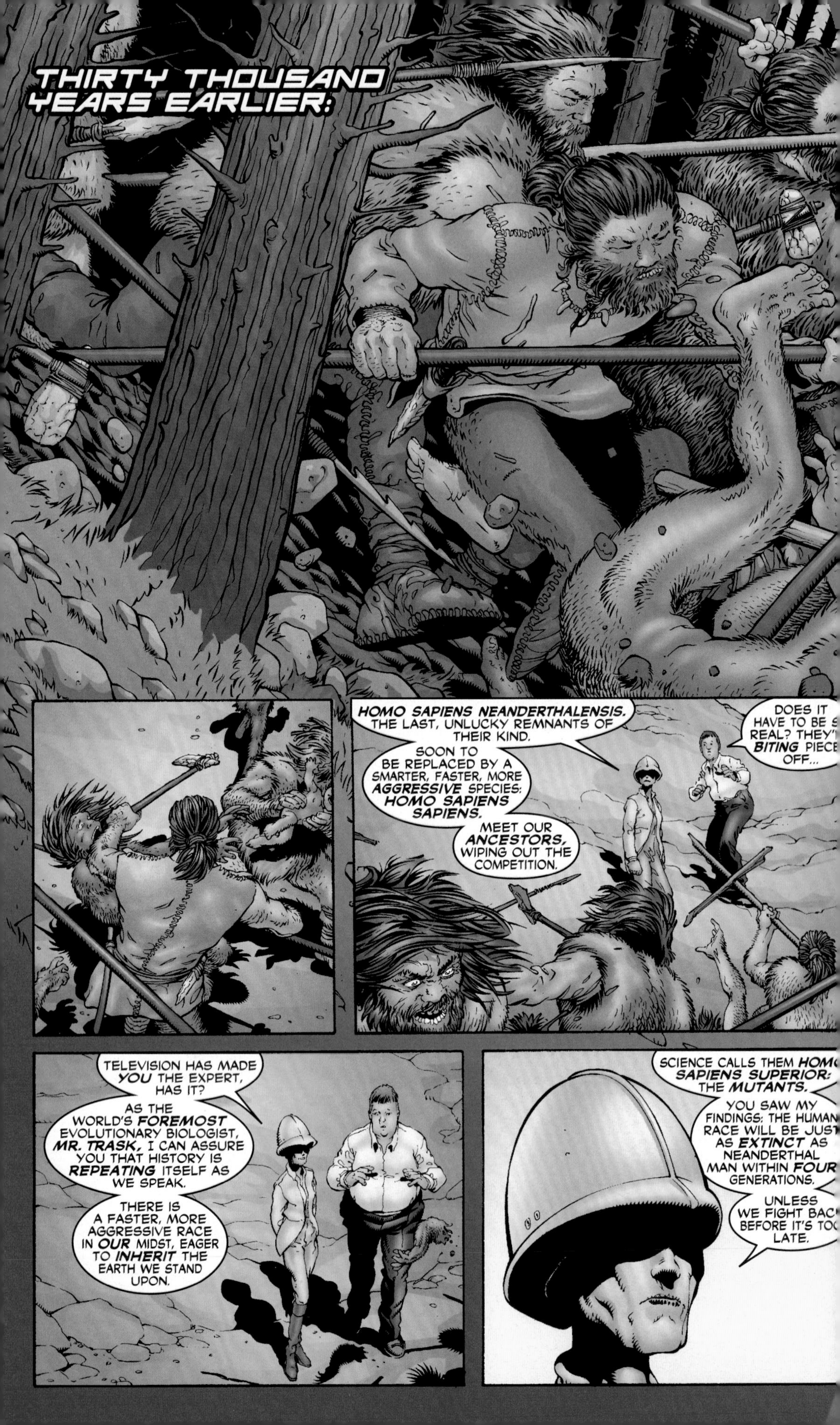
THIRTY THOUSAND YEARS EARLIER:
HOMO SAPIENS NEANDERTHALENSIS. THE LAST, UNLUCKY REMNANTS OF THEIR KIND.
SOON TO BE REPLACED BY A SMARTER, FASTER, MORE AGGRESSIVE SPECIES: HOMO SAPIENS SAPIENS.
MEET OUR ANCESTORS, WIPING OUT THE COMPETITION.
DOES IT HAVE TO BE S REAL? THEY' BITING PIECE OFF...
TELEVISION HAS MADE YOU THE EXPERT, HAS IT?
AS THE WORLD'S FOREMOST EVOLUTIONARY BIOLOGIST, MR. TRASK, I CAN ASSURE YOU THAT HISTORY IS REPEATING ITSELF AS WE SPEAK.
THERE IS A FASTER, MORE AGGRESSIVE RACE IN OUR MIDST, EAGER TO INHERIT THE EARTH WE STAND UPON.
SCIENCE CALLS THEM HOM SAPIENS SUPERIOR: THE MUTANTS.
YOU SAW MY FINDINGS: THE HUMAN RACE WILL BE JUST AS EXTINCT AS NEANDERTHAL MAN WITHIN FOUR GENERATIONS.
UNLESS WE FIGHT BAC BEFORE IT'S TO LATE.

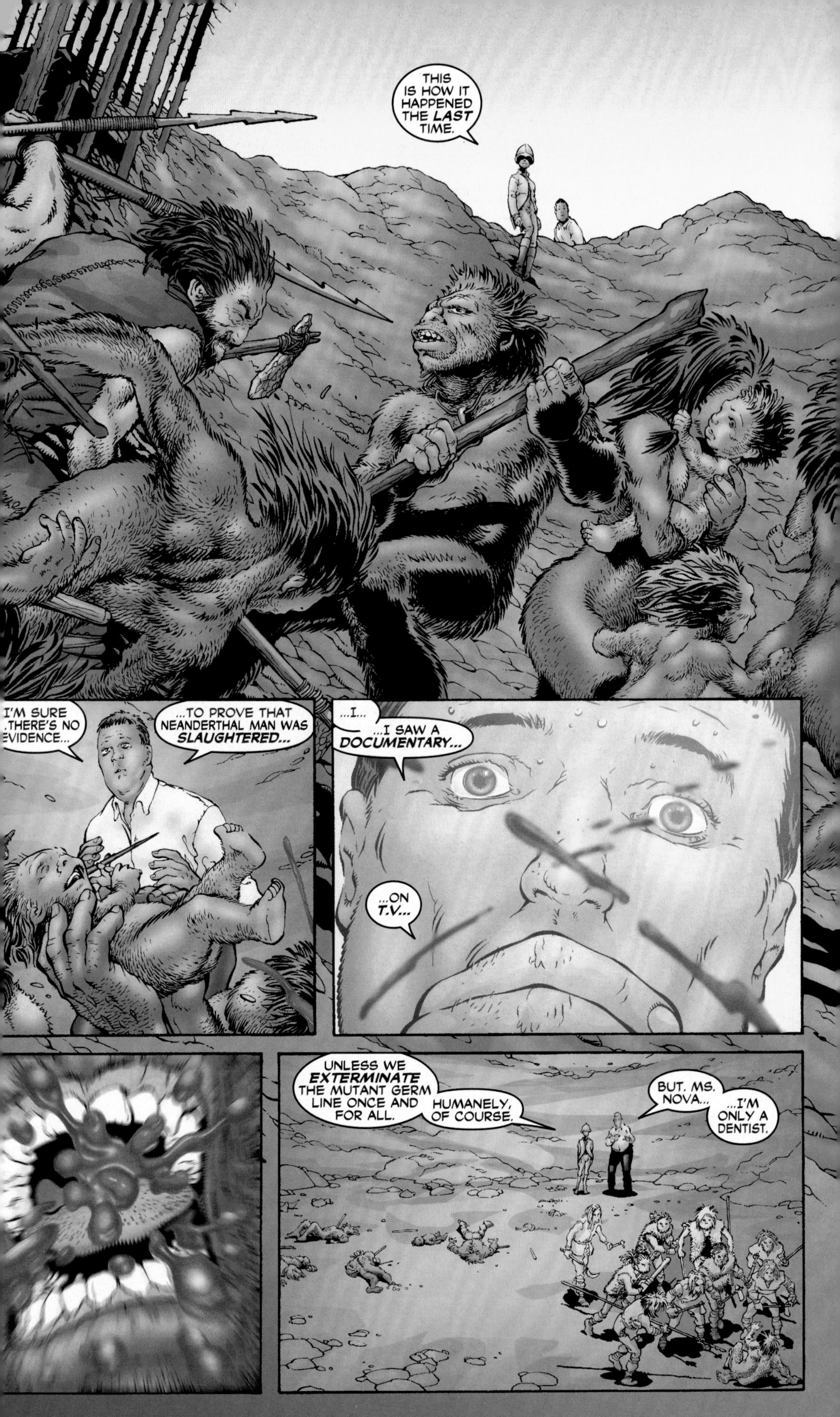
THIS IS HOW IT HAPPENED THE LAST TIME.
I'M SURE THERE'S NO EVIDENCE...
...TO PROVE THAT NEANDERTHAL MAN WAS SLAUGHTERED...
...I...
...I SAW A DOCUMENTARY...
...ON T.V...
UNLESS WE EXTERMINATE THE MUTANT GERM LINE ONCE AND FOR ALL.
HUMANELY, OF COURSE.
BUT, MS. NOVA...
...I'M ONLY A DENTIST.

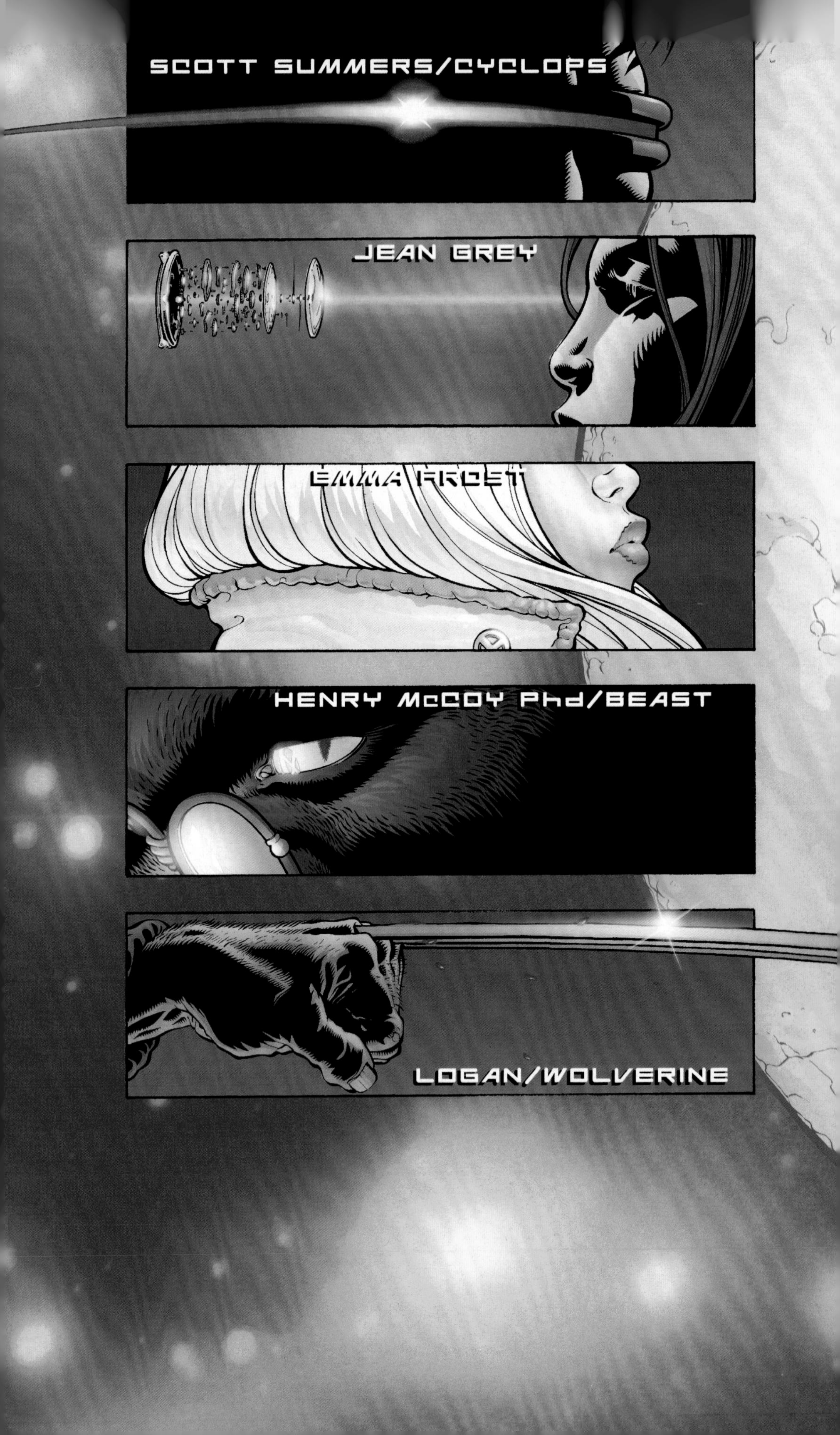
SCOTT SUMMERS/CYCLOPS
JEAN GREY
EMMA FROST
HENRY McCOY Phd/BEAST
LOGAN/WOLVERINE

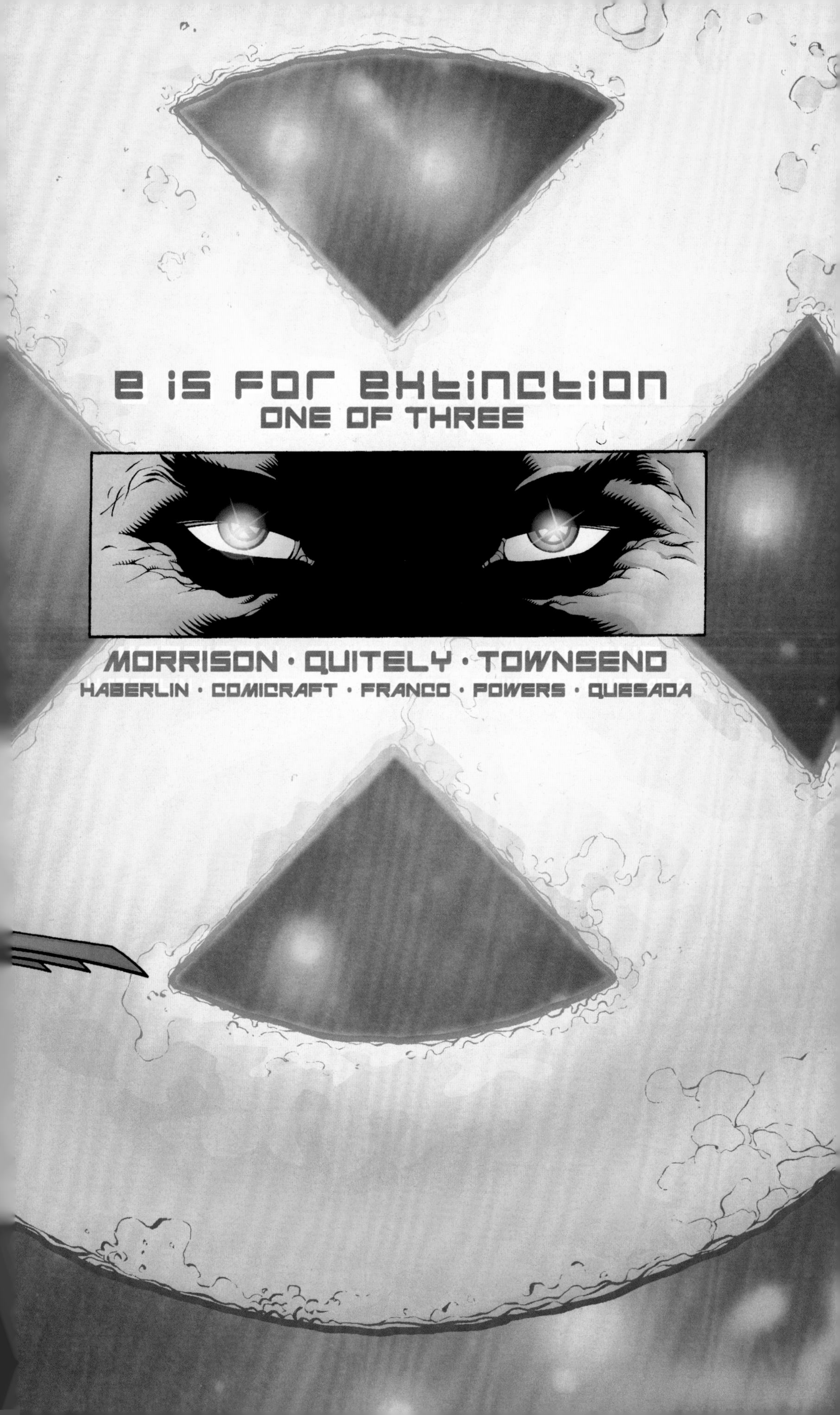
E IS FOR EXTINCTION
ONE OF THREE
MORRISON · QUITELY · TOWNSEND
HABERLIN · COMICRAFT · FRANCO · POWERS · QUESADA

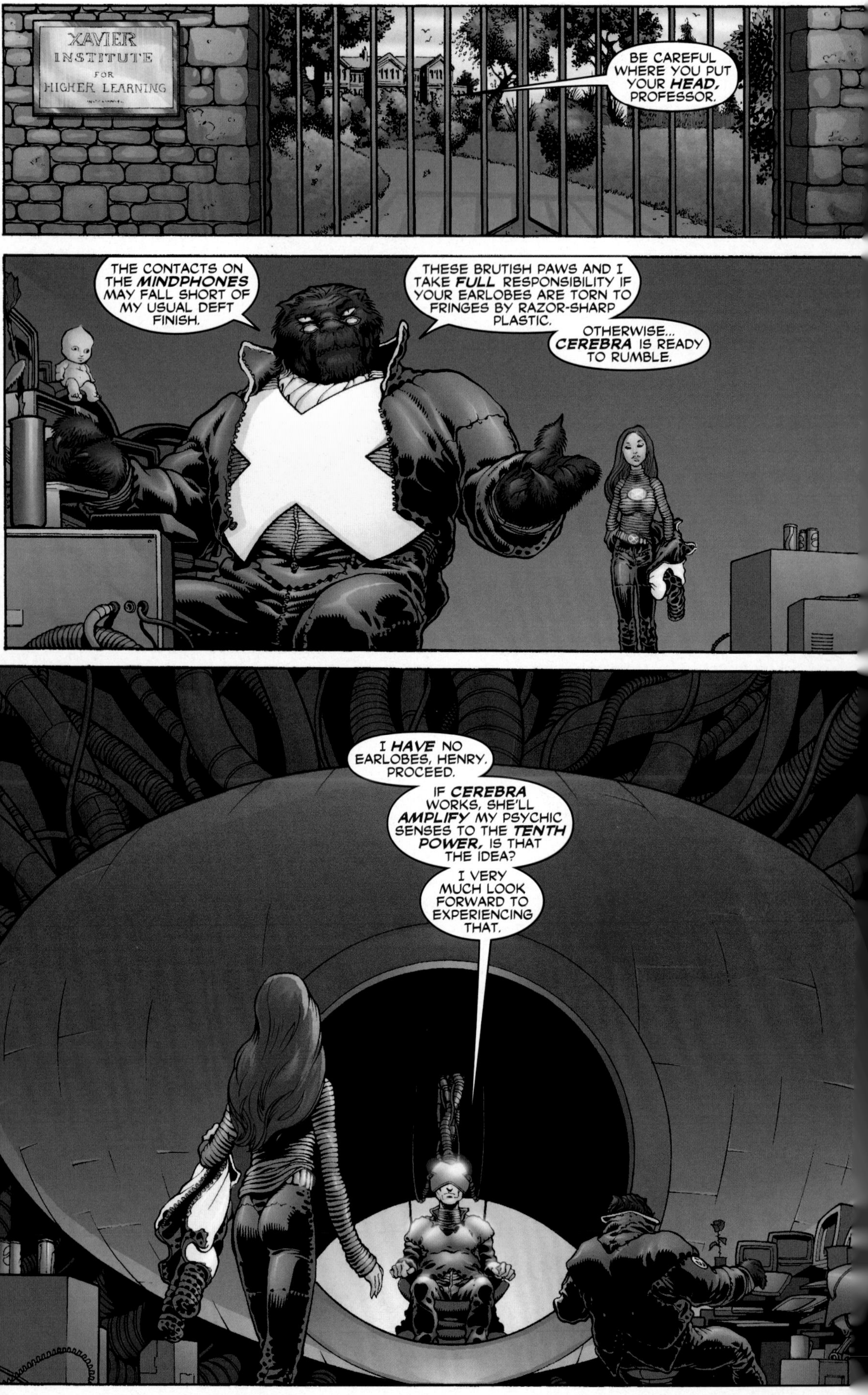
XAVIER INSTITUTE FOR HIGHER LEARNING
BE CAREFUL WHERE YOU PUT YOUR HEAD, PROFESSOR.
THE CONTACTS ON THE MINDPHONES MAY FALL SHORT OF MY USUAL DEFT FINISH.
THESE BRUTISH PAWS AND I TAKE FULL RESPONSIBILITY IF YOUR EARLOBES ARE TORN TO FRINGES BY RAZOR-SHARP PLASTIC.
OTHERWISE... CEREBRA IS READY TO RUMBLE.
I HAVE NO EARLOBES, HENRY. PROCEED.
IF CEREBRA WORKS, SHE'LL AMPLIFY MY PSYCHIC SENSES TO THE TENTH POWER, IS THAT THE IDEA?
I VERY MUCH LOOK FORWARD TO EXPERIENCING THAT.

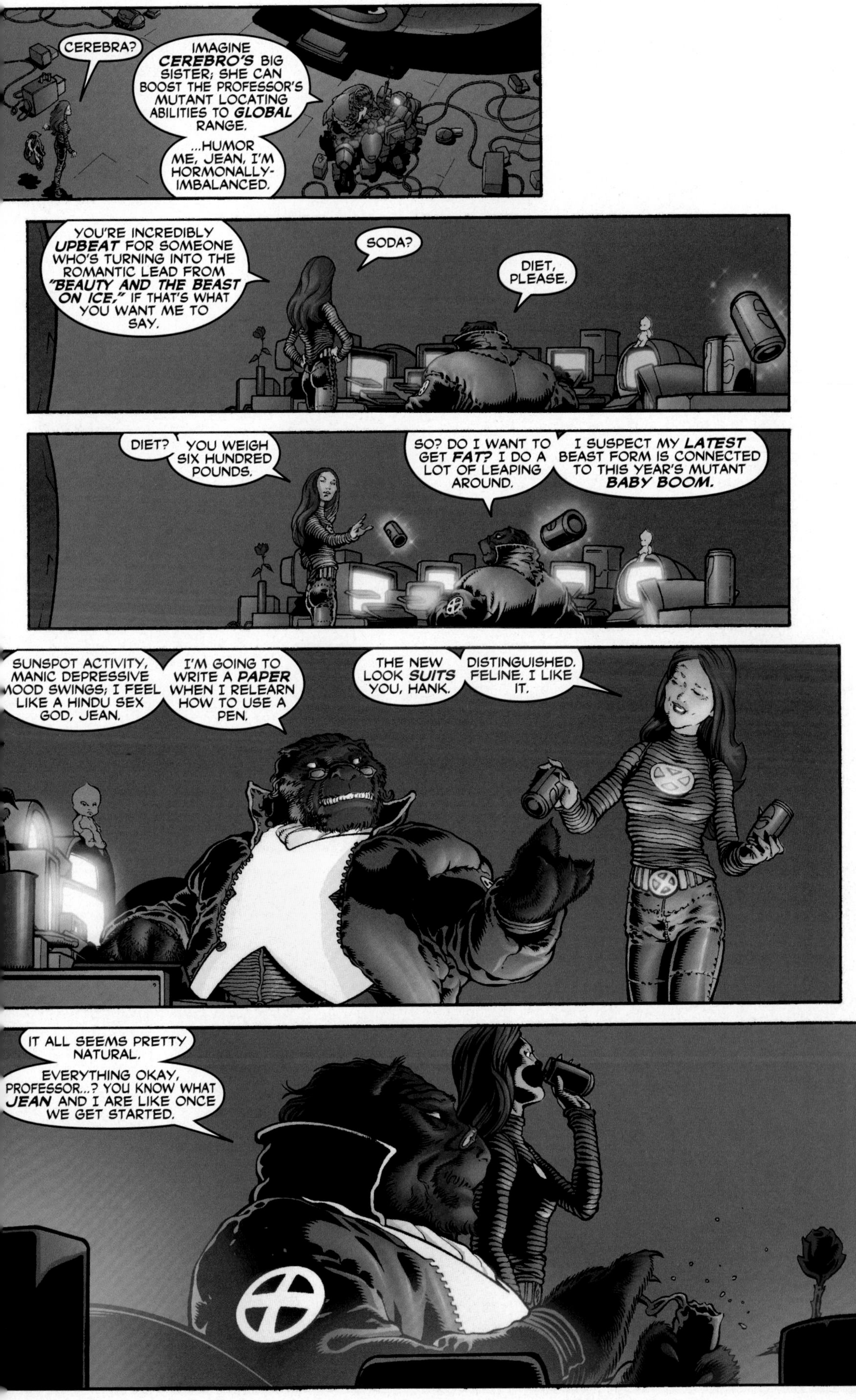

CEREBRA?
IMAGINE CEREBRO'S BIG SISTER; SHE CAN BOOST THE PROFESSOR'S MUTANT LOCATING ABILITIES TO GLOBAL RANGE.
...HUMOR ME, JEAN, I'M HORMONALLY-IMBALANCED.
YOU'RE INCREDIBLY UPBEAT FOR SOMEONE WHO'S TURNING INTO THE ROMANTIC LEAD FROM "BEAUTY AND THE BEAST ON ICE," IF THAT'S WHAT YOU WANT ME TO SAY.
SODA?
DIET, PLEASE.
DIET?
YOU WEIGH SIX HUNDRED POUNDS.
SO? DO I WANT TO GET FAT? I DO A LOT OF LEAPING AROUND.
I SUSPECT MY LATEST BEAST FORM IS CONNECTED TO THIS YEAR'S MUTANT BABY BOOM.
SUNSPOT ACTIVITY, MANIC DEPRESSIVE MOOD SWINGS; I FEEL LIKE A HINDU SEX GOD, JEAN.
I'M GOING TO WRITE A PAPER WHEN I RELEARN HOW TO USE A PEN.
THE NEW LOOK SUITS YOU, HANK.
DISTINGUISHED. FELINE. I LIKE IT.
IT ALL SEEMS PRETTY NATURAL.
EVERYTHING OKAY, PROFESSOR...? YOU KNOW WHAT JEAN AND I ARE LIKE ONCE WE GET STARTED.

I'M FINE. JOIN ME IN MY MIND AND TAKE A *LOOK* FOR YOURSELF, HENRY.

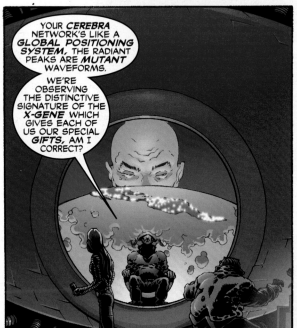

YOUR *CEREBRA* NETWORK'S LIKE A *GLOBAL POSITIONING SYSTEM*, THE RADIANT PEAKS ARE *MUTANT* WAVEFORMS.

WE'RE OBSERVING THE DISTINCTIVE SIGNATURE OF THE *X-GENE* WHICH GIVES EACH OF US OUR SPECIAL *GIFTS*, AM I CORRECT?

THIS IS *VERY* UNUSUAL, CHARLES.

YOUR THOUGHTS ARE ACTUALLY FORMING SOME KIND OF *CONDENSATION* ON THE WALLS ALL AROUND YOU.

I *MISSED* IT. THERE'S *SOMETHING*... AROUND COLOMBIA... *ECUADOR*, PERHAPS... I *THOUGHT* I FELT A TRACE, BUT...

ENHANCE X200.

IT MUST HAVE BEEN A TRICK OF THE TWINKLE IN YOUR EYES, HANK.

IT WAS LIKE A *FLARE*...A GENETIC *FLARE*...SOMEONE COULD BE IN TROUBLE.

I REALLY *DID* SE SOMETHING...

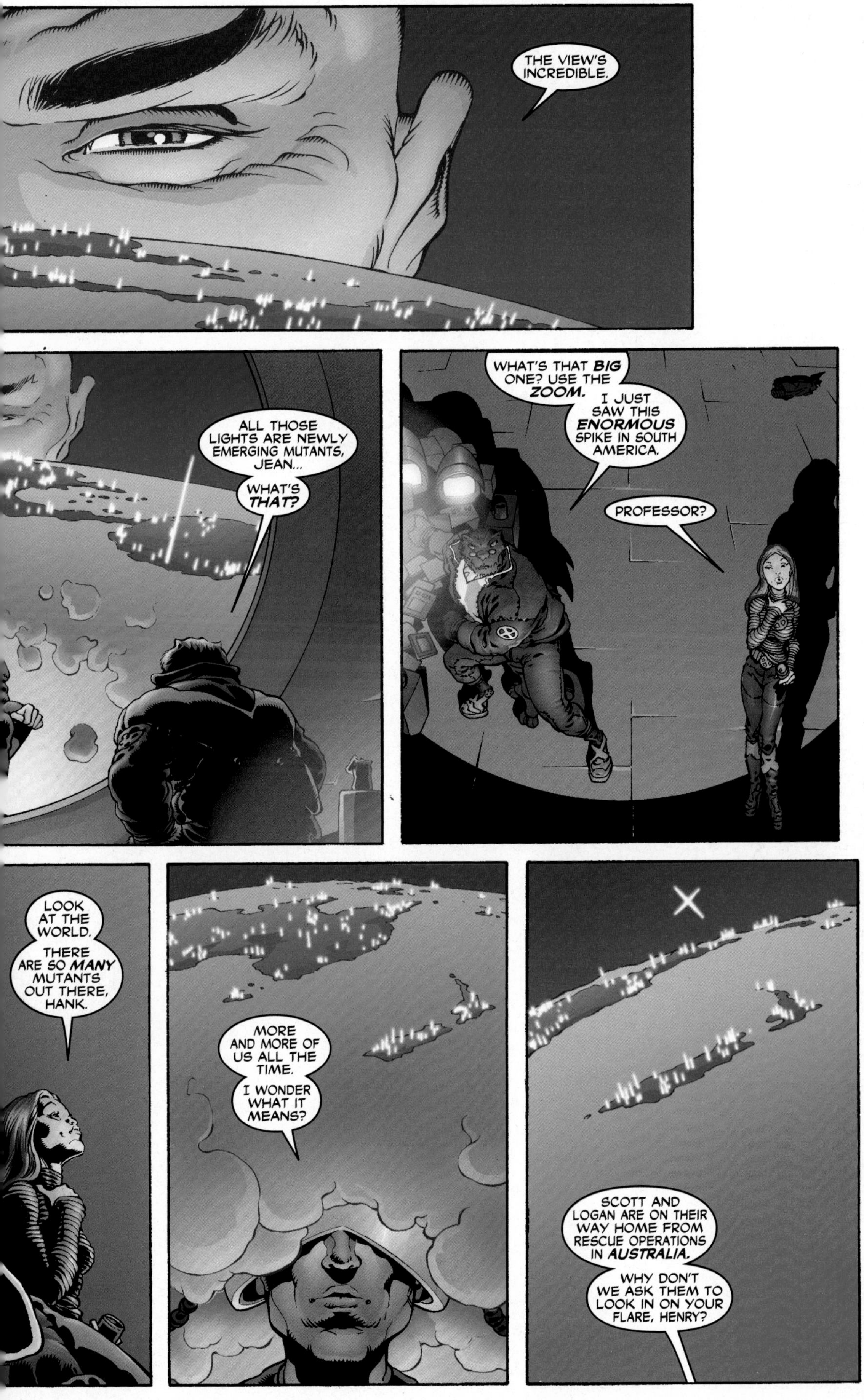
THE VIEW'S INCREDIBLE.
ALL THOSE LIGHTS ARE NEWLY EMERGING MUTANTS, JEAN...
WHAT'S *THAT?*
WHAT'S THAT *BIG* ONE? USE THE *ZOOM.*
I JUST SAW THIS *ENORMOUS* SPIKE IN SOUTH AMERICA.
PROFESSOR?
LOOK AT THE WORLD.
THERE ARE SO *MANY* MUTANTS OUT THERE, HANK.
MORE AND MORE OF US ALL THE TIME.
I WONDER WHAT IT MEANS?
SCOTT AND LOGAN ARE ON THEIR WAY HOME FROM RESCUE OPERATIONS IN *AUSTRALIA.*
WHY DON'T WE ASK THEM TO LOOK IN ON YOUR FLARE, HENRY?

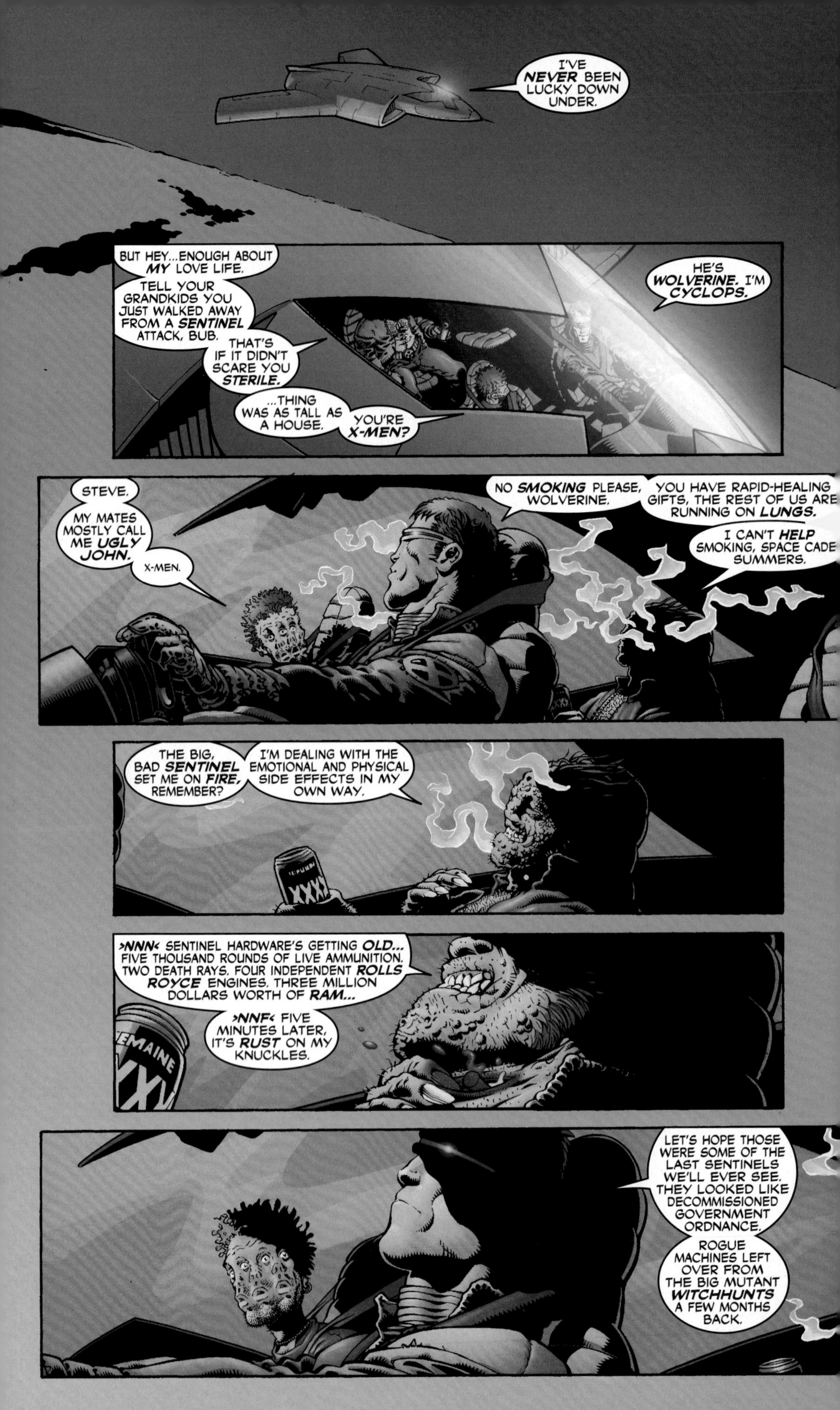
I'VE NEVER BEEN LUCKY DOWN UNDER.
BUT HEY...ENOUGH ABOUT MY LOVE LIFE.
TELL YOUR GRANDKIDS YOU JUST WALKED AWAY FROM A SENTINEL ATTACK, BUB.
THAT'S IF IT DIDN'T SCARE YOU STERILE.
...THING WAS AS TALL AS A HOUSE.
YOU'RE X-MEN?
HE'S WOLVERINE. I'M CYCLOPS.
STEVE.
MY MATES MOSTLY CALL ME UGLY JOHN.
X-MEN.
NO SMOKING PLEASE, WOLVERINE.
YOU HAVE RAPID-HEALING GIFTS, THE REST OF US ARE RUNNING ON LUNGS.
I CAN'T HELP SMOKING, SPACE CADE SUMMERS.
THE BIG, BAD SENTINEL SET ME ON FIRE, REMEMBER?
I'M DEALING WITH THE EMOTIONAL AND PHYSICAL SIDE EFFECTS IN MY OWN WAY.
XXXX
>NNN< SENTINEL HARDWARE'S GETTING OLD... FIVE THOUSAND ROUNDS OF LIVE AMMUNITION. TWO DEATH RAYS. FOUR INDEPENDENT ROLLS ROYCE ENGINES. THREE MILLION DOLLARS WORTH OF RAM...
>NNF< FIVE MINUTES LATER, IT'S RUST ON MY KNUCKLES.
LET'S HOPE THOSE WERE SOME OF THE LAST SENTINELS WE'LL EVER SEE. THEY LOOKED LIKE DECOMMISSIONED GOVERNMENT ORDNANCE.
ROGUE MACHINES LEFT OVER FROM THE BIG MUTANT WITCHHUNTS A FEW MONTHS BACK.

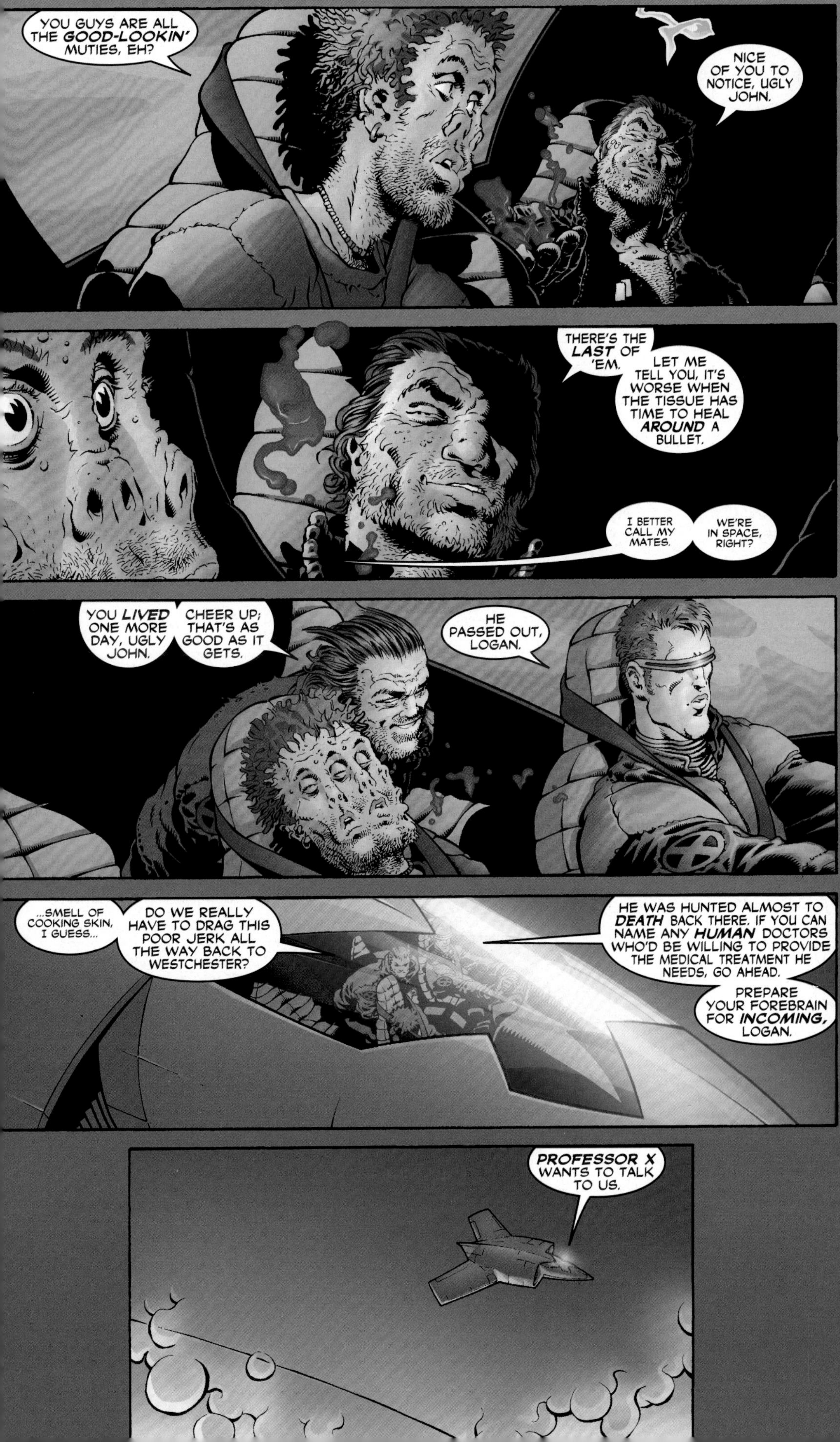

YOU GUYS ARE ALL THE GOOD-LOOKIN' MUTIES, EH?
NICE OF YOU TO NOTICE, UGLY JOHN.
THERE'S THE LAST OF 'EM.
LET ME TELL YOU, IT'S WORSE WHEN THE TISSUE HAS TIME TO HEAL AROUND A BULLET.
I BETTER CALL MY MATES.
WE'RE IN SPACE, RIGHT?
YOU LIVED ONE MORE DAY, UGLY JOHN.
CHEER UP; THAT'S AS GOOD AS IT GETS.
HE PASSED OUT, LOGAN.
...SMELL OF COOKING SKIN, I GUESS...
DO WE REALLY HAVE TO DRAG THIS POOR JERK ALL THE WAY BACK TO WESTCHESTER?
HE WAS HUNTED ALMOST TO DEATH BACK THERE. IF YOU CAN NAME ANY HUMAN DOCTORS WHO'D BE WILLING TO PROVIDE THE MEDICAL TREATMENT HE NEEDS, GO AHEAD.
PREPARE YOUR FOREBRAIN FOR INCOMING, LOGAN.
PROFESSOR X WANTS TO TALK TO US.

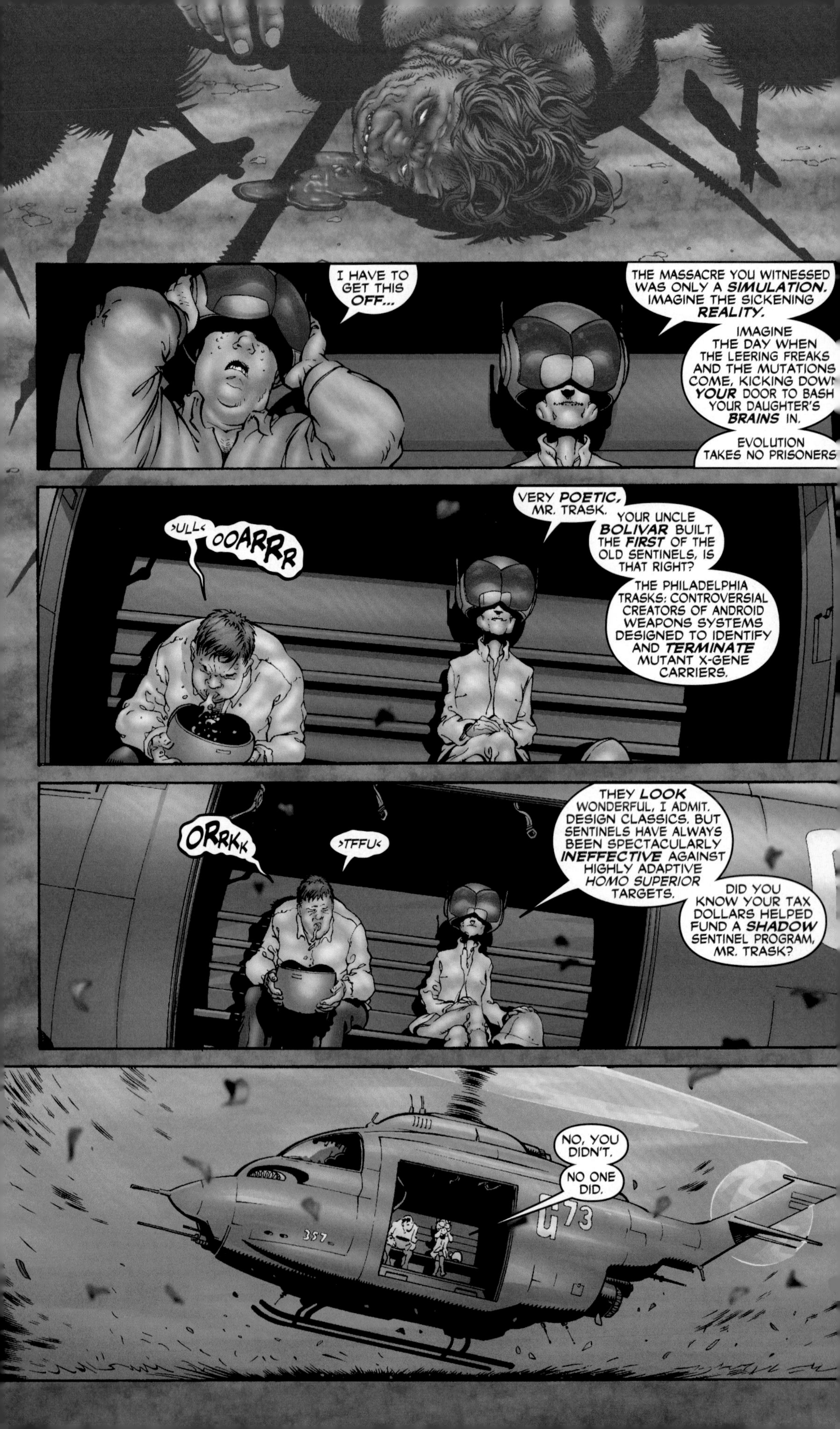

I HAVE TO GET THIS OFF...
THE MASSACRE YOU WITNESSED WAS ONLY A SIMULATION. IMAGINE THE SICKENING REALITY.
IMAGINE THE DAY WHEN THE LEERING FREAKS AND THE MUTATIONS COME, KICKING DOWN YOUR DOOR TO BASH YOUR DAUGHTER'S BRAINS IN.
EVOLUTION TAKES NO PRISONERS
>ULL< OOARRR
VERY POETIC, MR. TRASK.
YOUR UNCLE BOLIVAR BUILT THE FIRST OF THE OLD SENTINELS, IS THAT RIGHT?
THE PHILADELPHIA TRASKS: CONTROVERSIAL CREATORS OF ANDROID WEAPONS SYSTEMS DESIGNED TO IDENTIFY AND TERMINATE MUTANT X-GENE CARRIERS.
ORRKK
>TFFU<
THEY LOOK WONDERFUL, I ADMIT. DESIGN CLASSICS. BUT SENTINELS HAVE ALWAYS BEEN SPECTACULARLY INEFFECTIVE AGAINST HIGHLY ADAPTIVE HOMO SUPERIOR TARGETS.
DID YOU KNOW YOUR TAX DOLLARS HELPED FUND A SHADOW SENTINEL PROGRAM, MR. TRASK?
NO, YOU DIDN'T.
NO ONE DID.

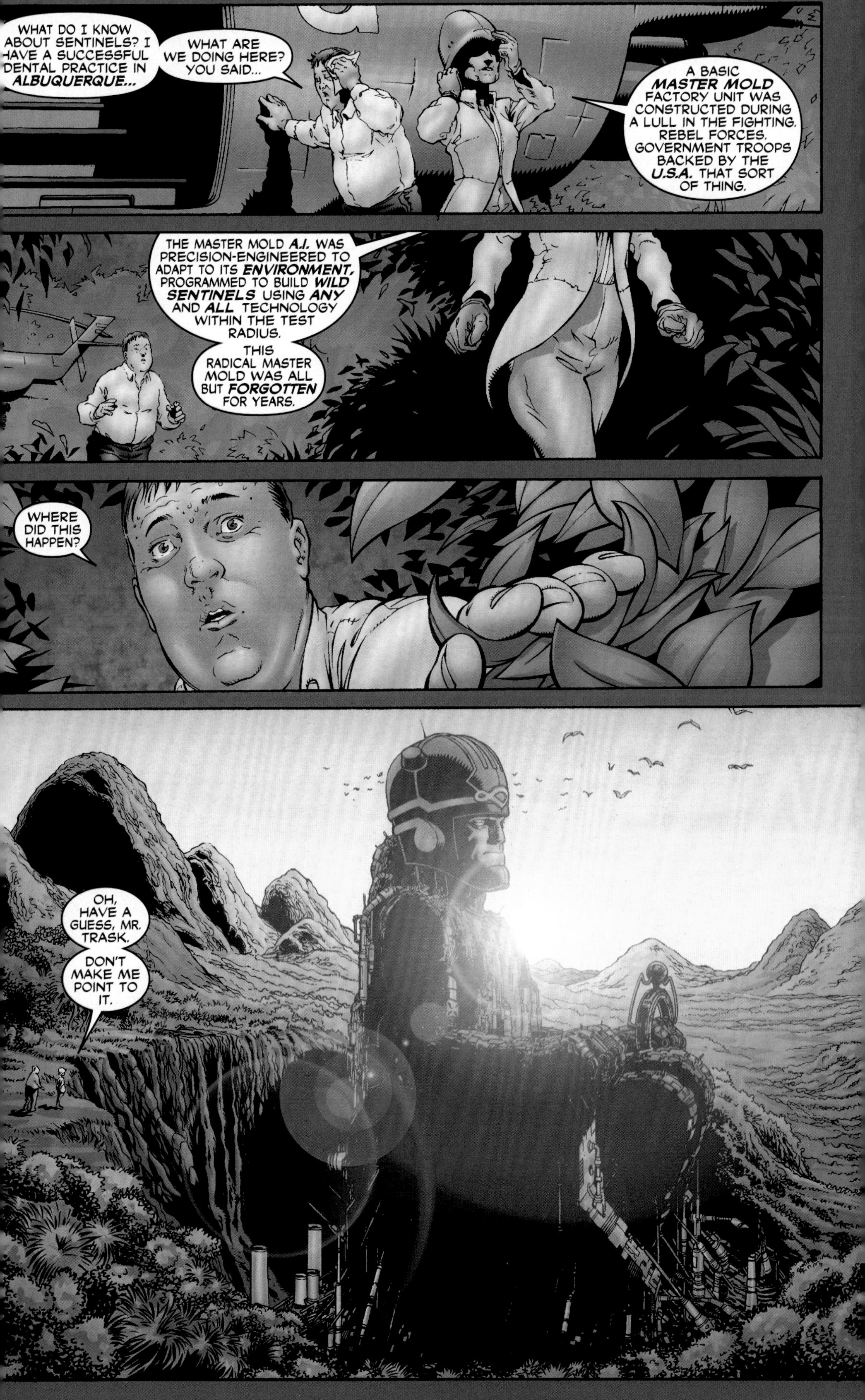
WHAT DO I KNOW ABOUT SENTINELS? I HAVE A SUCCESSFUL DENTAL PRACTICE IN ALBUQUERQUE...
WHAT ARE WE DOING HERE? YOU SAID...
A BASIC MASTER MOLD FACTORY UNIT WAS CONSTRUCTED DURING A LULL IN THE FIGHTING. REBEL FORCES. GOVERNMENT TROOPS BACKED BY THE U.S.A. THAT SORT OF THING.
THE MASTER MOLD A.I. WAS PRECISION-ENGINEERED TO ADAPT TO ITS ENVIRONMENT, PROGRAMMED TO BUILD WILD SENTINELS USING ANY AND ALL TECHNOLOGY WITHIN THE TEST RADIUS.
THIS RADICAL MASTER MOLD WAS ALL BUT FORGOTTEN FOR YEARS.
WHERE DID THIS HAPPEN?
OH, HAVE A GUESS, MR. TRASK.
DON'T MAKE ME POINT TO IT.

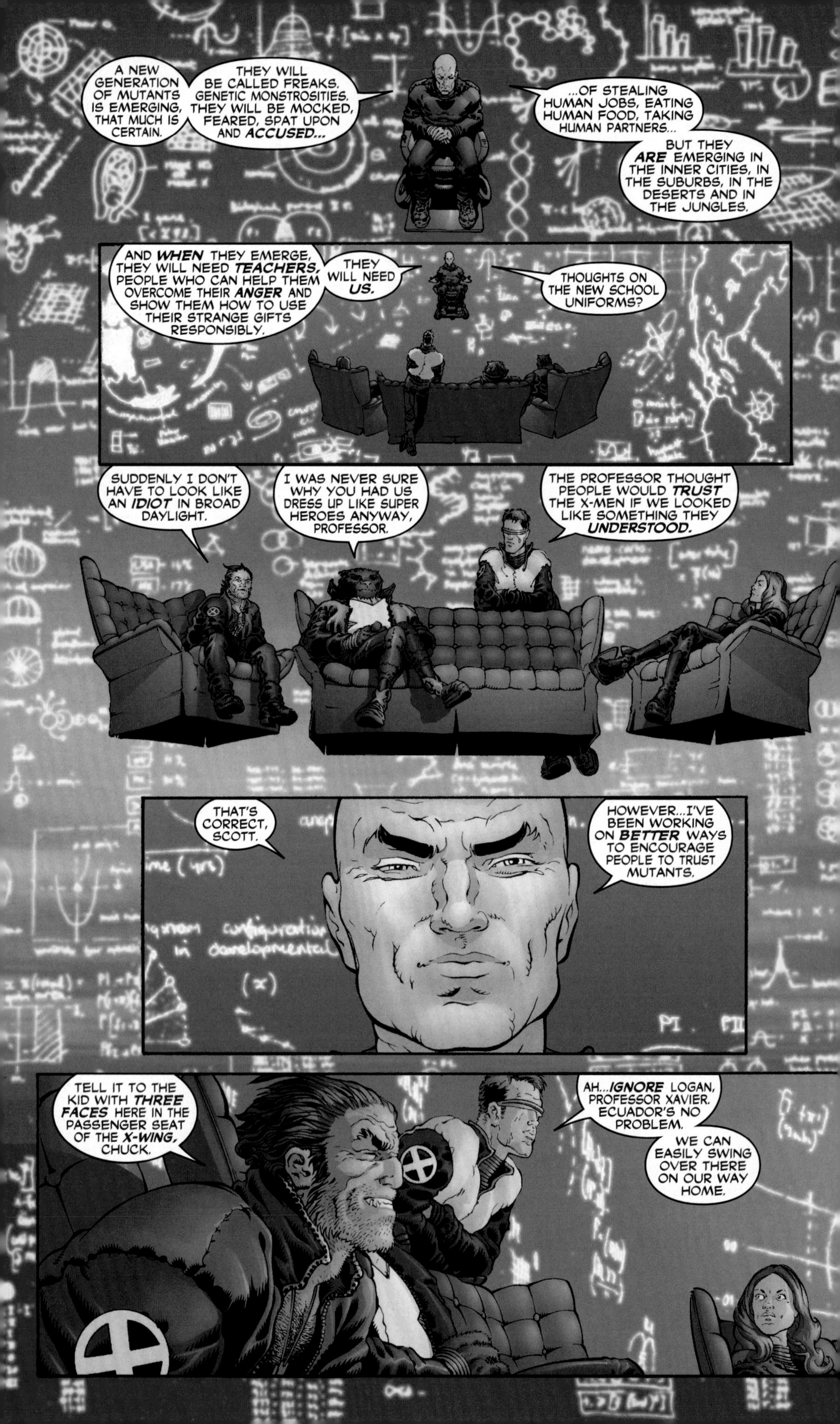
A NEW GENERATION OF MUTANTS IS EMERGING, THAT MUCH IS CERTAIN.
THEY WILL BE CALLED FREAKS. GENETIC MONSTROSITIES. THEY WILL BE MOCKED, FEARED, SPAT UPON AND ACCUSED...
...OF STEALING HUMAN JOBS, EATING HUMAN FOOD, TAKING HUMAN PARTNERS...
BUT THEY ARE EMERGING IN THE INNER CITIES, IN THE SUBURBS, IN THE DESERTS AND IN THE JUNGLES.
AND WHEN THEY EMERGE, THEY WILL NEED TEACHERS, PEOPLE WHO CAN HELP THEM OVERCOME THEIR ANGER AND SHOW THEM HOW TO USE THEIR STRANGE GIFTS RESPONSIBLY.
THEY WILL NEED US.
THOUGHTS ON THE NEW SCHOOL UNIFORMS?
SUDDENLY I DON'T HAVE TO LOOK LIKE AN IDIOT IN BROAD DAYLIGHT.
I WAS NEVER SURE WHY YOU HAD US DRESS UP LIKE SUPER HEROES ANYWAY, PROFESSOR.
THE PROFESSOR THOUGHT PEOPLE WOULD TRUST THE X-MEN IF WE LOOKED LIKE SOMETHING THEY UNDERSTOOD.
THAT'S CORRECT, SCOTT.
HOWEVER...I'VE BEEN WORKING ON BETTER WAYS TO ENCOURAGE PEOPLE TO TRUST MUTANTS.
TELL IT TO THE KID WITH THREE FACES HERE IN THE PASSENGER SEAT OF THE X-WING, CHUCK.
AH...IGNORE LOGAN, PROFESSOR XAVIER. ECUADOR'S NO PROBLEM.
WE CAN EASILY SWING OVER THERE ON OUR WAY HOME.

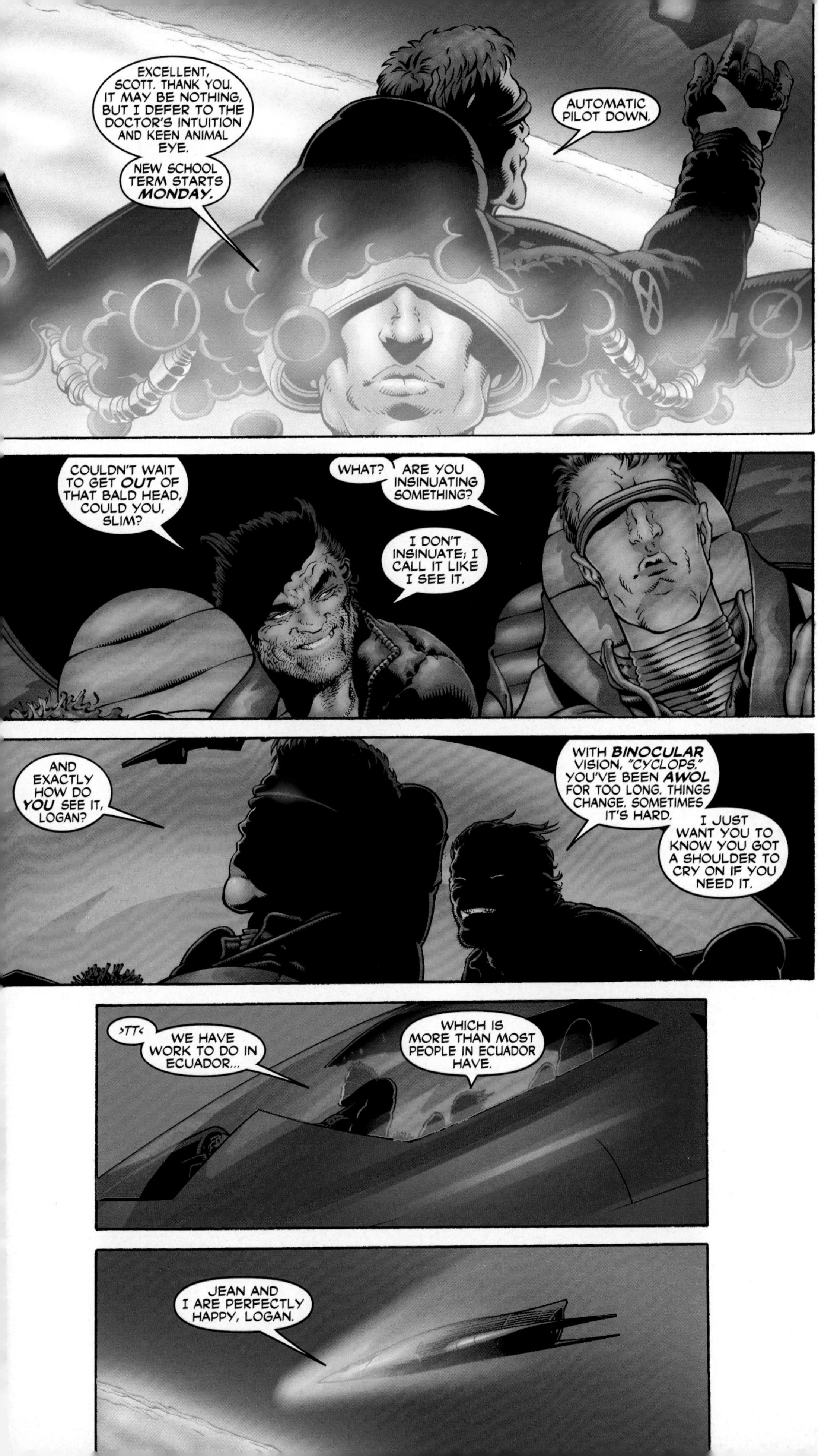

EXCELLENT, SCOTT. THANK YOU. IT MAY BE NOTHING, BUT I DEFER TO THE DOCTOR'S INTUITION AND KEEN ANIMAL EYE.
NEW SCHOOL TERM STARTS MONDAY.
AUTOMATIC PILOT DOWN.
COULDN'T WAIT TO GET OUT OF THAT BALD HEAD, COULD YOU, SLIM?
WHAT?
ARE YOU INSINUATING SOMETHING?
I DON'T INSINUATE; I CALL IT LIKE I SEE IT.
AND EXACTLY HOW DO YOU SEE IT, LOGAN?
WITH BINOCULAR VISION, "CYCLOPS." YOU'VE BEEN AWOL FOR TOO LONG. THINGS CHANGE. SOMETIMES IT'S HARD.
I JUST WANT YOU TO KNOW YOU GOT A SHOULDER TO CRY ON IF YOU NEED IT.
>TT<
WE HAVE WORK TO DO IN ECUADOR...
WHICH IS MORE THAN MOST PEOPLE IN ECUADOR HAVE.
JEAN AND I ARE PERFECTLY HAPPY, LOGAN.

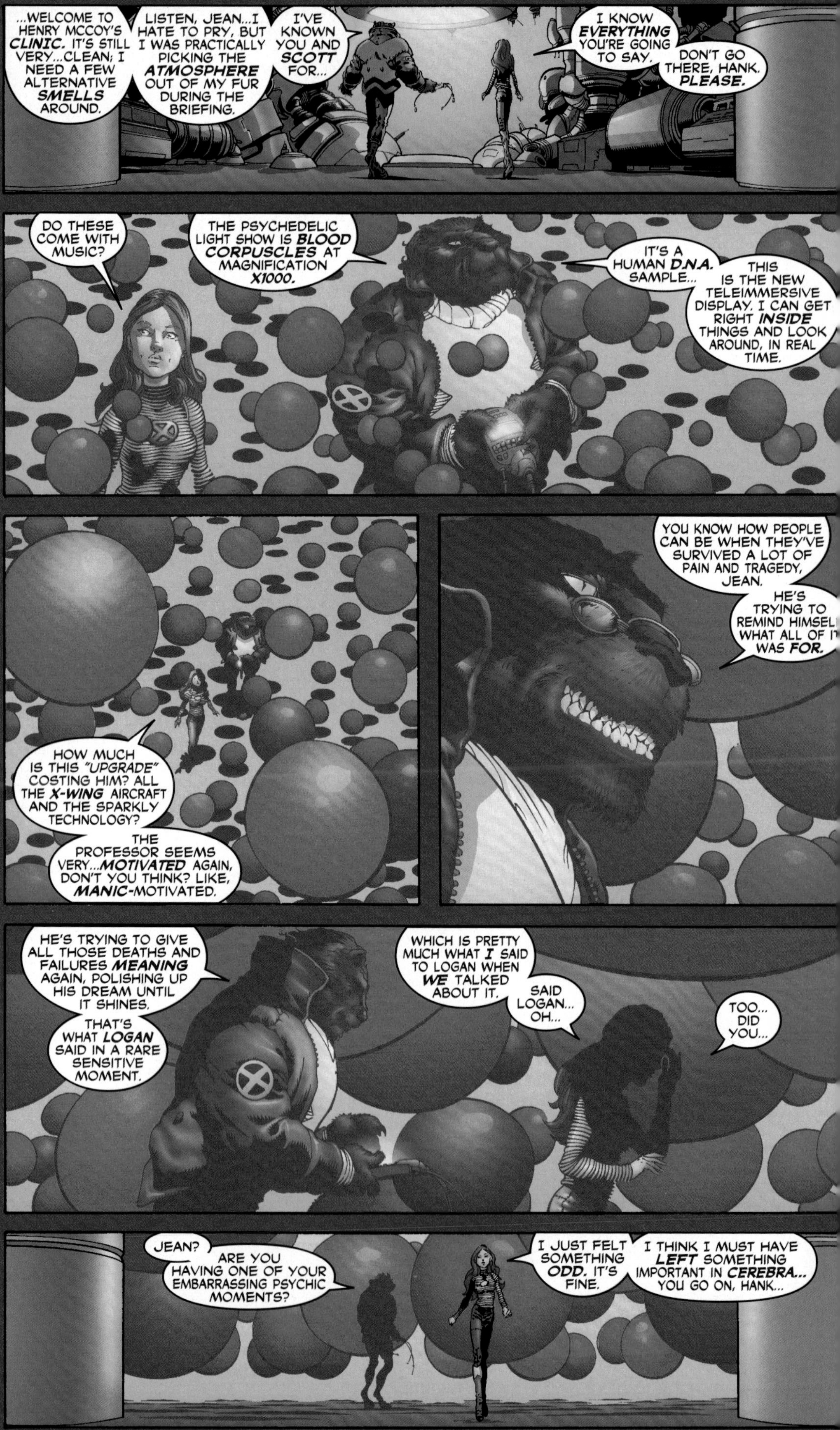
...WELCOME TO HENRY MCCOY'S CLINIC. IT'S STILL VERY...CLEAN; I NEED A FEW ALTERNATIVE SMELLS AROUND.
LISTEN, JEAN...I HATE TO PRY, BUT I WAS PRACTICALLY PICKING THE ATMOSPHERE OUT OF MY FUR DURING THE BRIEFING.
I'VE KNOWN YOU AND SCOTT FOR...
I KNOW EVERYTHING YOU'RE GOING TO SAY.
DON'T GO THERE, HANK. PLEASE.
DO THESE COME WITH MUSIC?
THE PSYCHEDELIC LIGHT SHOW IS BLOOD CORPUSCLES AT MAGNIFICATION X1000.
IT'S A HUMAN D.N.A. SAMPLE...
THIS IS THE NEW TELEIMMERSIVE DISPLAY. I CAN GET RIGHT INSIDE THINGS AND LOOK AROUND, IN REAL TIME.
HOW MUCH IS THIS "UPGRADE" COSTING HIM? ALL THE X-WING AIRCRAFT AND THE SPARKLY TECHNOLOGY?
THE PROFESSOR SEEMS VERY...MOTIVATED AGAIN, DON'T YOU THINK? LIKE, MANIC-MOTIVATED.
YOU KNOW HOW PEOPLE CAN BE WHEN THEY'VE SURVIVED A LOT OF PAIN AND TRAGEDY, JEAN.
HE'S TRYING TO REMIND HIMSEL WHAT ALL OF IT WAS FOR.
HE'S TRYING TO GIVE ALL THOSE DEATHS AND FAILURES MEANING AGAIN, POLISHING UP HIS DREAM UNTIL IT SHINES.
THAT'S WHAT LOGAN SAID IN A RARE SENSITIVE MOMENT.
WHICH IS PRETTY MUCH WHAT I SAID TO LOGAN WHEN WE TALKED ABOUT IT.
SAID LOGAN... OH...
TOO... DID YOU...
JEAN?
ARE YOU HAVING ONE OF YOUR EMBARRASSING PSYCHIC MOMENTS?
I JUST FELT SOMETHING ODD. IT'S FINE.
I THINK I MUST HAVE LEFT SOMETHING IMPORTANT IN CEREBRA... YOU GO ON, HANK...

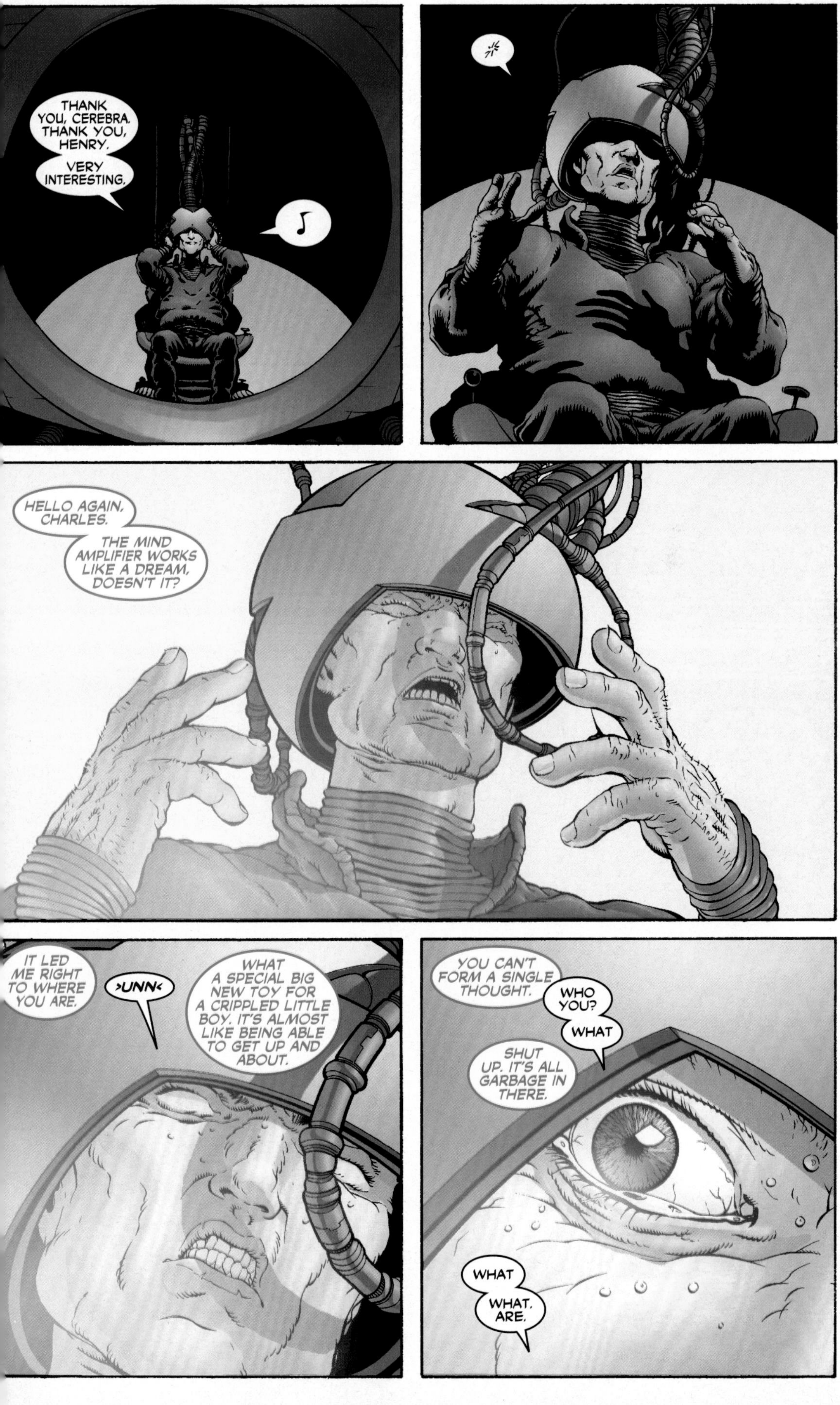
THANK YOU, CEREBRA. THANK YOU, HENRY.
VERY INTERESTING.
HELLO AGAIN, CHARLES.
THE MIND AMPLIFIER WORKS LIKE A DREAM, DOESN'T IT?
IT LED ME RIGHT TO WHERE YOU ARE.
>UNN<
WHAT A SPECIAL BIG NEW TOY FOR A CRIPPLED LITTLE BOY. IT'S ALMOST LIKE BEING ABLE TO GET UP AND ABOUT.
YOU CAN'T FORM A SINGLE THOUGHT.
WHO YOU?
WHAT
SHUT UP. IT'S ALL GARBAGE IN THERE.
WHAT
WHAT. ARE.

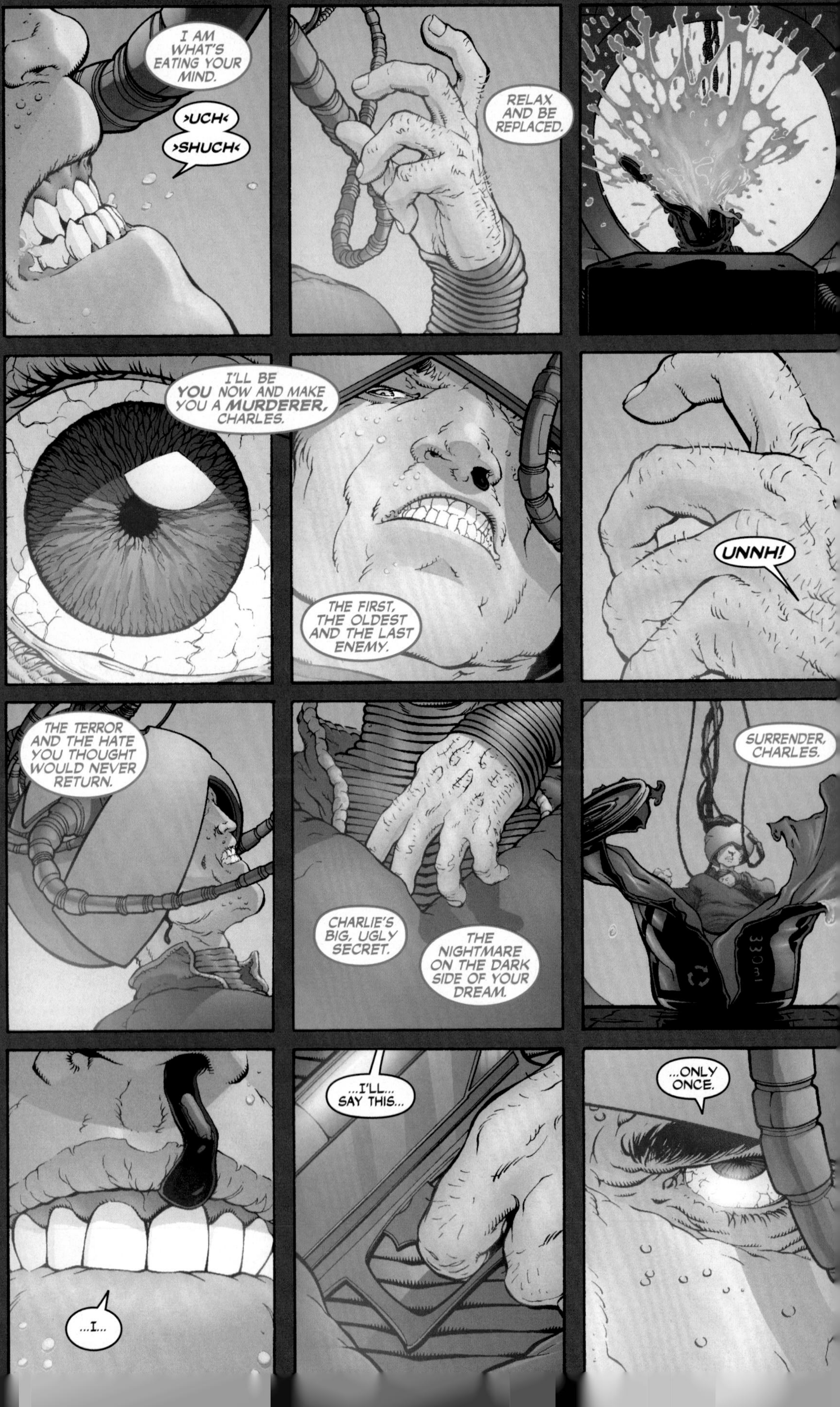
I AM WHAT'S EATING YOUR MIND.
>UCH<
>SHUCH<
RELAX AND BE REPLACED.
I'LL BE YOU NOW AND MAKE YOU A MURDERER, CHARLES.
THE FIRST, THE OLDEST AND THE LAST ENEMY.
UNNH!
THE TERROR AND THE HATE YOU THOUGHT WOULD NEVER RETURN.
CHARLIE'S BIG, UGLY SECRET.
THE NIGHTMARE ON THE DARK SIDE OF YOUR DREAM.
SURRENDER, CHARLES.
...I...
...I'LL... SAY THIS...
...ONLY ONCE.

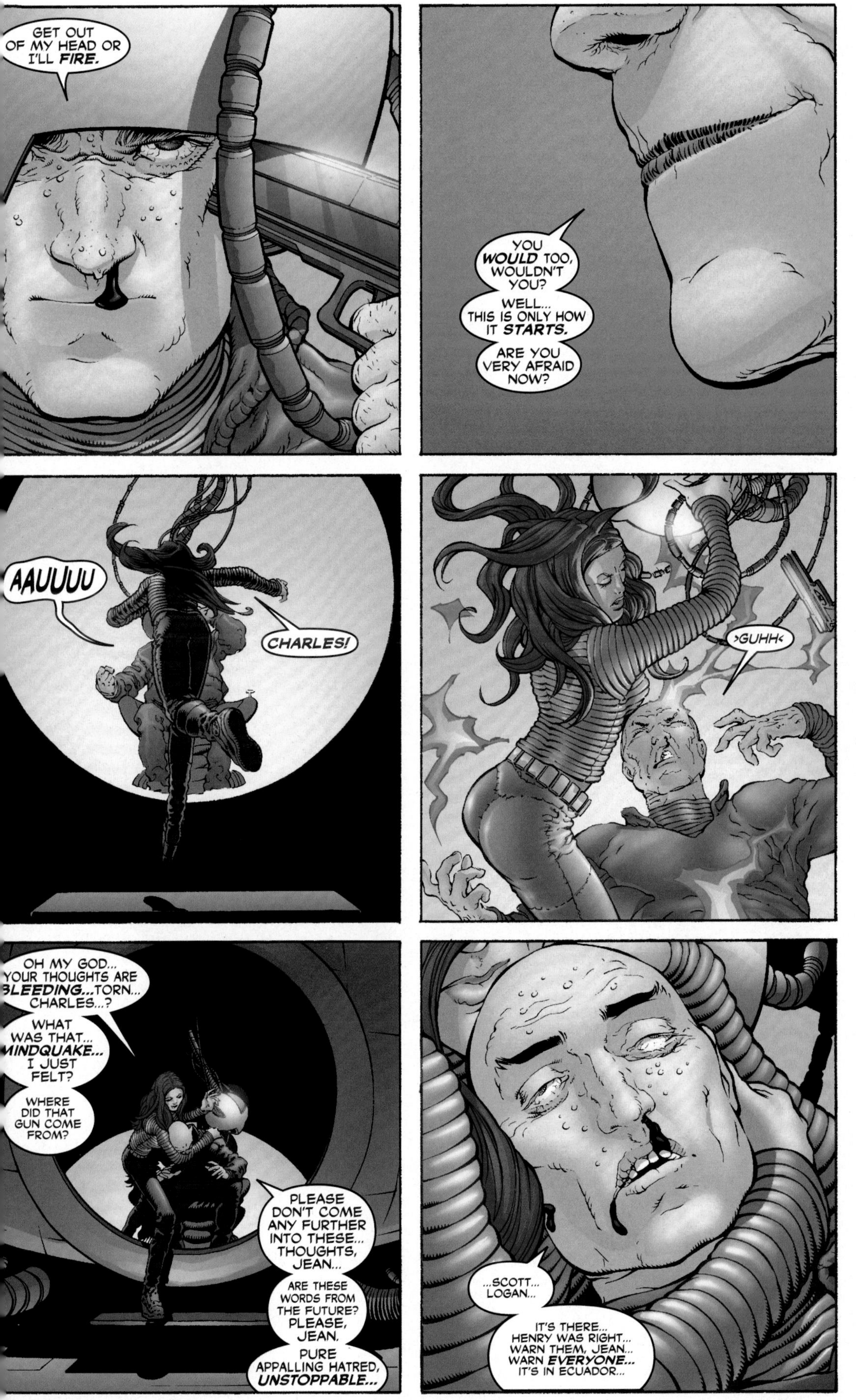
GET OUT OF MY HEAD OR I'LL FIRE.
YOU WOULD TOO, WOULDN'T YOU?
WELL... THIS IS ONLY HOW IT STARTS.
ARE YOU VERY AFRAID NOW?
AAUUUU
CHARLES!
>GUHH<
OH MY GOD... YOUR THOUGHTS ARE BLEEDING...TORN... CHARLES...?
WHAT WAS THAT... MINDQUAKE... I JUST FELT?
WHERE DID THAT GUN COME FROM?
PLEASE DON'T COME ANY FURTHER INTO THESE... THOUGHTS, JEAN...
ARE THESE WORDS FROM THE FUTURE? PLEASE, JEAN.
PURE APPALLING HATRED, UNSTOPPABLE...
...SCOTT... LOGAN...
IT'S THERE... HENRY WAS RIGHT... WARN THEM, JEAN... WARN EVERYONE... IT'S IN ECUADOR...

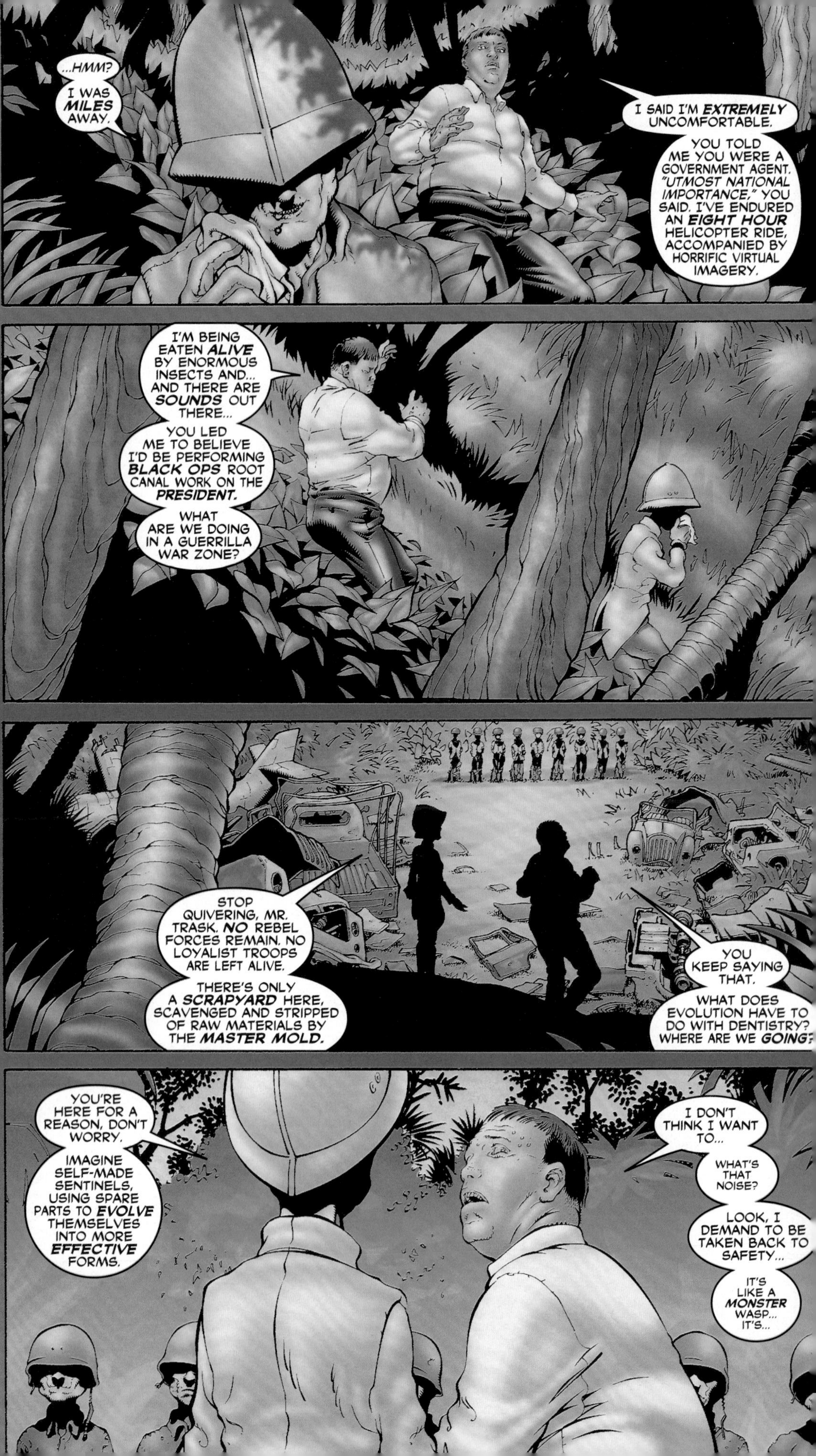
...HMM? I WAS MILES AWAY.
I SAID I'M EXTREMELY UNCOMFORTABLE.
YOU TOLD ME YOU WERE A GOVERNMENT AGENT. "UTMOST NATIONAL IMPORTANCE," YOU SAID. I'VE ENDURED AN EIGHT HOUR HELICOPTER RIDE, ACCOMPANIED BY HORRIFIC VIRTUAL IMAGERY.
I'M BEING EATEN ALIVE BY ENORMOUS INSECTS AND... AND THERE ARE SOUNDS OUT THERE...
YOU LED ME TO BELIEVE I'D BE PERFORMING BLACK OPS ROOT CANAL WORK ON THE PRESIDENT.
WHAT ARE WE DOING IN A GUERRILLA WAR ZONE?
STOP QUIVERING, MR. TRASK. NO REBEL FORCES REMAIN. NO LOYALIST TROOPS ARE LEFT ALIVE.
THERE'S ONLY A SCRAPYARD HERE, SCAVENGED AND STRIPPED OF RAW MATERIALS BY THE MASTER MOLD.
YOU KEEP SAYING THAT.
WHAT DOES EVOLUTION HAVE TO DO WITH DENTISTRY? WHERE ARE WE GOING?
YOU'RE HERE FOR A REASON, DON'T WORRY.
IMAGINE SELF-MADE SENTINELS, USING SPARE PARTS TO EVOLVE THEMSELVES INTO MORE EFFECTIVE FORMS.
I DON'T THINK I WANT TO...
WHAT'S THAT NOISE?
LOOK, I DEMAND TO BE TAKEN BACK TO SAFETY...
IT'S LIKE A MONSTER WASP... IT'S...

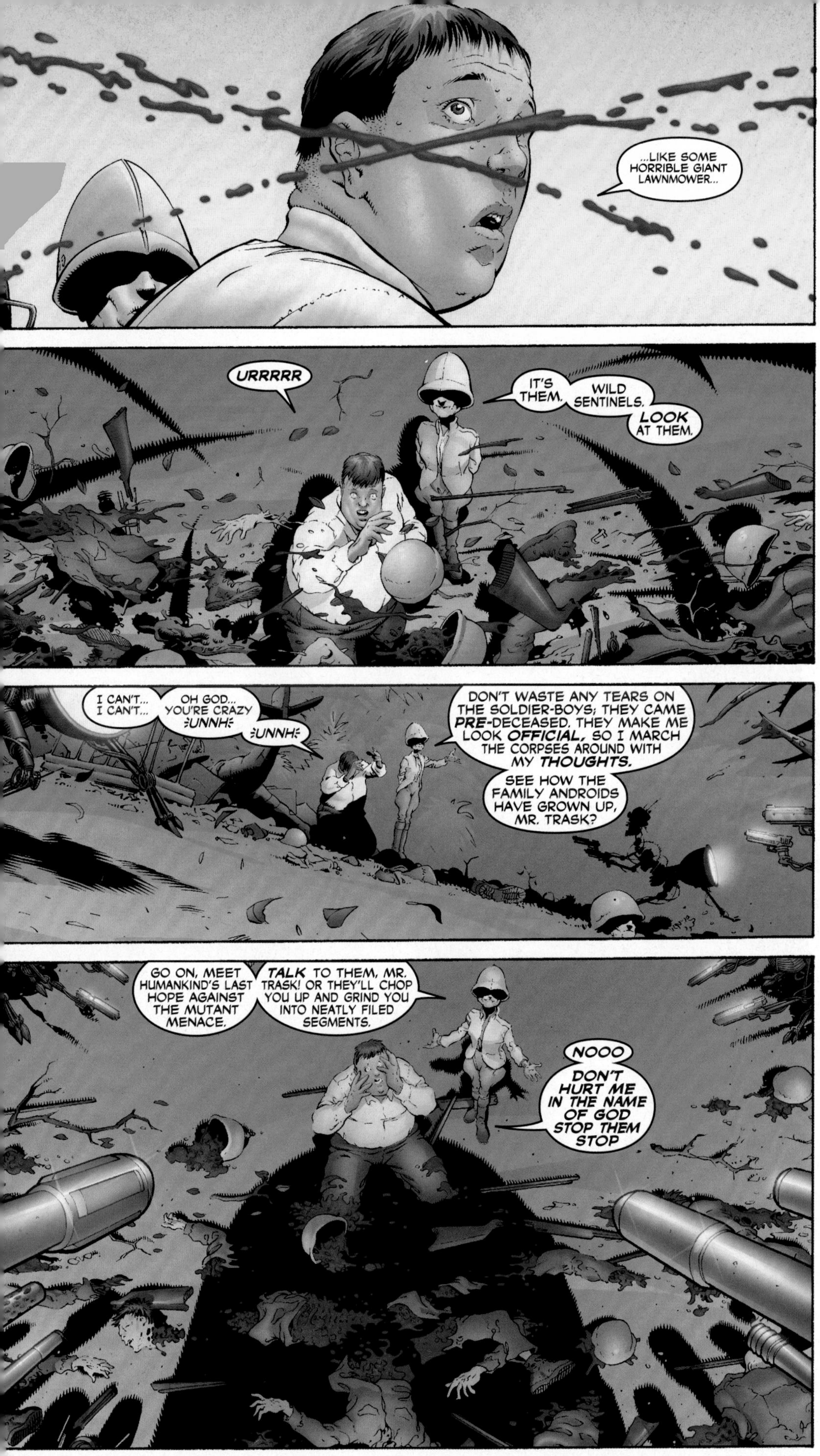
...LIKE SOME HORRIBLE GIANT LAWNMOWER...
URRRRR
IT'S THEM.
WILD SENTINELS.
LOOK AT THEM.
I CAN'T... I CAN'T...
OH GOD... YOU'RE CRAZY
UNNH
UNNH
DON'T WASTE ANY TEARS ON THE SOLDIER-BOYS; THEY CAME PRE-DECEASED. THEY MAKE ME LOOK OFFICIAL, SO I MARCH THE CORPSES AROUND WITH MY THOUGHTS.
SEE HOW THE FAMILY ANDROIDS HAVE GROWN UP, MR. TRASK?
GO ON, MEET HUMANKIND'S LAST HOPE AGAINST THE MUTANT MENACE.
TALK TO THEM, MR. TRASK! OR THEY'LL CHOP YOU UP AND GRIND YOU INTO NEATLY FILED SEGMENTS.
NOOO
DON'T HURT ME IN THE NAME OF GOD STOP THEM STOP

AMM

AH

ANH

VOCAL IDENTIFICATION: TRASK.

PRIME COMMAND PROTOCOLS SEARCH: ONLINE.

RUNNING PROTOCOLS: STOP.

PRESERVE TRASK D.N.A.

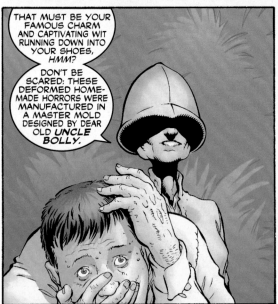

THAT MUST BE YOUR FAMOUS CHARM AND CAPTIVATING WIT RUNNING DOWN INTO YOUR SHOES, HMM?

DON'T BE SCARED: THESE DEFORMED HOME-MADE HORRORS WERE MANUFACTURED IN A MASTER MOLD DESIGNED BY DEAR OLD UNCLE BOLLY.

PRESERVE TRASK D.N.A.

THEY'LL DO ANYTHING YOU SAY, MR. TRASK. I BROUGHT YOU HERE IN MY CAPACITY AS A BIOLOGIST BECAUSE I FEEL IT'S YOUR DUTY TO SAVE THE HUMAN SPECIES.

THEY'RE NOT ATTACKING YOU.

WHY BE THE SMALL MAN WHEN YOU COULD BE THE SCOURGE AND DESTROYER OF MONSTERS?

THESE ANDROID ASSASSINS HAVE OBVIOUSLY REACHED THE LIMITS OF THEIR ABILITY TO EVOLVE IN THIS ENVIRONMENT.

WITH A WORD, YOU CAN EXTEND THEIR REACH.

WITH A WORD, YOU CAN EXTERMINATE HOMO SUPERIOR IN ITS INFANCY...WHILE THE SPECIES IS STILL TOO YOUNG TO FIGHT BACK.

SO LOWER THAT ONCE-COMMANDING VOICE OF YOURS A FEW OCTAVES.

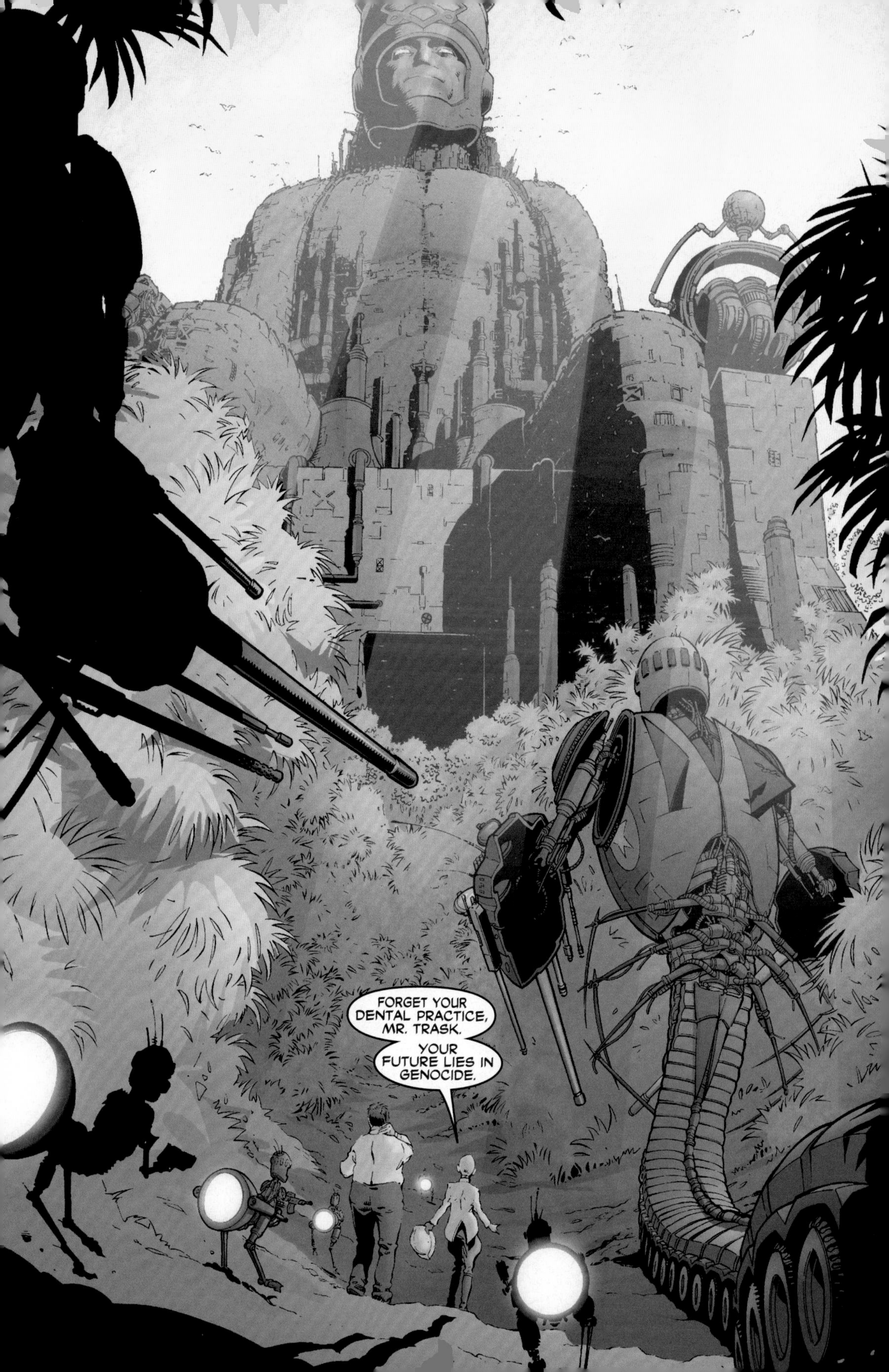
FORGET YOUR DENTAL PRACTICE, MR. TRASK.
YOUR FUTURE LIES IN GENOCIDE.

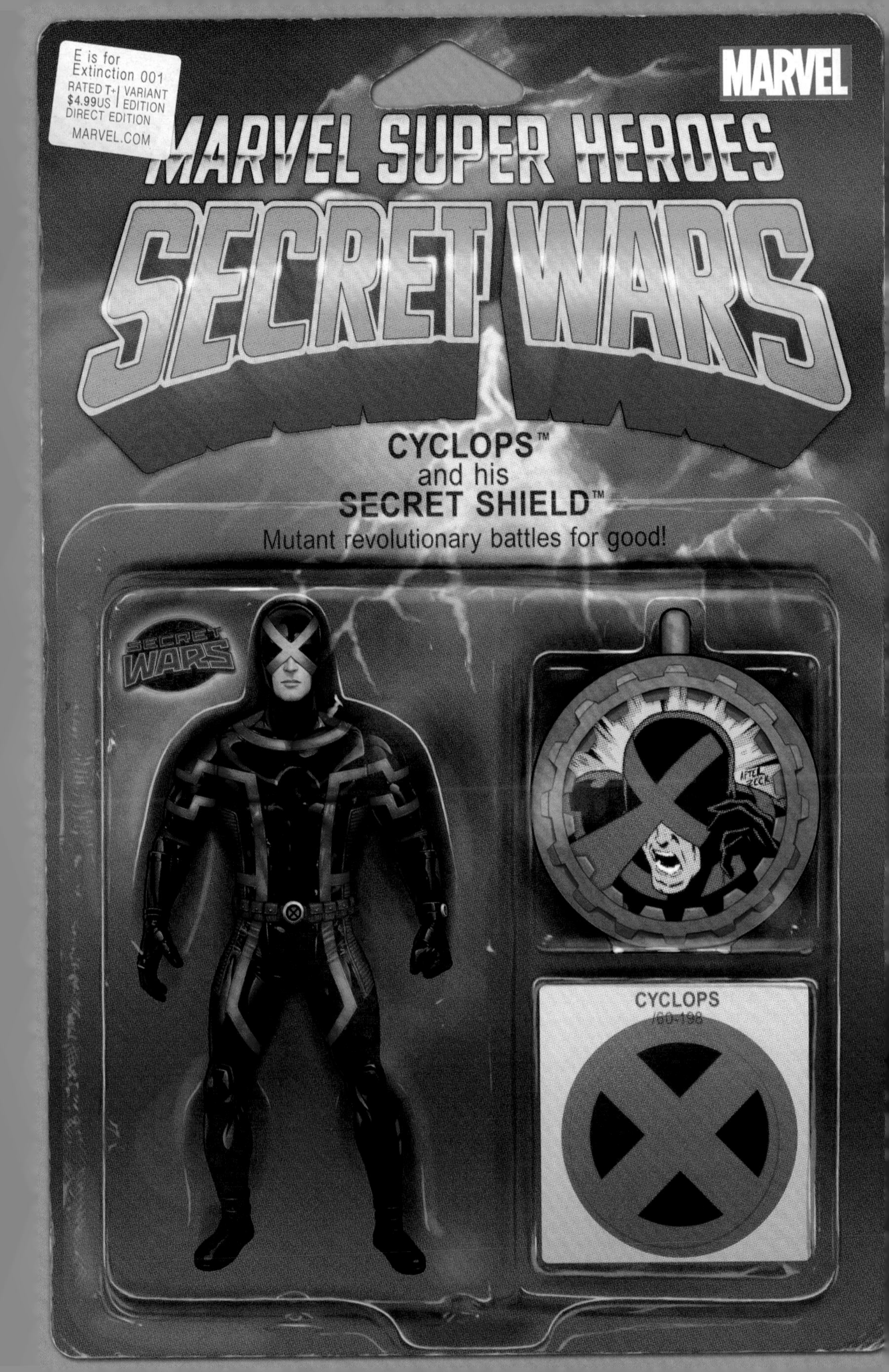
E is for Extinction 001
RATED T+
$4.99US
DIRECT EDITION
VARIANT EDITION
MARVEL.COM
MARVEL
MARVEL SUPER HEROES
SECRET WARS
CYCLOPS™
and his
SECRET SHIELD™
Mutant revolutionary battles for good!
SECRET WARS
CYCLOPS

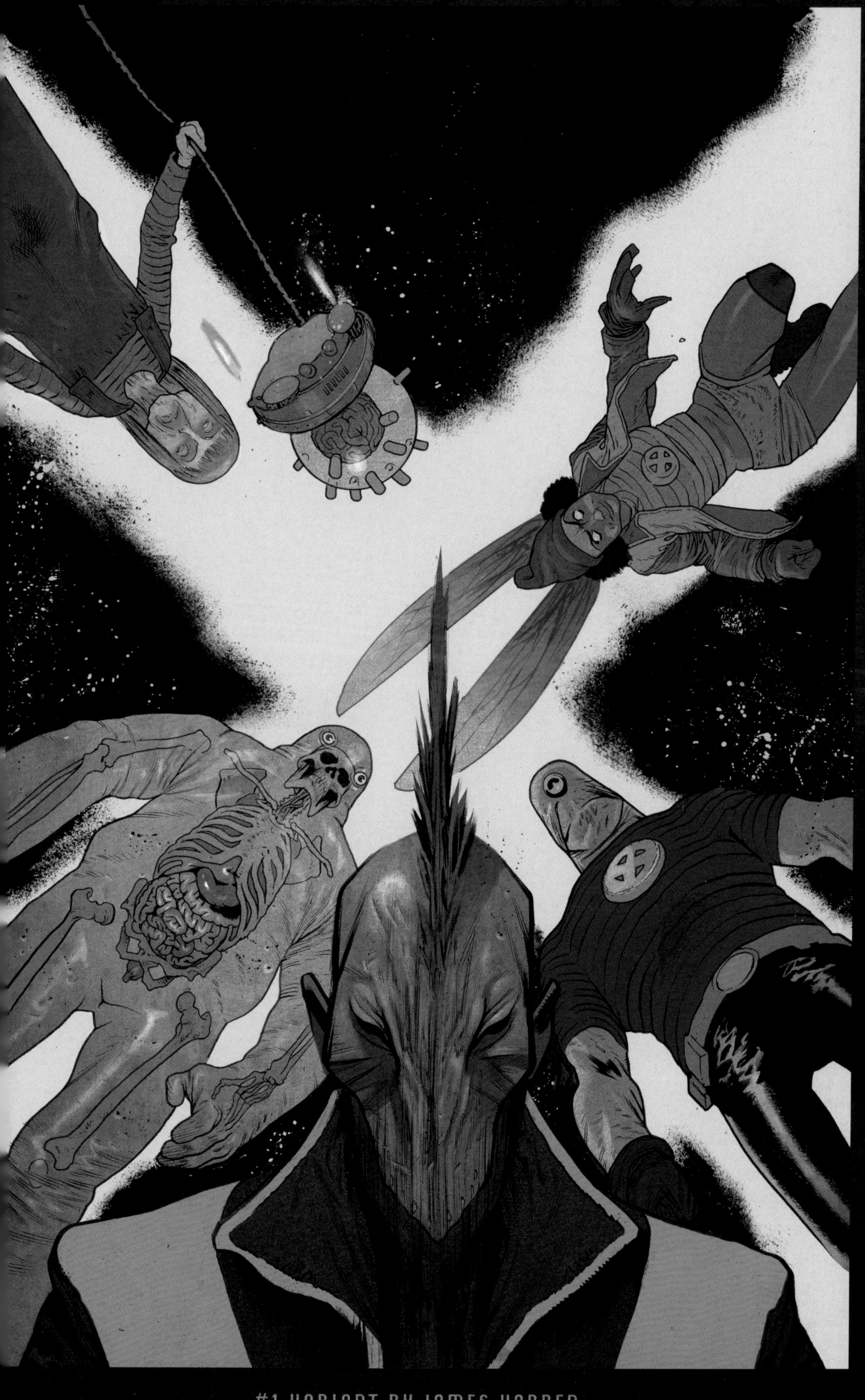

#1 VARIANT BY JAMES HARREN

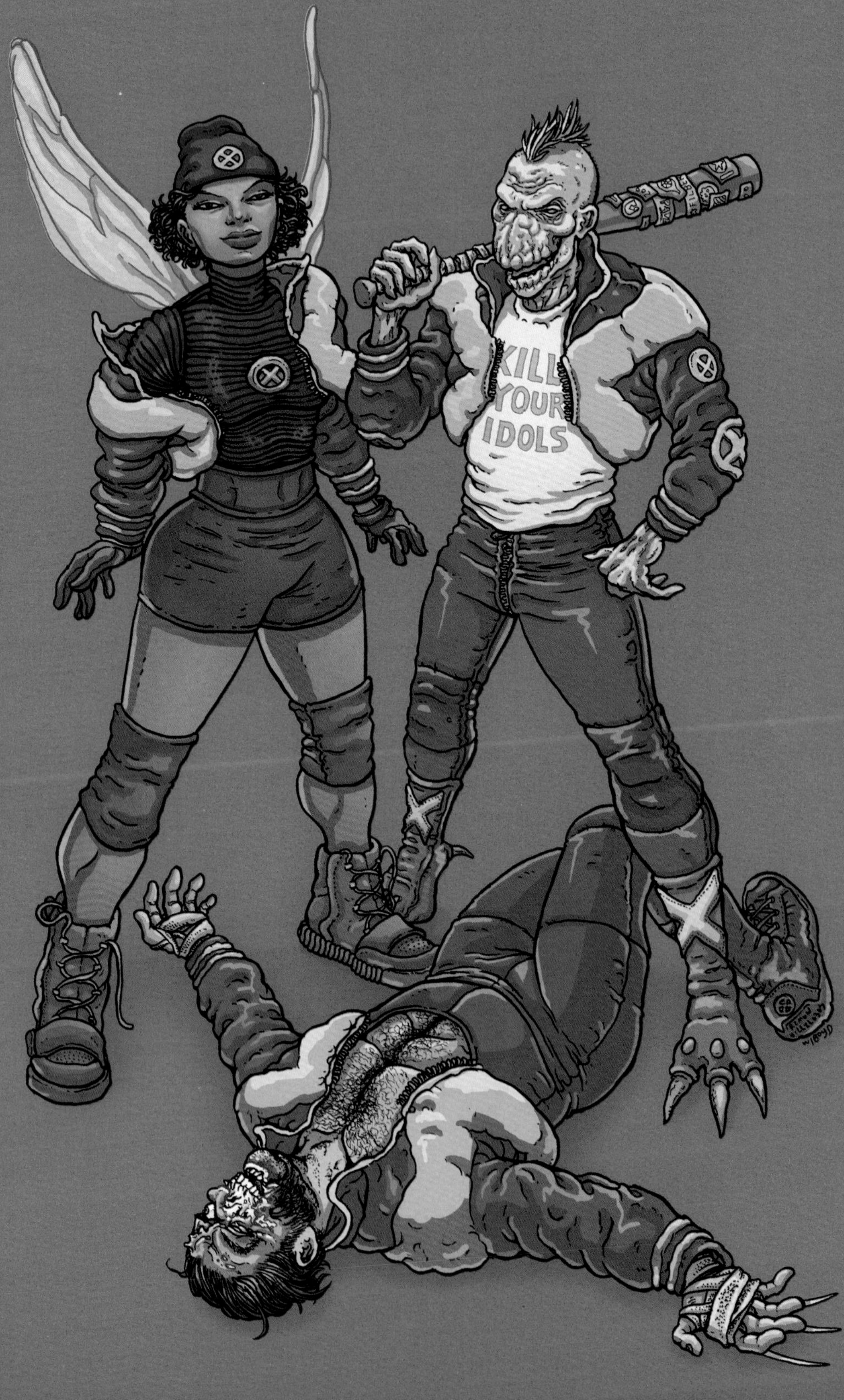
KILL YOUR IDOLS

#2 VARIANT BY RAMON VILLALOBOS & JORDAN BOYD

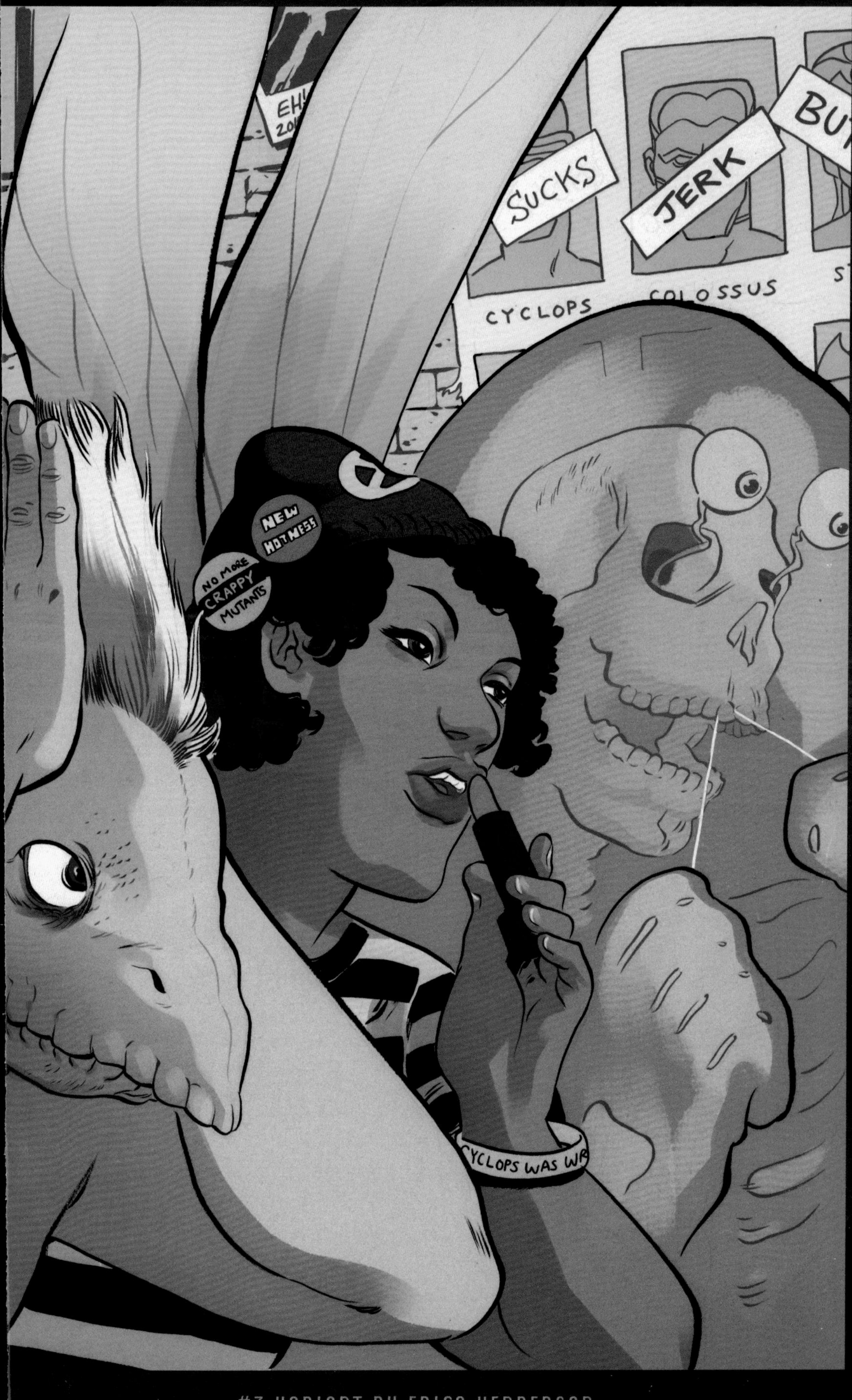
SUCKS
JERK
CYCLOPS
COLOSSUS
NEW HOTNESS
NO MORE CRAPPY MUTANTS

#3 VARIANT BY ERICA HENDERSON

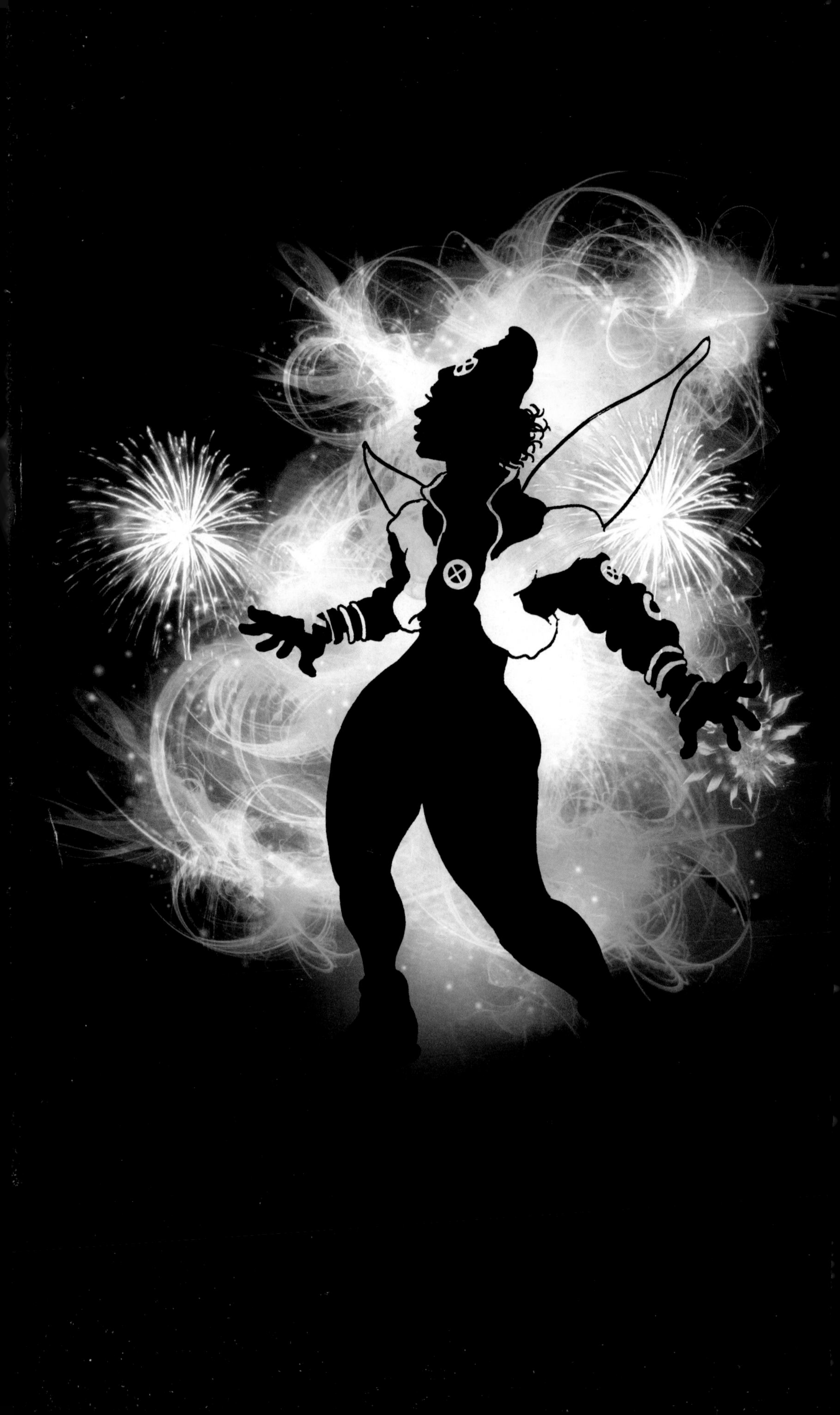